Painfully Rich

×200

PAINFULLY

RICH

THE OUTRAGEOUS FORTUNE AND
MISFORTUNES OF THE HEIRS OF J. PAUL GETTY

John Pearson

ST. MARTIN'S PRESS ✿ NEW YORK

Production Editor: David Stanford Burr
Design: Sara Stemen

Library of Congress Cataloging-in-Publication Data

Pearson, John.
    Painfully rich : the outrageous fortune and misfortunes of the heirs of J. Paul Getty / John Pearson.
        p.   cm.
    ISBN 0-312-13579-3
    1. Getty family.   2. Getty, J. Paul (Jean Paul), 1892–1976—Family.   3. Millionaires—United States—Biography.
I. Title.
CT274.G48P43   1995
929'.2'0973—dc20   95-32434
                                                             CIP

First Edition: November 1995

10   9   8   7   6   5   4   3   2   1

for Peter and Pamela Evans—

the best of friends

"Money is the last enemy that shall never be subdued. While there is flesh there is money— or the want of money; but money is always on the brain, so long as there is a brain in reasonable order."

—Samuel Butler, *Note Books*

Contents

George Franklin II
(July 9, 1924–June 6, 1973)
= [1] Gloria Gordon (m. 1951; div. 1967)
= [2] Jacqueline Riordan (m. May 1971)

Jean Ronald
(b. December 19, 1929)
= Karin Seibl (m. 1964)

Anne Catherine
(b. October 9, 1952)
= Erhardt

Claire Eugenia
(b. August 8, 1954)
= [1] Mazzota
= [2] Perry

Caroline Marie
(b. June 14, 1957)

Christopher Ronald
(b. July 23, 1965)
= Pia Miller

Stephanie Marie
(b. February 24, 1967)
= Alexander Weibel

Isabel

Maria Theresa

Sara   Nicholas

Jean Paul III
(b. November 4, 1956)
= Gisela Marline Zacher (m. September 1974)

Aileen
(b. July 14, 1957)
= Christopher Wilding

Paul Balthazar
(b. January 22, 1975)

Caleb Wilding

Andrew Wilding

Beau Maurizio George Getty-Mazzota
(b. 1979)

Byron Perry

Somerset Perry

Sebastian Perry

George Franklin Getty = Sarah Catherine McPherson Risher
(1855–May 31, 1930) | (1852–December 26, 1941)

Gertrude Lois
(1880–1890)

Jean Paul
(December 15, 1892–June 6, 1976)
= [1] Jeanette Demont (m. October 1, 1923; div. September 22, 1927)
= [2] Allene Ashby (m. October 27, 1926; div. 1928)
= [3] Adolphine Helmle (m. December 1928; div. August 1932)
= [4] Ann Rork (m. December 2, 1932; div. March 7, 1936) = [2] Douglas Wilson
= [5] Louise Dudley "Teddy" Lynch
(m. November 17, 1939; div. May 29, 1958)

Donna Wilson

Eugene Paul (Jean Paul, Jr.)
(b. September 7, 1932)
= [1] Gail Harris (m. 1956; div. 1964)
= [2] Talitha Pol (m. December 10, 1966)
(d. July 12, 1971)

Gordon Peter
(b. December 20, 1933)
= Ann Gilbert (m. 1964)

Timothy Ware
(June 15, 1946 – August 17, 1958)

Cecile Karin Margarita
(b. August 25, 1970)

Christina Therese
(b. August 14, 1975)

Tara Gabriel Galaxy Gramaphone
(b. May 30, 1968)

Mark
(b. July 9, 1960)
= Domitilla Harding (m. 1982)

Ariadne = Justin Williams
(b. July 23, 1962)

Natalia   August

Alexander
Joseph
Julius

Gordon Peter, Jr.
(b. July 29, 1965)

Andrew Rork
(b. July 1, 1967)

John Gilbert
(b. September 7, 1968)

William Paul
(b. June 6, 1990)

Acknowledgments

TO write a book as complex as the story of the Gettys is to incur countless debts of gratitude to those whose generosity with time and memory helped to make it possible; so as well as thanking Gordon Getty for permission to quote from his poem, "My Uncle's House" on page 204, and E. L. Doctorow for permission to quote from *Ragtime* on page 67, I would like to thank the following for talking to me: Aaron Asher, Adam Alvarez, Brinsley Black, Michael Brown, Lady Jean Campbell, Josephine Champsoeur, Craig Copetas, Duff Hart Davis, Penelope de Laszlo, Douglas and Martha Duncan, Harry Evans, Malcolm Forbes Jr., Lady Freyberg, Stephen Garrett, Gail Getty, Gordon Getty, Mark Getty, Ronald Getty, Christopher Gibbs, Judith Goodman, Lord Gowrie, Dan Green, Priscilla Higham, James Halligan, Dr. Timothy Leary, Robert Lenzner, Donna Long, John Mallen, Jonathan Meedes, David Mlinaric, Judge William Newsom, Juliet Nicolson, Geraldine Norman, Edmund Purdom, John Richardson, John Semepolis, June Sherman, Mark Steinbrink, Claire Sterling, Alexis Teissier, Lord Christopher Thynne, Briget O'Brien Twohig, Vivienne Ventura, Jacqueline Williams.

Paul Shrimpton, kindliest of bankers, managed my overdraft with rare compassion; Julie Powell, my local computer genius saved me when Word Perfect failed me; Oscar Turnhill checked my facts and punctuation; and Edda Tasiemka of the miraculous Hans Tasiemka Archive found me press reports that no one else so much as knew existed.

But my greatest thanks must go, firstly, to my friend, Peter Evans, for making me laugh and for so much wise advice over everything from *le mot juste* to the title of this book, and secondly to my perfect wife, Lynette, who has been my inspiration, and my consolation and who coped so well with being painfully poor as I wrote about the painfully rich.

Painfully Rich

Introduction

JEAN Paul Getty was eighty-three and had had three facelifts, the first at sixty; but the last had failed, making him look inordinately old. He was reputedly the richest American alive, but recently all he had wanted was to hear Penelope read him G. A. Henty's Victorian boys' adventure stories. Penelope—he called her Pen—was a tall, good-looking woman who had been his closest friend for more than twenty years, and she read well, in the no-nonsense voice of the upper-class Englishwoman she was. Getty had a large collection of the works of G. A. Henty. Possibly they made him think of a daring boyhood he had never had— and a life of physical adventure he wished that he had led.

Getty believed in reincarnation but dreaded dying. Convinced that he had been the Roman emperor Hadrian in an earlier life, and having been so fortunate in this, his present one, he feared that the third time around he might not be so lucky. Getty reincarnated as a coolie, as the child of a Calcutta slum? Could God have such a twisted sense of humor? All too possible, and the prospect daunted him.

His youngest surviving son, accompanied by his wife, had flown to London from California and had been with him at the house for several days, trying to persuade him to "go home" with them by chartered Boeing. "Home" was Getty's ranch-house overlooking the Pacific Ocean at Malibu, but the old man was terrified of flying and had not seen Malibu or his native United States, for over twenty years. What sort of home was that?

"You know what, Pen? They want to take me back because they think I'm dying."

He stated the fact in his flat midwestern voice, which seemed to count the cost of every syllable, then closed the subject as a bookkeeper closes an account. J. Paul Getty, billionaire, was staying put.

He was also refusing now to go to bed.

"People die in bed," he said, making it clear that he had no intention of doing so if he could help it. Recently he had taken to living in his armchair with a shawl around his shoulders.

Death is harder for the rich to face than it is for humbler mortals, the rich having so much more to lose and leave behind them—this great drafty house, for instance. Built between 1521 and 1530 by Sir Richard Weston, a courtier of Henry VIII, Sutton Place had been one of Jean Paul Getty's many bargains when he prized it from a hard-pressed Scottish duke (Sutherland) in 1959. It was the nearest thing to a real home that he had ever had, and for all its discomfort and inconvenience he truly loved this red-brick Tudor pile with its twenty-seven bedrooms, its timbered hall complete with minstrels' gallery, its home farm, and its resident ghost (of Anne Boleyn; who else?), all set in bijou Surrey countryside twenty miles by motorway from London.

Then there was Getty's lion, Nero, growling in his cage outside the house. The old man loved Nero as much as he permitted himself to love almost anyone, and since he fed him personally, Nero would miss him.

After Nero came Getty's women.

"Jean Paul Getty is priapic," Lord Beaverbrook once warned his granddaughter Lady Jean Campbell.

"What does that mean, Grandpapa?" she asked him.

"Ever ready," he replied.

Getty had always been that way. Ever since his adolescence in Los Angeles, women had been the one luxury the old miser had never denied himself. How he had enjoyed them in his time! Young and old, fat and fashionably thin, drum majorettes and duchesses, streetwalkers, stars, and socialites. Until quite recently he had been taking vitamins in massive doses, together with the so-called sex drug, H3, to maintain his potency. But now all that was over, and it was no longer sex but the rumor of his imminent departure that brought his mistresses to Sutton Place.

He would not be lavish with them, any more than he was lavish with himself. He was courteous to women, but rarely became emotionally involved for long.

Had all his money brought him happiness? There is a certain consolation in the thought of the very rich deriving little pleasure from their wealth, and much of Getty's undoubted popularity originated in that look of crucified affliction with which he had schooled himself to face the world.

As Getty's onetime chief executive, the celebrated Claus von Bülow, put it, he always looked as if he were attending his own funeral. But clever Claus was swift to add that behind that rainy countenance his boss was secretly enjoying life, and that this contrast formed what he saw as the essential comedy of Getty's whole existence. Von Bülow may have had a somewhat special sense of humor, but according to him, Getty always saw the funny side of things. Perhaps he did, and we will never know what risible delights the old nocturnal joker found in a balance sheet in the stillness of the Surrey night.

For his fortune had achieved surreal proportions, and since most of it was carefully invested and busily creating yet more money, not even J. Paul Getty ever knew precisely how rich he was. Suffice it to say that his fortune was almost as great as the annual budget at that time of Northern Ireland, where his forebears originated; more than the national debt of Belgium; more than any human being could exhaust in a lifetime of indulging the most extravagant desires. Getty could have given every man, woman, and child in the United States a ten-dollar bill and still been rich.

Few things, of course, would have been less likely, for unlike John D. Rockefeller, who habitually dispensed a freshly minted dime to each child he met, Jean Paul was disinclined to acts of random generosity. Indeed, he was disinclined to generosity, period. But his celebrated stinginess was not exactly what it seemed.

"That's how he got so rich," people used to say. But they were wrong. Avarice alone could never have accounted for a fraction of a fortune such as his, and Getty's stinginess was less the cause of his exaggerated wealth than a symptom of something more intriguing.

The truth was that Jean Paul Getty was a man of passion, which he had channeled single-mindedly into the creation of his massive fortune much as a great composer pours his soul into a symphony. Getty's true love was money, and he had proved himself a faithful and romantic partner during his lifelong love affair with wealth, jealously acquiring it and making it increase in massive quantities over more than sixty years.

His avarice was an incidental aspect of this love. How can one bear to waste the object of one's adoration? How could he squander that delightful substance which, with death approaching, offered him his greatest hope of immortality?

Wealth surrounded Jean Paul Getty like a nimbus, conferring upon him godlike qualities not vouchsafed to poorer mortals. Through money he was able to create continual movement round the world. His security guards with fierce German shepherds patrolling the darkness near the house, his oil refineries working round the clock, his tankers plowing distant oceans, and his oil wells pumping wealth from the depths of the sea and the farthest reaches of the desert.

But there are limits to the godlike powers that wealth bestows on mortal billionaires, and nothing could relieve Getty of the final act required of him. He had always been a quiet, lonely man, and during the night of June 6, 1976, still sitting in his favorite chair, silently and quite alone, he died.

DEATH is a great diminisher, and it was strange how insignificant America's richest man appeared once he was dead. In accordance with his wishes his body was laid out in state in the great hall of Sutton Place like a Tudor nobleman. "He always liked to think he was Duke John of Sutton Place," one of his mistresses remarked. But a dukedom was one thing even his enormous fortune could not buy, and the only mourners watching by the bier were security men making sure that, even now, the body wasn't kidnaped.

Later, and again in accordance with his wishes, a memorial service was held at the chic Anglican Church of St. Mark's, on North Audley Street in Mayfair. As an event it was curiously in character. Another duke (Bedford this time) delivered the address to a dry-eyed, fashionable congregation; just one of Getty's surviving sons, though suffering severe effects of heroin and alcohol addiction, managed to attend; and the vicar never got his service fee.

Not that one could blame Jean Paul for that, for by then he had made the journey he had always dreaded—by air freight in his coffin in a Boeing's cargo hold to California—and he was currently residing in Hollywood's Forest Lawn cemetery while the family and the Los Angeles authorities argued over where to bury him.

But there still remained one area where the vital force of this inscrutable old man was very much alive: in his last will and testament, which had been duly published by his London lawyers. It was a fascinating document, as much for what it left out as for what it stated, and it served to emphasize the mystery of the whole baroque relationship between the dead man, his enormous fortune, and the members of his very scattered family.

A will is an opportunity to deliver those one loves a final judgment before going off to meet one's own. It was an opportunity Jean Paul appreciated, having lived his life in the shadow of the will made by his father half a century before. And, like his papa, he made the most of it.

For the past ten years, whenever his lawyer, energetic, white-haired Lansing Hays, flew in to see him from Los Angeles, Getty would want to make some change to the fearsome document. There was always somebody to add to or angrily subtract from, the list of legatees. Getty was a man of some precision, and his will became a fine-tuned expression of his wishes.

He had never bothered much with humble people, and the humble people in his life received scant crumbs from America's richest table. Léon Turrou, his trusted security adviser, and Tom Smith, the masseur Getty had relied on to relieve his pains in his last years, both said he had promised to remember them—and both were bitter when they discovered they had been forgotten. The gardeners at Sutton Place got three months' wages, the butler, po-faced Bullimore, six, and his faithful secretary, Barbara Wallace, who had mother-henned him for some twenty years, was lucky to receive $5,000.

Remembering him, she is more generous than he was with her.

"That's how he was," she says. "I loved him, and what counted was not the money but the memory of working with the most extraordinary character I've ever known."

Others were less charitable, for he also used his will to make clear what he thought about the women in his life. His legal adviser, the chaste Robina Lund, received $200 a month—possibly to put on record what he thought of chastity. But the unchaste Nicaraguan Mrs. Rosabella Burch fared little better, so he may have had some other reason.

The only female friend who did well was Penelope Kitson, who received some $850,000 worth of Getty Oil stock. When the value of the stock doubled in the early eighties, she become the only person to become a dollar millionaire from reading G. A. Henty.

Again, the frugality of these personal bequests was totally in character, and was probably intended to emphasize the big surprise within this deeply pondered document. For in one untypically grand gesture, Jean Paul Getty had decided to dispose of the mass of his personal fortune in its entirety, unconditionally and without the faintest reservation.

He'd always been a man for sly surprises, and apart from Lansing Hays had given nobody the slightest hint of how he would be opening the sluices on this vast amount of money to benefit one unsuspecting legatee: the modest J. Paul Getty Museum in Malibu, which he had been quietly creating on the grounds of his ranch house but had never dared to visit.

In museum terms the legacy was vast. At Getty's death his personal assets were computed at nearly $1 billion (equivalent to at least $2 billion today, allowing for inflation). With that money, the strange museum, which he had had meticulously built in the form of an ancient Roman villa on the shores of the Pacific Ocean, became overnight the most richly endowed institution of its kind in modern history.

According to the old man's personal assistant, Norris Bramlett, "This was his hope of immortality. He wanted the Getty name to be remembered as long as civilization lasted."

The bequest was also, as he knew quite well, a highly tax-efficient way of disposing of a large amount of capital. In California, the museum counted as a charity, and provided its directors spent 4 percent of the value of the capital on acquisitions every year, the U.S. Internal Revenue Service would not assess taxes on it. Getty had always been viscerally opposed to paying taxes—and, unlike simpler citizens who feel the same, he rarely had.

Beyond these facts, the will gave not the barest explanation of why he had disposed his money as he had or of why no conditions were imposed upon the way the museum trustees spent it. When Getty's rival oilman Armand Hammer created his own much smaller museum in Los Angeles, he tied up everything in minutest detail. The steel baron Henry Clay Frick had almost made it legally impossible to change so much as an aspidistra in the atrium of the Frick Collection in New York. But should the trustees of the J. Paul Getty in their wisdom suddenly decide to sell the whole collection, using the assets to create a bicycle museum, a bicycle museum is what the J. Paul Getty Museum will irrevocably become.

But just as the will shed little light upon the old man's reasons for bequeathing everything like this, so it also left obscure a more intriguing mystery: the financial fate of the members of his family, or, as he liked to call them, the Getty dynasty—the children and grandchildren of three of his five failed marriages. Since the will made little mention of them, what of their future? Had he simply forgotten them, or had they been collectively disinherited?

Archaeologists unearthing the tombs of some of the richest pharaohs sometimes found, concealed behind the burial chamber, a further chamber crammed with still more splendid objects where the spirit of the dead resided.

Something similar had happened with the money left by Jean Paul Getty, for it was typical of the old man's covert nature that behind his personal fortune, which he bequeathed to his museum, he had been slowly building up a second, even greater fortune, which resided in a trust not covered by his will.

This massive trust had always been completely separate from Getty's personal fortune, and had grown with winnings from the secret game he had been playing with the world for over forty years. The trust was where he stacked away the vast amounts of money that, according to the complex rules by which this game was played, some of his descendants would inherit—and some, emphatically, would not.

Although this trust had suited Getty's purposes as a sort of monster tax-proof money box, it was originally created as a so-called spendthrift trust to placate his formidable, stone-deaf mother, Sarah, who had known him well enough to distrust his motives. It was she who established the trust in the mid-1930s to protect the financial interests of her grandchildren from what she saw as Getty's spendthrift tendencies, and appropriately it bore her name, the Sarah C. Getty Trust.

It was strange to have the century's richest miser publicly proclaimed a spendthrift. Stranger still was the way he seemed obsessively compelled to go on adding to the trust, creating this prodigious pile of untaxed capital. When finally split between its beneficiaries in 1986, the trust was valued in excess of $4 billion; since then, the resultant capital has more than doubled yet again in value.

One might have thought, as Sarah presumably did, that this spendthrift trust would guarantee her descendants all the benefits and pleasures wealth can bring to those who journey down the rocky road of life: freedom from anxiety and care; the best of everything, faithful friends; and—dare one whisper it?—happiness. Reader, think again!

THE great unanswered mystery of the Getty fortune is why it has apparently devoured so many of its beneficiaries.

Why should this massive reservoir of wealth have proved to be not just the largest but probably the most destructive major fortune of our time? And why, when millions die for want of money, and countless millions slave, scheme, murder, labor, subjugate themselves for such pathetic glimpses of the stuff, should something as pleasurable as money bring such misery and havoc as it has to Getty's heirs?

The human wreckage started piling up within the old man's lifetime. One son had killed himself three years before Jean Paul died. By then another son appeared intent on doing much the same through alcohol and heroin addiction. A third son, disinherited at birth, had grown increasingly embittered at the way his father had treated him. Only the fourth and youngest son was currently enjoying what by normal standards one might term a reasonably fulfilling life—but at the cost of cutting himself off from anything to do with Getty Oil or his father's other businesses.

By the time the old man died, the blight was starting to afflict the next generation, too. Getty's eldest grandson had been kidnaped by the Italian Mafia, losing his right ear in the process; he then embarked on a life of drug addiction, drink, and dissipation, which would end by almost totally destroying him. Later, his sister would end up suffering from AIDS.

Indeed, in the years following Jean Paul Getty's death, there were times when the family itself appeared intent on self-destruction, as brother battled through the courts with brother over this vast and poisoned legacy. As one journalist put it, by the 1980s the name of Getty had become "a synonym for family dysfunction."

Great fortunes can clearly have disastrous effects upon the heirs, generally by swamping them with too much money at an early age. But undiluted lucre was never at the root of all the Getty family's misery. None of J. Paul Getty's sons was raised in pampered luxury, or even in the expectation of inheriting enormous wealth. Nor were the grandchildren. Rather the contrary.

Balzac, who was fascinated by great fortunes, and the havoc that he saw them bring to the nouveaux riches families of France's Second Empire, believed that "behind every great fortune lies a great crime."

But the Gettys would have baffled him. For although there may have been a modicum of dirty work and double-dealing in the creation of the Getty fortune, there was no actual crime to put one's finger on—and certainly no "great" one.

There was, however, something more intriguing, which Balzac would have loved: the infinitely complex character of Getty himself. The story of his fortune is essentially the story of his life, and the contradictions and obsessions of this most eccentric Californian always played a crucial role in his achievement. They played an even greater part in the troubled heritage he left behind him, so much so that what happened to his children and his children's children also forms a part of Jean Paul Getty's legacy. Some were destroyed by it; some, though badly scarred, have come to terms with it; and some of the younger generation, all too well aware of what occurred, are seeking to offset the dangers for the future.

How all this happened forms an extraordinary chronicle of the effect of vast amounts of money on a group of very vulnerable human beings. To understand it, one must begin with the strange creation of the fortune, and the character of the solitary, frightened, womanizing puritan who made himself the richest human being in America.

PART ONE

CHAPTER ONE

Father and Son

JEAN Paul Getty was no novice to great wealth and the problems it could bring to its possessors. He was in fact a second-generation million-aire himself, whose father, George Franklin Getty, started the family fortune with profits from the Oklahoma oil boom of 1903. But just as it is hard to picture the sapling out of which a great tree grew, so the vastness of Jean Paul Getty's fortune almost totally obscures the lesser fortune that preceded it. It also obscures the fact that without his father and *his* fortune, the Getty billions could never have existed.

When Jean Paul was already in his sixties, rich as Croesus, and immensely proud to be sleeping with a duchess, with the sister of a duke, and with a distant cousin of the tsar of Russia, one of his odder habits was to recite part of Lincoln's Gettysburg Address, which he knew by heart, to those he particularly wanted to impress. On concluding, he would casually mention that Gettysburg happened to derive its name from an ancestor of his, one James Getty, who bought the site of the historic town from William Penn in person and endowed it with his name.

It might seem odd that the richest American felt obliged to produce this sort of ancestral credit rating. What is odder is that the story was totally untrue. Gettysburg got its name from a family called Gettys, and Jean Paul's ancestors had no connection with the place at all.

More to the point, his father's history, far from requiring phony enhancement of the sort sometimes indulged in by the English aristocracy, was one of those tales of achievement of which any son, particularly an American, might well have been extremely proud. But then, Jean Paul had reasons of his own to feel ambivalent about his father, and about the part their curious relationship had played in the whole bizarre creation of his fortune.

*

JEAN Paul himself was born in Minneapolis in 1892. His father, a powerful, godly man, was thirty-seven at the time. His mother, Sarah, née Risher—dark eyes, tightly piled-up hair, and the down-turned mouth of the dissatisfied character she was—was three years older, of distant Dutch and Scottish origins. The Gettys themselves originated in Northern Ireland, arriving in America at the end of the eighteenth century. George began life as the offspring of poor farming folk in Maryland. His father died when George was six, leaving the boy to labor with his mother in the fields, until his uncle Joseph Getty, famous as a local hellfire temperance preacher, sent him to school in Ohio.

George was a strong, hardworking boy, and the adversity following his father's death left him with an iron resolution to raise himself from poverty. Meanwhile, from Uncle Joe he learned the rigid precepts of fundamentalist Christianity, together with a lifelong hatred of the demon drink and a steadfast faith in the saving grace of God to lift humanity from poverty and sin.

While he was at Ohio University, studying to become a teacher, George caught the eye of Sarah Risher. She had no intention of spending her life married to a schoolmaster, so she made George promise to become a lawyer, offering the money from her dowry to pay his way through law school.

It is appropriate that Sarah Getty's name is still enshrined within the massive trust that came to dominate the fortunes of her family, for throughout the marriage sharp-eyed Sarah was the mover, egging on her dutiful, hardworking younger partner to make money and succeed.

Within a year of their marriage in 1879 George had already earned his law degree at the University of Michigan, and Sarah was urging them to move to thriving Minneapolis, where her husband turned his legal talents to the insurance business and began to prosper. By their early thirties, George and Sarah owned their own house in the most fashionable part of Minneapolis, drove a coach and pair, and were people of substance and promise in the booming capital of the North Star State, Minnesota.

FAR from weakening their religious ideals, success made both Gettys stronger in the faith. From his uncle Joe, George had imbibed a Calvinistic sense of good and evil; worldly wealth was seen as evidence of heavenly favor. According to this practical belief, God rewarded those who hearkened to his word, and he smiled on those who forswore the devil and his works.

As zealous Methodists, George and Sarah were serious and self-denying. Having signed the pledge in his early twenties, George remained a lifelong and dedicated teetotaler. And until he reached the age of thirty-five his life had seemed a storybook example of the benefits that flow from Christian conduct. He had hearkened to the word of God. He had labored in the vineyard. Now the time had come for George, like Job, to face his period of tribulation.

WHEN he was being hailed as his country's richest human being, one of the few possessions Jean Paul Getty genuinely treasured was a sepia photograph of a small girl he had never seen. She had ringlets, a large bow in her hair, and soulful eyes foreshadowing her imminent demise.

This was his sister, Gertrude Lois Getty, who was born in 1880, soon after George and Sarah's marriage, and who died in the typhoid epidemic that swept Minnesota in the fall of 1890. Sarah also caught this fearsome illness; although she recovered, she was left with hearing loss that steadily grew worse, making her virtually deaf at fifty.

For George and Sarah, the taking of their only child, "the sunbeam of the family," tried their faith as Christians. Of the two, George appeared the more affected; he underwent a deep religious crisis, for a while turning to spiritualism in an attempt to find his daughter.

When he finally emerged from this crisis he was more steadfast in the faith than ever, and actually abandoned Methodism for the stricter creed of Christian Science, whose principles he adhered to firmly for the remainder of his life.

As if to show that God approved this change of creed, George shortly afterward received a sign. In her fortieth year Sarah, who had conceived but once before, discovered she was pregnant. And the arrival of a son on December 15, 1892, was like an early Christmas present to replace their daughter.

In their gratitude to God, how could the Gettys fail to treasure such a child? And George had further reasons for rejoicing in the newborn Jean Paul Getty. Here was an heir at last to carry on the name and inherit the money that was steadily accruing from the lucrative insurance business of the thriving cities of the Midwest.

SARAH named the child after her husband's Getty cousin, John, but it was very much in character that she also had to give the boy a touch of European sophistication by making the name not John but Jean. With time the name would be compressed to the bare initial J. and within the family its owner would be generally referred to as Paul. But there was something more prophetic than Sarah can have realized in her bestowal of this personal connection with Europe. Europe and its culture were to act as magnets to her son and many of the members of his family.

DESPITE the Gettys' middle-class prosperity, life with two straitlaced, aging parents who were haunted by a vanished daughter offered little in the way of sociability or mirth, and Paul, though cosseted and protected, had a lonely and loveless childhood. His mother actively discouraged contact with other children, for fear of fresh contagion. And while overprotective with her son, she was careful not to show him too much love, in case she lost him as she had lost his sister.

Years later Paul told his wife that as a child he was never cuddled, nor did he have a birthday party or a Christmas tree. His one great interest was his postage stamp collection, his closest friend a mutt called Jip.

Undoubtedly this claustrophobic childhood put its mark on him; he would always be a loner, wary of his fellows and keeping his thoughts and feelings to himself. "I have long been able to exercise a considerable degree of control over my display of emotions," he proudly wrote when he was over eighty.

But the tedium of childhood in this rigid little family clearly affected him in other ways as well. Instead of passively accepting the gray horizons of puritanical nineteenth-century America, he secretly rebelled; throughout his life, part of him would always struggle to escape the boredom and restriction of humdrum domesticity. He would never be entirely at ease within a family. Instead, he would be always on the move, and until the onset of old age would never settle anywhere for long. Left to his own devices, Jean Paul Getty would have been a wanderer.

WITH business booming, God appeased, and his home in Minneapolis in order, George Franklin Getty had every reason to be happy—particularly when he suddenly received a further sign of heavenly approval.

In 1903, when Paul was ten, the Lord directed George to Bartlesville, a one-horse town in what was legally still Indian territory in Oklahoma, to settle an insurance claim. At the time he had no way of knowing the stupendous outcome of this unexciting journey. Bartlesville was buzzing with the beginnings of the Oklahoma oil bonanza. Under its barren landscape lay some of the largest oil reserves in the United States. And George had arrived just in time to benefit from them.

"There are men," wrote his son, "who seem to have an uncanny affinity with oil in its natural state. I am inclined to think that my father had a touch of this himself."

Perhaps he had; but, to start with, it was little more than passing speculation that led George to invest $500 for a lease on the oil rights to "Lot 50," 1,100 acres of virgin prairie outside Bartlesville.

But the Lord had directed George aright. When drilling started on Lot 50 that October, it almost instantly struck oil, and one year later, George had six wells in production. The price of crude was 52 cents a barrel at the time; Lot 50 was averaging 100,000 barrels every month.

Apart from heavenly guidance, more prosaic factors also contributed to George's rapid creation of a fortune. He had already saved considerable reserves of capital from the insurance business; he knew the law; and he conducted his affairs in an honest and self-denying way.

Within the next three busy years, George propelled his company, which he called Minnehoma Oil (a name derived not from some romantic Indian maiden, but from the businesslike elision of the two words "Minnesota" and "Oklahoma") into a thriving company. By 1906, George Getty was a millionaire.

CHAPTER TWO

A Solitary Childhood

PAUL was ten when he arrived in Bartlesville and got his first glimpse of George's famous Lot 50 oil well. He was deeply disappointed. Knowing that Bartlesville was in Indian territory, he had gone there expecting "redskins," squaws, and wigwams. Instead he saw a makeshift boomtown, reeking of oil, and peopled with men in grimy overalls.

But it was a formative experience for any boy to watch his father suddenly grow rich so very easily, and this was something Jean Paul would not forget. Having this intimate entrée to the oil business, he would not find it difficult to do the same, should he ever need to. And from the start of Minnehoma, George took it for granted that his son would naturally join him in the company and ultimately succeed him at its head. He even encouraged his young son to use his pocket money to buy two Minnehoma shares. "Now I have to work for you," he told him, handing him the share certificates.

George had a habit of dispensing nuggets of his homespun wisdom. "A businessman is only as good as his sources of information" was one such; "Let your deeds speak louder than your words" another. But throughout childhood and adolescence, Paul stayed obtusely uninspired by his father's words—and by the oil business, having interest of his own to occupy his time.

Later in life, he would always speak of George with considerable piety and reverence. "He was a great man, and a genuine philosopher," the son solemnly intoned. "He taught me everything I know." But in fact, Jean Paul taught himself everything he needed, and father and son would often clash with one another. According to his cousin Hal Seymour, "Paul and his father just seemed to get in one another's way when they were together in the house."

In character Paul was closer to his mother than to stolid George. He had inherited her down-turned mouth, her restlessness, her locked-in nature; then, as he grew, further similarities between them revealed

16

themselves. Sarah's deafness made her particularly isolated, and Paul began to emulate her solitariness. Even his voice was to bear the traces of their close relationship. The measured diction that became a sort of Getty trademark was something that he learned from talking with a mother who was hard of hearing. And like his mother, Paul increasingly relied upon his own company. Cousin Hal remembered him as being "exceptionally solitary, even for an only child."

Unlike his parents, Paul found little pleasure in the joys of Christianity; his one true passion was for reading. By the age of ten he had discovered those works of G. A. Henty which he would be enjoying in his eighties.

As a boys' adventure writer, Henty had inspired a generation of Victorian schoolboys, transporting them from the boredom of the dusty schoolroom to the most colorful periods of history, peopled with its most exciting characters. *Under Drake's Flag, With Clive in India, With Moore at Corunna*: Even the titles were an invitation to a solitary only child to escape from a closed-in Christian home in Minnesota to the richer, more exciting world outside.

NOW that George was rapidly becoming rich, and was frequently away in Oklahoma, Sarah decided it was time for one more move: from the flat farmlands and freezing winters of Minnesota to sunny California. She claimed that her health was delicate and that she needed warmth and a change of scenery. As usual, George agreed with her.

After visiting San Diego, which they thought provincial, the Gettys decided on a plot of land on newly laid-out South Kingsley Drive, on the corner of the still-unsurfaced stretch of Wilshire Boulevard beyond the Los Angeles city limits. There they built themselves a house.

As a family the Gettys had few close friends, and the move had cut them off from those they had. They drank not, neither did they sin, and Sarah's growing deafness heightened the family's sense of isolation. In the days before efficient hearing aids, it was hard for any family with a parent suffering this most antisocial of afflictions to be open and at ease with those around them. So now more than ever the Gettys were thrown back upon their own resources. Their self-sufficiency and reclusiveness were habits Paul learned early, practiced all his life, and passed on to his children.

George tried to be as strict with his son as with himself, but the more exacting George became, the more sullen was his son's reaction. Paul was willful, as solitary children often are; and George, as parents often do, imagined that the cure was discipline. So, shortly after the Gettys moved to Los Angeles, Paul was sent as a day boy to the local military school—which he inevitably hated. Drill, marching, uniforms, and discipline were not for him. He stayed for nearly four years, acquired few friends, showed zero aptitude for soldiering, and when he finally escaped, was grateful for the peace and privacy of his own room in the house on South Kingsley.

IT used to be a commonplace of educational theory that teenage boys who read too much and were left to their own devices were particularly at risk of sexual temptation. This certainly applied to Paul, and the hearty discipline of the military school had failed to cure him. As something of a bookworm—he was known to his classmates as Dictionary Getty—he had remained stolidly resistant to "healthy" group activities such as marching, military style exercises, and team games of all types. The result was predictable. Together with his love of reading went an obsession with the opposite sex that stayed with him for life. In matters sexual he had finally discovered something he was good at.

Perhaps this was because of his manner, which was always courteous and charming with the other sex. ("Paul never said no to a woman— or yes to a man," as somebody remarked.) Or possibly it was simply because he knew what he wanted, which in matters sexual as in those of business tends to bring results. At all events, by his fourteenth birthday Paul was apparently boasting of losing his virginity. If so, it was more of an achievement for a boy from a rich Christian family in California than it would be today. By Getty standards, it was also seriously sinful, placing him on collision course with all those strictly held and practiced beliefs solemnly maintained by George and Sarah.

PAUL was increasingly getting on his father's nerves, and vice versa. A period supposedly studying economics at the University of Southern California in Los Angeles was followed by a further period supposedly studying law at Berkeley. But universities, it seemed, were not for Jean Paul, and as a thoroughly discontented seventeen-year-old he soon returned to South Kingsley Drive.

By now Jean Paul was very much his mother's precious only child, the gift of God and consolation for her deafness and advancing years. So rather than lose him totally, she schooled herself to overlook his faults and tended to support him in his battles with his father. As something of a bait—and a way of keeping him at home—she also arranged that he should have a private entrance to his room, with his own latchkey.

It was typical of Sarah that having done this, she was soon objecting to the friends he started bringing home, but there was little she could do about them—any more than she and George could really interfere with their son's developing interest in the nightlife of Los Angeles. Without telling his parents, Paul began borrowing his father's car, an impressive four-door Chadwick tourer, which he would silently roll out of the garage when his parents were asleep, and use to tour the local nightspots with his friends to pick up girls.

One night, after Paul had visited a roadhouse with companions Sarah would have disapproved of—and met some girls she would have disapproved of even more—disaster struck. One of the girls spilled red wine on the car's upholstery, and although the teenagers did their best to mop it up, nothing could remove the stains. When George saw what had happened, he must have realized the truth: that Paul was not just borrowing the family barouche for reasons of nocturnal pleasure, but indulging in his father's particular bête noir, the demon drink itself.

But George's reaction set an important precedent for future relations in the Getty family. No bellow of paternal rage disturbed the peace at South Kingsley Drive. As usual when it came to Paul, Sarah almost certainly restrained George, and not a word was said about the incident.

George had ways of registering paternal disapproval. The next time Paul tried borrowing the car when his parents were in bed, he found the back wheel firmly padlocked to a ring cemented to the garage floor.

WHEN Sarah made the family migrate two thousand miles southwest from frozen Minneapolis to radiant Los Angeles, this stretch of southern California had yet to become the overpopulated paradise at the far end of the great American rainbow. Its golden landscape was unsullied, its ocean unpolluted, and its perfect year-round climate was still unaffected by the products of the oil industry that was making George's fortune.

The Gettys were early émigrés from the East in search of happiness, but even in California happiness eluded them. The outdoor pleasures of the Golden State were not for George and Sarah. As far as George the dedicated oilman was concerned, life still centered on the Oklahoma oilfields over a thousand miles by railroad to the east. And Sarah found Los Angeles sadly deficient in culture and amenities. Thus it was very much in character that the house the couple built was more of a harking back to Old World memories than a celebration of the new.

In his mid-sixties Paul would finally succumb to the lure of owning a permanent home, the stately Tudor pile of Sutton Place. And here, among the orange groves off rural Wilshire Boulvard, was surely its precursor: a Tudor-style mansion with mullioned windows, picturesque gables, and freshly stained "Elizabethan" beams. As a house it presumably belonged to the distant world of another imagined Getty ancestor. Nostalgia was its keynote.

A few years later, when George felt rich enough to take Paul and Sarah off on their first extended holiday together, they unsurprisingly traveled to Europe.

This was still the period when the heroes and heroines of novelists like Henry James and Edith Wharton were taking it for granted that only in Europe could they discover a truly civilized existence. Europe, in those far-off days, remained the fountainhead of history, art, and serious sophistication for the American élite.

But this obsession with Europe was far more typical of East Coast millionaires than of Californian nouveaux riches like George and Sarah. And it is interesting that at the very moment when expatriate New York moviemakers just up the road from them in the Hollywood Hills were beginning a counterculture that would conquer Europe with a homegrown vision of America, the Gettys should have undertaken this laborious journey to New York, then on to Europe for a carefully planned three-month tour by road of all the major capitals. From this moment it was the Old World, rather than the New, that captured the imagination of Jean Paul Getty.

As so often in the family, the push to make this journey came from Sarah. Left to his own devices, George would have been content to mind the store in Oklahoma. But Sarah was insistent, and so off they went—shipping the famous Chadwick tourer with them, collecting a chauffeur in Liverpool whose accent they could barely comprehend, then driving on rapidly to France, determined to experience and see as much as possible.

The Gettys were energetic rather than luxurious travelers, setting yet another pattern that their son would copy. In Paris they enjoyed a fortnight at the Hôtel Continentale, a haunt of bourgeois businessmen and traveling salesmen, rather than the Ritz, which George could easily have afforded. Then it was off along the dusty roads to Monte Carlo, Rome, Geneva, Amsterdam, before heading back across the Channel, seeing London, and returning on the liner *Aquitania* to New York.

For the young man with the wavy hair and the practiced pale blue eye for any girl he saw, this bumpy journey was a formative experience. He loved travel, and he positively enjoyed hotels, being excited by the richness and the possibilities of adventure in these European cities. But he must have felt inhibited by the presence of two aged parents, one a strict Methodist with hearing problems and the other a teetotaling, moralistic, born-again Christian Scientist. Eighteen-year-old Jean Paul Getty couldn't wait to return to Europe and start enjoying all these fascinating places on his own.

BACK on South Kingsley Drive, Sarah was happy that her restless son evinced such interest in European culture, and despite her fears of losing him, seems to have supported his ambition to return to Europe once he told her that he wished to study at Oxford University.

George was less enthusiastic. Oxford's dreaming spires were not for him, but Sarah talked him into granting Paul an adequate allowance— in the form of a banker's draft for $200 a month—and in August 1912, after a brief trip to Japan, the twenty-year-old son and heir was once more crossing the Atlantic—this time on his own.

He traveled in considerable style, for this was very much the journey of the indulged scion of an American millionaire, with echoes, however faint, of those European grand tours on which English aristocrats once dispatched their offspring to obtain some culture and knowledge of the world before returning home to their inheritance. This European trip would affect Paul profoundly, but not exactly in the way his parents were expecting.

From the start it was a considerable undertaking for a solitary, more or less philistine young American to make such a journey on his own. But just as with his women, Paul was distinctly knowledgeable and self-assured when it came to getting what he wanted.

He had already talked George into obtaining him a letter of introduction from one of his former legal cronies, the lawyer William Howard Taft, who now happened to be the Republican President of the United States. And once in Europe he grandly purchased a secondhand Mercedes tourer, ordered several suits from Savile Row tailors, and then set out for the unlikely object of his journey. He arrived at Oxford that November, when the term had already started.

Oxford before the First World War was very much a closed society, and this unknown, unconnected young American, who had failed to take a degree at either Los Angeles or Berkeley, had little in the way of learning to commend him.

Luckily this hardly mattered, as the standard of education among most Oxford undergraduates of the period was lamentably low, and Paul was anyway not in Oxford on a quest for learning. Like Jay Gatsby, he wanted something quite different: the right to call himself an Oxford man. This, with customary single-mindedness, he more or less obtained.

The letter from the President of the United States provided his introduction to the president of fashionable Magdalen College, the comfortable classicist Dr. Herbert Warren, who spent some time with this self-possessed young Californian, and ended by recommending someone in his college to "tutor" him in economics. Paul also became a non-collegiate member of the St. Catherine's Society, which was not yet a fully accredited Oxford College, but which permitted him to attend lectures if he wished—something rarely done by the majority of undergraduates at the time. And he had little difficulty finding lodgings in the center of the city.

But although he later claimed that while at Oxford he had "more or less lived at Magdalen," and though he insisted that "the men at Magdalen accepted me as one of their number," he was not a member of Magdalen College or of Oxford university. Not that this ever kept him from tacitly implying that he was—and in later years he always made great play of how his time at Magdalen had subtly infiltrated him into the bosom of the British upper classes.

"The first close friend I made at Magdalen," he would fondly reminisce, "was the brother of the present Earl of Portarlington, George Dawson-Damer." Running George a gilded second was His Royal Highness, the Prince of Wales, who also chanced to be at Magdalen. "We always called each other 'David' and 'Paul,' " said Getty casually, "and formed a close, warm friendship that was to endure for almost half a century."

It was never very clear how long Paul actually spent at Oxford or whether he did obtain the "diploma" that he claimed—nor how really "close and warm" was that lifelong friendship with the future king of England—but little of this really mattered. What *was* important was that here at Oxford, Paul had seen at last a world he thoroughly admired and envied. Some of his Magdalen friends invited the rich young Californian home to enjoy that fashionable institution, the Edwardian weekend; later, Getty was to write nostalgically of how the houses he had visited were "frequently stately country manors which, in that last blaze of the Edwardian era, were still at the height of their splendour."

Here, in vivid contrast with simple sunny California and the grimy oil wells of Oklahoma, was a world of titled aristocrats, stately homes, grandiose art—and wonderfully sophisticated women. Here was a world that would haunt Paul Getty for the remainder of his life.

There are essentially two sorts of snobs: insiders attempting to keep the vulgar out, and spellbound outsiders trying to convince themselves that they are in. Paul was emphatically in the second category—and henceforth one important part of his ambition would be the desire to stake his claim within that illusory yet sacred zone of titles, deference, ancient wealth, and European royalty which he had glimpsed at Magdalen during that golden time before the lamps went out all over Europe.

AFTER Oxford, Paul was in no hurry to return to California. He was becoming a compulsive traveler, seriously intent upon escape, and rather than become immersed in the tedium of South Kingsley Drive, he was soon at the wheel of the Mercedes en route to what he had decided was his favorite city, Paris. Summer was spent in Russia, autumn in Berlin, and just before Christmas he was in Vienna, planning to spend the beginning of 1914 on the sights of Egypt.

But money had become a problem—which inevitably brought him into conflict with his father. Two hundred dollars a month meant fairly basic travel, and requests for more produced a sour response from George, who was becoming increasingly exasperated by this European "gallivanting" of his wayward son.

By now Paul had been in flight for more than a year, and it was on the eve of his twenty-first birthday—which was spent aboard a rusty coaster, sailing to Alexandria—that his requests for money finally exploded into bitter conflict with his father.

Thoroughly annoyed by what he saw as his son's "continuing extravagance and self-indulgence," George informed him that he was taking back 15,000 shares which he had placed in Paul's name in Minnehoma Oil. This produced a venomous riposte from Paul, showing something of the anger and resentment that, when thwarted, he could summon up against his father.

After a sharp demand to be permitted to retain the shares, Paul attacked George for his stinginess to his only son, reminding him that when William Randolph Hearst reached twenty-one, *his* father had actually presented him with the *San Francisco Examiner*, together with the newspaper building, which was worth at least $3 million. Paul bitterly continued that he had no intention of being "cheated out of my birthright," and ended by saying that his father's attitude left him no alternative "but to deal with the matter as I would with an opponent."

Once more it seems that Sarah smoothed things over. Soon she was writing affectionately to Paul, saying how much she wished that she could "fly to see him," and by early summer she had even persuaded

George to make another transatlantic crossing so that they could meet their wayward son in Paris, relish the reunion, and travel home together.

June 1914 saw the Gettys reconciled and staying once again at the Hôtel Continentale; it was there that Paul disclosed his real ambition for the future. Since he had every intention of continuing to travel and indulge in cosmopolitan society, he was going to become a diplomat—or, failing that, a writer.

Sarah appears to have supported him. George said nothing.

DESPITE his limitations, George Getty was not stupid, and in some ways he understood his son better than Paul understood himself.

Instead of squandering precious time and money touring Europe, George felt Paul should be safely settled in the one place where a son of his should obviously be: the family business, where he would learn the ropes, make decisions, and be groomed as his father's successor.

Great events were now on George's side. With France and Germany on the brink of war, Paul could not return to Europe as he hoped in the autumn of 1914 to start learning diplomatic French and German. This gave George his chance to offer a deal, which he knew that Paul would not refuse.

This was a straightforward business proposition: George proposed to supply Paul with a stake of $10,000 for Paul to seek his fortune in the Oklahoma oil fields as George had done himself eleven years before. George emphasized that this was not a gift, but an investment by Minnehoma, Inc. Any profit would accrue to the company, and Paul would be entitled to a 30 percent commission. Paul agreed.

Conditions had grown tougher than when George arrived at Bartlesville and stumbled into the Oklahoma oil bonanza. Competition had increased, large companies such as Standard Oil were moving in, and it was that much harder for the individual wildcatter to find his plot of oil-rich land, lease the mineral rights, and make his fortune. But since Oklahoma was a massive area, containing one of the largest natural oilfields in the United States, there were still discoveries—and fortunes—to be made by anyone sufficiently determined. George was sure that once Paul had his first real taste of money and success, he had him hooked.

CHAPTER THREE

The First Million Dollars

FOR a young man with a ruthless disposition, a little capital, and a resilient physique, the oil industry was the bargain basement of the twentieth century. Ford would produce its millionth motorcar by the end of 1914, and war in Europe made the demand for oil increase dramatically. Then as the century progressed, America's thirst for oil would go on growing, and the oil industry would inevitably grow with it.

Paul arrived in Tulsa, in the heart of Oklahoma's oil-rich territory, to try his luck in the late autumn of 1914. In his pale gray suit, starched collar, and fedora hat, the soft-spoken Oxford man from California must have been an unlikely figure among the speculators, drillers, engineers, and drifters who thronged the lobby of the newly built Tulsa Hotel.

Despite his manner and appearance, Paul was not as soft and overcivilized as he seemed. At twenty-two he measured five feet ten inches and was extremely strong and conscious of his body. As a loner he had continued his hatred of team sports, but he was obsessive in strengthening his physique. He swam a lot, lifted weights, and practiced judo; around this time he was also confident enough as a boxer to go several rounds with a friend, the future world heavyweight champion Jack Dempsey.

Heavyweights in training often like to take on lighter fighters to improve their speed, and Dempsey's verdict was that Paul was "well built, pugnacious by nature, and quick. I've never met anyone with such intense concentration and willpower—perhaps more than is good for him."

During that winter and the spring of 1915, Paul needed all these qualities as he drove the length of Oklahoma in his battered Ford, searching for the plot of oil-rich land that would make his fortune. He had great determination, spurred on by his desire to match his father's original achievement.

It was nearly a year before he succeeded. In August 1915, after bluffing several other would-be purchasers, he secured his first oil lease for a rock-bottom $500. His luck held. His well on the so-called Nancy Taylor Lease was soon producing over 1,000 barrels daily, and with crude-oil prices reaching $3 a barrel late that autumn, his capital began accruing. Encouraged by success, he started buying further leases, which proved even more productive, and by the summer of 1916, Paul's percentage of the profit he had made for Minnehoma passed the magic figure of $1 million.

He was all of twenty-three—and a millionaire. Convinced that there were more important things in life than oil, he decided to retire.

THIS should have been the moment he was waiting for: the precious time to realize his true ambitions. And but for the war he might have done so, sailed for Europe, and the Getty story would have had a different ending.

War was making Europe inaccessible. Paul always claimed that around this time he volunteered to be a flier, and that while he waited for his papers to arrive (they never did) he had no alternative but to return to South Kingsley Drive.

His old room with its private entrance was awaiting him, crammed with his personal possessions lovingly tended by his mother. Rather to his surprise, he found himself enjoying being home. As he later wrote, "Southern California was an ideal place for anyone seeking to enjoy himself. It had a wonderful climate, spectacular scenery, and then as later, it abounded with exceedingly attractive, largely unattached young women."

It was those "largely unattached young women" who particularly appealed to him, and during the summer of 1916, with a million dollars in the bank, he made the most of their presence. "In my experience," he used to say, "money is the only absolutely certain aphrodisiac"— but a snazzy car also helped, and he bought several in succession: a Cadillac convertible, an early Chrysler, a bright red Duesenberg.

At South Kingsley Drive, with his private key, he came and went exactly as he pleased, and sometimes even brought his women home there for the night. "Rather the 'deep deep bliss of the double bed' at South Kingsley Drive, than the 'hurly-burly' of the backseat of a Duesenberg," as Mrs. Patrick Campbell might have said.

*

GEORGE and Sarah must have known what was going on; according to their own strict principles, their son had now become a hopeless sinner. But had they told him so, they would have run the risk of losing him— and that was something Sarah wouldn't contemplate. So George and Sarah kept their feelings to themselves; Paul continued down the primrose path—and peace and harmony obtained on South Kingsley Drive.

For Paul there was now one all-important factor in this pleasant situation: the fact that he had made himself a millionaire. Thanks to his money he had also made himself completely independent, and George was effectively deprived of any power to tell him what to do. This meant that Paul was able to enjoy his early twenties in a sort of extended spoiled childhood, indulged by his mother, tolerated by his father, and enjoying all the pleasures of a rich and thoroughly emancipated modern adolescent.

This lesson in the moral power of money would have a significant effect on Paul and on his parents. Money effectively removed the moral imperative from everyday existence, and thanks to his money, Paul could live a virtual double life—which clearly suited him. On the one hand, he no longer needed to assert himself against his puritanical papa; nor would he ever cease to be, at least in theory, the devoted only child of "Beloved Mama" either. Never needing to grow up, he would protest his love for them both most touchingly until they died.

At the same time he could also be a sort of licensed puritan, making the most of many things his parents disapproved of—fast cars and faster women, nightclubs and bootleg gin, high life and low company.

As a result, the moral sense of Jean Paul Getty seemed strangely contradictory, and he followed several lines of least resistance—eager for freedom yet anxious for his parents' love, essaying all manner of escapes yet always returning like a wayward child to the house on South Kingsley Drive.

AS a Christian, George was presumably counting on the fact that his son's unedifying life of sin could not go on forever. This was the time for Christian patience. God in his wisdom would surely make his presence felt, just as he did to the Apostle Paul on the Damascus road. Once this happened, his benighted son would see the error of his ways and become reborn in Christ; then George and Sarah could finally rejoice in one more sinner saved.

It was an optimistic theory, and to a point it was correct. Jean Paul's idle, hedonistic life could not continue. Something had to bring it to a close. But when that something happened, it was certainly not what George had bargained for—and Jean Paul failed to react as his parents prayed he would.

The girl's name was Elsie Eckstrom, and she claimed in court that she had been a virgin before Paul plied her with alcohol, drove her home, and forcibly deflowered her at South Kingsley Drive.

Paul's lawyer counterclaimed that Elsie was no virgin but an habitué of roadhouses and nightclubs, who drank and danced and slept around and got no more than she deserved.

The truth about the events is no longer particularly important—but what nobody denied in court was that sexual intercourse took place beneath the parental rafters of the Getty residence on South Kingsley Drive, and that a baby daughter born in 1917 was christened Paula.

After much unwelcome publicity, with banner headlines in the *Los Angeles Times* during September 1917, Paul reluctantly produced $10,000 for Miss Eckstrom and the baby, and the child who was presumably the first offspring of the man destined to become his country's richest citizen vanished from the scene, along with any further scandal. To this day the Getty family has heard no more of her.

What was intriguing was that, as in the Sherlock Holmes story of the dog that didn't bark in the night, there was still no outburst, no disclaimer, no evident reaction from the Getty family. Shortly afterward, however, Paul left his life of idleness in California and returned to work for Minnehoma in the oil fields of Oklahoma.

George Getty could console himself with the thought that his son, although a sinner, was clearly dedicated to the family business and showing extraordinary flair in the oil industry. He had energy and drive and vision, was a tougher businessman than George had ever been, and would make an admirable successor at the head of Minnehoma when George decided to retire.

In fact Paul was already showing signs of taking over as the driving force in Minnehoma. During 1919, he had the idea of extending the company's operations from Oklahoma to the freshly discovered coastal oil fields of California. Initially George was not enthusiastic, but Paul insisted, and Minnehoma's California operation proved highly profitable, more than doubling the capital value of the company. (This in turn led to the restructuring of Minnehoma under the new name of George Getty Oil, Inc.)

Now, too, Paul showed signs of actively enjoying life on the oil fields—learning the skills of the oil engineer, proving himself against the toughest workers on the rigs, boozing and whoring with them in the evenings, and fighting with his fists when necessary. It was a man's life, and this onetime would-be intellectual found himself thoroughly enjoying it. No more was heard of literature or diplomacy. "Nothing," Paul would write, "can adequately describe the emotion and triumph one experiences when he [sic] rings in his first producing well."

Despite this, George was far from happy with his son. Paul had not repented of his trespasses, nor did he show the slightest sign of doing so. George also had his doubts about Paul's probity; he watched Paul taking risks and underwriting deals that he personally would not have sanctioned. There may have been an element of jealousy as well—the professional jealousy of the older man who fears his son displacing him, and the sexual jealousy of the aging puritan who glimpses, in his son's behavior, something of the fun he might have had himself.

For with the end of the war Paul was growing restless, and had started taking longer holidays and traveling abroad—first to Mexico and then to his beloved Europe. It was not hard to imagine what he was doing on his travels, and George and Sarah must have felt that their son's last chance of salvation lay in finding a good wife, settling down in California, and raising a family.

CHAPTER FOUR

Marital Fever

ON emerging from adolescence, young girls possess a special kind of beauty and, though no longer children, are briefly free of the demands that come so swiftly with maturity. It was this fragile, transitory stage of femininity that seems to have excited Jean Paul Getty in his thirties.

Not only did he like young virgins, but being very rich he could afford them. They flattered his ego, kept him young, and were far less exacting in their expectations than were older women. (Living life exactly as he wanted, Paul was never very sympathetic to the emotional demands of others.) An important factor in his sexuality, this taste for Lolita-style nymphets was also a cause of many subsequent dramas and disasters in the family. It led him into five failed marriages, all with women almost young enough to have been his daughters.

The first began in 1923, when at thirty he suddenly proposed to seventeen-year-old Jeanette Dumont, a dark-eyed, half-Polish high school beauty. Acting not unlike an anxious adolescent himself, he kept the romance secret from his parents, and it was not until he and his child bride returned to Los Angeles from a secret wedding at Aventura, Mexico, in October, that he broke the news to them that he was married.

In fact they were delighted, and rapidly became extremely fond of their schoolgirl daughter-in-law. They helped to find the newlyweds an apartment close to South Kingsley Drive, and when Jeanette discovered she was pregnant, they did all they could to make their son feel happy at the prospect of a family.

But a family was the last thing Paul desired. Nor did he desire Jeanette once the virginal bride turned into a pregnant and dependent wife. Far from approaching parenthood with joy, he bucked away, and like the spoiled only child he was, made angry efforts to escape.

With his precious freedom under threat, the aggressive side of Getty's nature—which his old sparring partner Jack Dempsey had noticed—

soon became apparent. Gravid Jeanette was cruelly neglected as he returned to the nightlife of Los Angeles with more responsive partners. When she complained, bitter rows ensued. According to subsequent divorce-court testimony it was now that he yelled at her, "I'm sick and tired of you, sick and tired of being married." According to the same source, he later "beat and bruised her," even threatening to kill her. Then he left her.

But despite these ructions, it was somehow typical of Paul that when the son he didn't want was born, on July 9, 1924, he proudly named him George Franklin Getty II—in honor of his father.

GEORGE meanwhile was far from well. Early in 1923, at the age of sixty-eight, he suffered a major stroke on the Brentwood golf course in Los Angeles. It affected his speech and the right side of his body.

With his father out of action, Paul took charge of the company. Later he would always claim that, due to bad management and the squandering of capital on unprofitable oil leases, George Getty Oil, Inc., was actually running at a loss. But by saying so and trying to increase efficiency, he made few friends among the old guard in the company. When the senior Getty gamely struggled back to work some six weeks later, he was greeted by numerous complaints about "the boy" from old employees, angry at the way they had been treated in his absence.

During his period in charge of the family company, Paul had also been pondering the future—and envisaging George F. Getty Oil, Inc., growing from a relatively simple oil-producing operation into a conglomerate capable of refining and marketing a range of petroleum products for the rapidly expanding U.S. market. This was clearly where the future lay—but it was not what his father or his senior directors wished to hear.

Then, finally, George's gathering resentment turned to anger when, on top of everything, people told of how Paul had been behaving to Jeanette.

"That boy deserves a spanking" was his astonishing reaction. For George could barely shuffle round the office with a stick, let alone administer his burly son a spanking. Which did not keep his rage from increasing even further when he heard that Paul, having summarily walked out on wife and baby, was about to get himself involved in a scandalous divorce.

Even Sarah turned against her son now, confiding to a friend that she seriously believed that Paul had been "taken over by the Devil."

*

FAR from being cured of marriage by Jeanette and all the trouble that had followed, Paul remained firmly in the throes of what he later called "Marital fever." Like an alcoholic on a bender, he was more enthusiastic for the married state than ever.

The truth was that he loved marrying but hated marriage. Marrying was exciting and romantic, but marriage brought the obligations and restrictions of a family, and he had been escaping from obligations and restrictions almost all his life. None of this prevented him from getting firmly entangled once again—even before he was even legally disentangled from Jeanette.

The beginning of 1926 found him back in Mexico in the bright red Duesenberg, hot on the trail of oil concessions in the Gulf of Mexico in the intervals between studying Spanish at the university in Mexico City.

At the university he became involved with two pretty students, Belene and Allene Ashby, daughters of a Texas rancher; amative as ever, he conducted love affairs with both at once. Belene was the prettier, but Allene was just seventeen, and the chance of marrying another nymphet proved too much for the nympholeptic J. Paul Getty.

So that October he and Allene Ashby drove to Cuernavaca in the Duesenberg and married. In his enthusiasm he seems to have overlooked the fact that, since his divorce from Jeanette was still not finalized, he had not only landed in a second marriage, but had also committed bigamy.

Mexico being Mexico, no one mentioned this or seemed to notice. And unlike her predecessor, Allene not only avoided pregnancy, but quickly changed her mind about being Mrs. J. Paul Getty. Paul was developing cold feet too; they parted swiftly, painlessly, and fairly amicably.

But Paul was too well known by now to marry incognito—even in Cuernavaca, Mexico. Somehow the news seeped back to South Kingsley Drive, and early that December George Franklin Getty called his lawyer.

ONE of the qualities George Getty shared with Paul was a marked ability to hide his feelings. During this period, despite his weakened health, he had managed to disguise his anger at his son's behavior, and amity was apparently restored within the Getty family—so much so that after the drama when he left Jeanette, Paul must have felt that he had been forgiven.

But with illness, George's religious views were manifestly hardening.

In 1913 he had already advanced from membership in the Third Church of Christ, Scientist in Los Angeles and joined the worldwide organization of the First Church, in Boston, Massachussetts. Now illness had evidently made him take his church's teachings more seriously than ever, for that autumn he had become a "class-taught student of Christian Science," attending a concentrated two-week instruction course on the message of the church's founder, Mary Baker Eddy. Within the teachings of that formidable lady, George would have discovered the most damning condemnation of his son's behavior.

"Infidelity to the marriage covenant is the social scourge of all races," wrote Eddy. "It is 'the pestilence that walketh in darkness, the destruction that wasteth at noonday.' " And, she added: "The commandment, 'Thou shalt not commit adultery,' is is no less imperative than the one, 'Thou shalt not kill.' "

Strong words. But for the dedicated Christian Scientist there was no evading them.

George must, however, have confined his feelings to his lawyer and himself. Certainly he didn't criticize Paul openly; 1927 started with a seemingly united Getty family, as Paul and his parents happily embarked on a joint holiday to the continent of Europe.

Even in 1927 it was unusual for a twice-married man going on thirty-five years old to take a lengthy European holiday with his aged parents, but despite his philandering, Paul remained as deeply involved with them as ever. He was still the same dutiful, attentive son who had gone on holiday with them before the war, and the unlikely trio seem to have enjoyed themselves. They went to Rome, then traveled on to Switzerland and Paris, staying faithfully at the Hôtel Continentale. As usual, Sarah was happy to be back in Europe, but George's fragile health seems to have forced them into an earlier-than-planned return by transatlantic liner. Being in no hurry to return himself, Paul saw them off, then rented an apartment near the Eiffel Tower and remained in Paris. The loving son had done his bit. The sophisticated man of pleasure could now take over.

One can imagine the relief with which he set about enjoying Europe once he was free to travel, please himself, and follow any passing love affair that caught his fancy. Affairs had become his favorite means of exercise and relaxation, and from Paris he proceeded to Berlin, where the nightlife particularly appealed to him. He had started learning German, and there was no shortage of pretty women willing to help this rich foreigner learn their language.

But business called him back to California. His father was clearly losing his grip on the company, and Paul was needed as a troubleshooter, boosting production from various Getty properties in California. It was demanding work, and George effectively acknowledged this by offering to sell Paul a third of the capital of George F. Getty, Inc., for $1 million. It may have seemed odd for a father to be offering to *sell* his son part of a company he would presumably inherit, but doubtless there were tax advantages involved. Certainly Paul did not seem at all concerned over the arrangement, particularly as George permitted him to pay a quarter of the price in cash and the rest in promissory notes.

With much to do, it was not until early summer that Paul escaped again to Europe. His first stop was Amsterdam, for the 1928 Olympics, where he saw the Finnish runner Paavo Nurmi set a new Olympic record in the 10,000-meter races. Then it was time for rather different games.

Paul had always loved Vienna, but at first he barely recognized it as the city he remembered from before the war. Although the old prosperity had gone, he was reassured to find that, at the Grand Hotel at least, "the service, food, wines and furnishings were as superior as they had been before the war." He was just starting to enjoy them when a fresh attack of matrimonial fever hit him rather badly.

The object was another seventeen-year-old—a striking blue-eyed blonde this time, whom he saw dining with an older couple in the hotel restaurant. Afterward he tried his luck and sent a note inviting her to dinner two nights later. Since she was young and foolish, she accepted.

He soon discovered she was not the fast young woman he expected, but a schoolgirl barely out of a north German convent, who was holidaying with her parents and a friend in Vienna. Her father, Dr. Otto Helmle, was the distinguished head of the Badenwerk industrial complex in Karlsruhe. Her name was Adolphine, but everybody called her Fini.

Paul was now thirty-six, and after many years perfecting the courtship of young girls, he found his methods worked as well as ever. Instead of attempting to disguise his age, he played the sophisticated, sympathetic older man, speaking German with an accent that amused her.

Fini was intrigued. Her admirer was closer to her father's age than hers, but he was so much more polite and cultured than the few boys she had met. Since he was so amusing and attentive, she found it hard to refuse him when he suggested that they meet again. He was persistent—and soon there were other things she found it hard to refuse. They became lovers; when she returned to Karlsruhe he followed. When he spoke of marriage, she insisted he discuss it with her father. And in Fini's father, Jean Paul Getty met serious opposition.

An upright, old-style Catholic who loved his family and exemplified the bourgeois virtues, Dr. Helmle seems to have instantly disliked Paul—and vice versa. Faced with this divorced American who had clearly bewitched his beloved Fini, the Herr Doktor indignantly refused permission for the match. From that point on, the romance became less a love affair between Paul and Fini than a battle of wills between Paul and Dr. Helmle.

True to his nature, Paul set his heart on winning—and finally did so, persuading the infatuated Fini to ignore her father and elope with him to Cuba. In an attempt to save her daughter's reputation, Frau Helmle traveled with her, and Paul and Fini were duly married in December 1928, a few days after his divorce from Allene Ashby became final. From Cuba they went on to Los Angeles, where Paul introduced his latest wife to George and Sarah.

Hoping that Paul was settling down at last, they greeted Fini warmly, and were happy when the couple moved into a nearby apartment.

But just as with Jeanette, the reality of married life started to repel Paul once his wife was pregnant. He was increasingly absent and she was miserable and lonely. Soon she was suffering from morning sickness, then from homesickness. When her parents wrote suggesting she return to Germany to have her baby, Paul did nothing to prevent her going. But neither would he go with her.

Instead, he insisted on going to New York to witness at first hand the aftermath of the Wall Street crash of October 1929. It impressed him deeply as the death knell of a whole financial era. Pondering the future, he left for Germany, reaching Berlin in time to be with Fini when she had their baby. At first he was affectionate to her and it seemed as if the marriage would continue. They called the baby Ronald; for a few days Paul appeared excited by the prospect of a second son.

But not for long. Fini wished to take the child to see her parents back in Karlsruhe. Paul refused to go with her—and there, effectively, the marriage ended. For Dr. Helmle returned to the attack, insisting that his daughter stay in Karlsruhe and file for divorce. Paul made no objection, having found in a Berlin dance hall a pretty girl, whom he moved in to his apartment. But Dr. Helmle proved as tough as his son-in-law; advised by a prominent divorce lawyer, he was soon demanding heavy damages for his daughter.

At this point Paul decided it might be advisable to save the marriage. He had actually begun a fresh reunion with Fini in Montreux when, on April 22, he received news that sent him rushing back to California. George had had a second stroke and was dying.

IT took Paul nine days by train and transatlantic liner to return to South Kingsley Drive. He arrived to find his father just alive, but his deaf mother so distraught that she could only communicate in writing. As a dedicated Christian Scientist, George was refusing to have a doctor, and the sickbed squalor was considerable. This, at least, was something Paul was able to alleviate. He calmed his mother, insisted on summoning a doctor, and then for thirty days kept vigil by the sick man's bed.

George died on May 31, 1930, with Paul and Sarah at his bedside. Both were overcome with grief. It was, wrote Paul, "the heaviest blow, the greatest loss, I had suffered in my life." But worse was to come. The next day, when the will was read, Paul discovered that his father had bequeathed his fortune not to him, but to Sarah.

Control of the all-important Getty oil interests passed to the executors. Paul's son, the three-year-old George F. Getty, Jr., received $350,000. And although Paul was "remembered" with a derisory $250,000, his father had effectively disinherited him.

CHAPTER FIVE

Getty's Secret

AS was to be expected from a man who spent a lifetime developing the inscrutable expression of a Chinese poker player, Paul gave the outside world no sign of the extent of his disaster. Because of this, there has always been a mystery over what he really felt about the way his father treated him.

Outwardly he seemed completely unaffected, behaving almost as if the will had not been written. Since he'd been so close to both his parents, how could anything have altered? Dearest Papa had loved him, and he had loved Papa in return. That was all that mattered, and it could never change.

Two days after George's death Paul devotedly inscribed a note for the press praising his father's virtues. "His loving kindness and great heart, combined with a charming simplicity of manner made George F. Getty the idol of all who knew him. His mental ability was outstanding to the last. I, his son and successor, can only strive to carry on to the best of my ability, the life work of an abler man."

There is no reason to doubt Paul's sincerity in writing this. Forty years later he would still be piously insisting that "the love, respect, and admiration I had for my father were boundless. His death was a blow that only passing years have numbed."

But the "blow" was more than simple grief for somebody he loved. For if nothing else, the will had inflicted a serious financial injury on Paul—and dealt a grave setback to his personal ambitions.

It also came as a complete surprise. Until that moment when the will was read, Paul had been regarding himself as his father's inevitable successor, and with reason. For years he had been helping to enrich the family company. He had initiated some of its most profitable ventures, and even before he bought his third of its capital for $1 million, he had been permitting money that was really due to him to be plowed

37

back into George F. Getty Oil, Inc. He must have counted on the fact that this would all descend to him.

Thus George had inflicted a considerable punishment on his son; and however calm Paul may have seemed in public, it was not in his nature to accept punishment from anyone.

In fact, he was deeply angered at the way he had been treated. Many years later, Getty's then accountant, who was on close terms with him at the time, told the oilman's biographer Ralph Hewins that "when his father died, Paul was swindled and hurt, and has since built up a protective armour." Claus von Bülow, who became Getty's "chief executive," says much the same. He believes that after George's death, Getty spent the rest of his life proving himself against his father's judgment. "Dad was going to eat his words. And when that is your attitude," von Bülow added, "it becomes an obsession."

But why, if Getty had this deep obsession, did he always say how deeply he had loved his father?

DURING the days following George's death, Paul had clearly had to face a fact that he would never publicly admit: that his father had done more than simply disinherit him.

Through all those years of Paul's affairs and broken marriages, father and son had carefully avoided any real confrontation over that most sensitive of subjects, Paul's blatant "immorality." But suddenly pretense was over. In his will George had done what he had never dared do face to face—deliver judgment on his son in the strongest terms at his disposal. Mary Baker Eddy had declared adultery and the breaking of marriage bonds akin to murder. Now, by disinheriting his only son and heir, George was rejecting him as firmly as he might have done a murderer.

For Paul this rejection contradicted the very basis of the wonderfully seductive way of life he'd been perfecting since his early twenties. Thanks to his own precocious fortune, Paul had remained in the condition of a pampered child, immune to criticism and paternal pressure. In his role of spoiled only son he knew that however badly he behaved he could always count upon affection and forgiveness from his parents. But no longer. By disinheriting him, George had made it clear that Paul was not forgiven—which left the son with a serious problem.

His obvious reaction would have been indifference. George was dead; Paul was relatively young and still extremely rich, and he could live his life exactly as he wanted. Why agonize over the judgment of a father now departed?

From someone who appeared so cold and ruthless, indifference is certainly what one might have expected. But George would always mean too much to Paul to be forgotten. "Dearest Papa" would always be the keeper of his conscience.

This left Paul a second possibility: do what his father had clearly wanted him to do; repent, reform, and settle into a godly, moral life like George and Sarah's. But this was equally impossible. Paul was going on forty, far too old to give up all those harmless pleasures that for twenty years had made his life worth living.

But there remained a third solution. If he could reverse his father's judgment, and somehow make him posthumously "eat his words," his problems would be over. He would be free to live exactly as he wanted, travel as he had before, enjoy his women, treat his wives and children as he pleased, and still refuse to settle down.

The only way to do this was to make a fortune large enough to gainsay George's evident belief that Paul's immorality disqualified him from managing the affairs of George F. Getty Oil, Inc. For a conservative Christian like George Getty, godliness was closely linked to creditworthiness, just as making money was a sign of virtue. So Paul could still redeem himself by producing a financial triumph—and this was the origin of that continuing obsession which von Bülow would notice thirty years later. From now on this obsession was to drive him forward until he ended up creating the largest fortune in America.

IT is here that one discerns the uniqueness of Jean Paul Getty both as a businessman and as a human being. By any definition, he was something of a freak, a forbidding combination of relentlessly acquisitive business genius with the emotional development of a sex-starved adolescent.

Henceforth the businessman would operate in overdrive, always attempting to increase that stock of money which would provide the adolescent with his alibi before his parents. As a businessman he possessed formidable resources: originality, strength of will, and an obsessive mastery of detail.

Now all these qualities were ruthlessly applied to the task before him—and it was now that he also really started to enforce strict control over his own expenditure. He had never been lavish with himself—still less with others—but now every petty stinginess held a deeper meaning: to add, however insignificantly, to the all-important pile of wealth and quietly inform the ghostly keeper of his conscience that he was not the immoral profligate his father had rejected.

Similarly, any personal acquisition was decided henceforth strictly on a profit basis. As a strict Christian, George F. Getty had been a dedicated self-denier, so Paul set out to beat him here as well. He would permit himself no self-indulgence in the purchase of a place to live, a work of art, even a piece of furniture, unless he could convince himself that it would appreciate in value.

The result was a strangely dedicated life, with everything in it geared to one overriding purpose: the accumulation of ever larger quantities of capital. For then and only then could the adolescent in Paul be permitted to continue as he had before Papa's demise—pursuing his teenage girls, refusing to shoulder any real responsibility as husband or as father, always on the move, and always able to believe that he could count on his parents' love behind him.

AS a recipe for happy living, Jean Paul Getty's system left a lot to be desired, but as far as business was concerned, his quaint psychology became a real source of strength, soon setting him apart from the happy ranks of other massively successful multimillionaires. For past a certain point, the makers of all large fortunes face the problem of maintaining motivation. Why continue? Why bother with acquiring yet more money when one has all the impressionist paintings, private jets, and Park Lane mansions one can live with?

There inevitably comes a point where even the most driven wealth-acquirer needs some extra motive to continue—like buying political power, creating an art collection, building a great ancestral home, or even, if all else fails, using the money for philanthropy.

That mordant critic of the social scene, the economist Thorstein Veblen, in his classic *Theory of the Leisure Class*, invented a term for the way the great nineteenth-century American nouveaux riches like the Vanderbilts and Rockefellers employed their surplus wealth in competitive display. He called it "conspicuous consumption": the building of great Rhode Island mansions, which they barely used; the throwing of massive parties, which none but the hideously rich could equal. Driven by such sumptuary competition, they sometimes reached the point Veblen identified as "conspicuous waste": the spending of very large amounts of money simply to defeat their rivals in a war of pointless ostentation.

Such problems never troubled Jean Paul Getty. Far from requiring any outside interests, he had a perfect built-in system of obsessive motivation. Far from ever getting bored with money, he was more profoundly satisfied the more of it he had. He would have regarded conspicuous consumption as unthinkable, conspicuous waste a gross obscenity.

He personally required none of the outward trappings of success. On the contrary, he wanted privacy and quiet to enjoy the solitary game that he was playing. Just as he had no need for others to envy or applaud him, so he felt no obligation to share any of his winnings with the multitude. He was completely self-obsessed and self-sustaining. All he required to ensure that his father ate his words was money— and as much of it as possible. As long as he could go on making it, he could live his life exactly as he wanted. As long as he could make his father's ghost stay silent, his money would have served its most important purpose.

CHAPTER SIX

Maternal Trust

WHEN the directors of George F. Getty Oil made Paul their president, they did so in the evident belief that as a minority shareholder, owning only a third of the capital, he would have no power to make serious decisions. Thanks to George's will, the head of the company, with two thirds of the capital, was eighty years of age, stone deaf, overweight, and lonely—his mother, Sarah.

Luckily for Paul she loved him dearly—and he did his best to ensure that her love continued. She still called him "Dearest Child," and he referred to her as "Beloved Mama." Twice and sometimes thrice a week he used to call at the house on South Kingsley Drive to take her out. By now she could barely walk. An elevator had been installed to get her to her bedroom, and she required a servant on each arm to reach his Cadillac. Sometimes he drove her through the foothills of the Santa Monica hills, but what she really liked was to feed the sea lions that still basked along the beach at Malibu. It must have been a strange sight: sea lions barking from the water's edge, overweight widow dressed in black, and neatly suited middle-aged son throwing herrings to the beasts at her direction.

But still stranger must have been their conversation. For the sea lions offered Paul his finest chance to influence his mother and persuade her to transfer her power in the company to him.

There must have been a strong temptation for a tired old lady to agree. After all, she had had little experience of business. She was very lame and old, and Paul could be remarkably persuasive.

But Sarah had always been obstinate, and despite Paul's arguments, something held her back. In the first place she believed that George's wishes ought to be respected. Since he had seen fit to place her in this position of responsibility, she had a duty to accept it. Second, she knew her son. She loved him dearly. He was all she had, but she also knew how rash and harebrained he could be, and during such dangerous economic times as the early thirties, wildness could lead a company like Getty to disaster.

Worse still, if she understood him properly, Paul was suggesting the complete reversal of much that dear Papa had stood for. Papa had built the company by discovering oil, buying leases on the land it lay in, and then producing it. He was an oilman, not a smart financier, and he believed in sticking to the things the company did best. He had always had an honest Christian dread of debt. She could hear him now: "The last thing to do is borrow. The first thing to do is always to repay your debts."

It was over this that Sarah's arguments with Paul invariably began. Paul had set his heart on expansion, on extending the company into every branch of the oil business—refining, marketing, and finally creating a network of gasoline stations selling Getty products nationwide. When she asked him where the money was to come from, he replied that the company had capital in reserve, and he was perfectly prepared to borrow, too, if necessary. He had even coined a motto of his own, which he repeated when she mentioned his father's fear of debt. "Buy when everyone else is selling, and hold on until everyone else is buying."

In fact, Paul was convinced that the Wall Street crash of 1929, far from being a dire warning, was actually offering George F. Getty Oil the chance of a lifetime by changing the economic landscape of the industry. Since oil shares on the New York Stock Exchange had plummeted, now was the time to buy, thus picking up oil reserves at bargain prices through their undervalued shares.

For Paul this seemed more sensible than developing fresh oil fields as he himself had been doing in the past. It also offered an unrivaled opportunity to achieve his great ambition. By carefully acquiring shares in publicly quoted oil companies, he could slowly gain control of them. Some were highly vulnerable, and he had his strategy worked out for the companies he wanted. It was time to act before the bargains vanished.

When he explained this to his mother she sometimes became extremely agitated, but he knew exactly how to calm her down.

"Times change, and this is what dear Papa would do himself if he was here," he'd tell her.

Sarah would usually end by agreeing—but she was never totally convinced that he was right.

DURING the next three years, Paul pursued his strategy of acquisition with the energy and skill of a raiding general bent on plunder. Anxious

as ever to disprove his father, he became a most adroit financier. He
was patient, fearless, and extremely sharp, but behind each operation
lay the thoroughness with which he made his preparations. Everything
was checked and rechecked. Nothing was left to chance.

Even so, his first big stock deal ended in disaster. In September 1930
he finally persuaded a reluctant Sarah to agree to borrow from the
Security-First National Bank for the purchase of $3 million worth of
stock in Mexican Seaboard, a California company with leases in the oil-
rich Kettleman Hills whose shares he considered undervalued.

After the deal, Paul had to leave on a hurried trip to Europe and so
couldn't stop the panic when the shares continued dropping. Had he
been present, he would have urged his directors to sit tight—as they
should have done—but in his absence the bank insisted on selling the
shares to repay the loan before they sank still further, and thus lost
practically $1 million. On his return, Paul found the boardroom atmo-
sphere "decidedly chilly," as he put it, adding that at least "Mother was
vindicated."

This was the nearest Paul ever came to real disaster. It was a sobering
lesson, reminding him that to fail now would mean losing everything,
proving that his father had been right. He had no alternative but to
continue, even if this meant risking every penny he possessed and
calling on any source of credit he could muster.

Typically, instead of playing safe, at this moment he raised the stakes.
Using all his energy and everything he owned, he started bidding for
Pacific Western, one of California's biggest oil producers, whose shares
had fallen in the last twelve months from $17 to $3.

This time he succeeded. By the end of 1931 he was nearly bankrupt,
but he was also firmly in control of Pacific Western. His plans were
working. Next on his plan of battle was America's ninth-largest oil
company, the $200 million Tide Water Associated Oil Company. To
take it was a daunting proposition for a small unknown outsider, but
he needed something big to justify himself against his father, even if
this brought him into conflict with his mother.

To begin with, she was acquiescent, and he was able to sell off George
F. Getty Oil's San Joaquin Valley oil field for $4.5 million without
excessive opposition. This sum was to be the war chest with which he
financed his campaign.

By March 1932 Tide Water stock had slumped to a record low of
$2.50 a share. But Paul knew that overhasty buying could raise the
share price and alert the Tide Water management to the threat he
represented. It was time for stealth—one quality he had never lacked.
By the end of March Paul had somehow acquired a significant holding

in Tide Water without any one in the company knowing who he was, or being any the wiser.

DURING this period following his father's death, Paul's financial situation remained closely tied in with his private life. Had he lost his nerve, as well as that million dollars on the Mexican Seaboard deal, he would have been tacitly admitting that his father had been right to disinherit him. But since he had such faith in his own future, and since his plans were steadily maturing, he had no need to worry over any criticism from the grave on the subject of his "immorality."

As a result, the period following his father's death saw Paul as sexually adventurous as ever, and finally hit by a fresh attack of his old affliction: marital fever.

This time the cause was slightly older than before. But although Ann Rork was all of twenty-one when Paul became involved with her in the autumn of 1930, she had barely changed from the dimpled nymphet of fourteen he had attempted to seduce some eight years earlier. She must have been a precocious adolescent, for Paul had been taking her to bars and nightclubs even then—until angrily warned off by Sam Rork, Ann's anxious father, who had heard about Paul Getty's reputation.

Rork himself was an old-time Hollywood producer, faintly famous as the discoverer of that star of silent movies, Clara Bow the original "vamp." He adored his quick-tongued daughter and encouraged her ambition to become a star by giving her the juvenile lead in *The Blonde Saint*, a forgettable romantic drama starring the matinee idol Gilbert Roland. But by 1930, Rork, who was badly hit by the Great Depression, was more amenable when his daughter's multimillionaire admirer started calling her again—even if he was now thirty-seven, with three failed marriages behind him.

Paul had to break off the romance in the autumn of 1930 to get to Germany as fast as possible in order to contest the divorce from Fini. Since her father's lawyers in Berlin were still trying to extract punitive damages, Paul was determined to appear in court in person, but his appearance made little difference. Dr. Helmle was as difficult as possible. His detectives produced fresh evidence of yet another woman's living with Paul during his period in Berlin; unable to get the settlement he wanted, Dr. Helmle got the case postponed until such time as Paul agreed. As Paul would not agree, he had no alternative but to return to America still legally encumbered with Fini as his wife.

So marriage had to wait as far as dark-eyed, baby-faced Ann Rork was concerned. Not that it seemed to matter deeply. Ann was grateful to her rich protector, and since he insisted that he loved her, she was perfectly prepared to wait.

In August 1931, Paul moved her into an apartment in the New York Plaza Hotel and, telling her that he'd like to marry her, asked her if she felt the same. When she nodded, he said, "Fine. Then we'll get married here. Since we love each other we don't need anybody else, nor do we need a license or a ceremony."

And that, it seems, was that. Many years later Ann told Getty's biographer Robert Lenzner, "I really thought that Paul was God. His knowledge was so awesome. He was," she added, "my first lover, and a very considerate one at that. I was introduced properly. And I certainly hope I pleased him."

It seems as if she did, for the next few months saw them very much together, first in Germany and then, early in 1932, in Paris, where they stayed in Paul's old bachelor apartment near the Eiffel Tower. But as soon as Ann discovered she was pregnant, the idyll ended, and Paul behaved as he always did at the prospect of a family.

Four years later, Ann's divorce court testimony would catalogue grievances identical to those of all his wives: neglect, abuse, and the times he left her to go out with other women. She claimed that once she was so unhappy that she even tried to kill herself by swallowing iodine, which burned her throat, but otherwise failed to harm her.

As the unhappy lovers still weren't married, except in the eyes of J. Paul Getty's private deity, the relationship would presumably have ended there and then but for the child Ann was carrying. For though he hated families, Paul still had a superstitious sense of the importance of his offspring. Not that this meant that he possessed the faintest glimmerings of parental feeling or a minimal desire to have his children near him. He emphatically did not. But on a recent visit to San Simeon, William Randolph Hearst had lectured him on his responsibility to father several heirs to make a dynasty. Paul liked the idea of a dynasty, and Hearst's words appear to have impressed him.

There were problems, however. An heir needed to be born in wedlock, and although he was perfectly prepared to marry Ann, he was still legally joined to Fini, and getting old for a second bout of bigamy.

As summer ended Paul and Ann were on holiday in Italy, she heavily pregnant, he compulsively unfaithful. In Rome he was off to nightclubs, and in Naples he dragged her, puffing and protesting, to the very crater of Vesuvius. Then it was back by ship to Genoa; the ship was still at sea on September 7, when Ann presented her lover with his third son. When the ship called at the port of La Spezia, the baby, premature and extremely small, was registered as Eugene Paul Getty.

PAUL and Ann returned to California with the baby, taking an apartment in the hills of Santa Monica. At first Paul was wary of introducing Ann to Sarah as his wife, partly because she wasn't and partly because Fini had been Sarah's favorite. Paul's divorce from Fini had not been finalized until that August. Paul was ordered to pay heavy damages and Fini was given custody of two year-old Ronald, who would spend the next few years with her in Switzerland. Paul was deeply resentful over what he thought a grave injustice and a dreadful waste of money, and he would never forgive Dr. Helmle—nor forget what happened.

But at least the divorce meant that he and Ann could now legitimize their child by marrying, which they did in Paul's favorite marital rendezvous of Cuernevaca, in December 1932. This also meant that Ann was finally allowed to meet Sarah.

Understandably perhaps, the two women never cared for each other, and in later years Ann blamed Sarah for the breakup of her marriage. But in the meantime, Paul had done what he'd never done before. He had bought himself a beach house facing the sea at Malibu, where he and his young family could all live happily together—except that they didn't. Paul was as firmly bound as ever to his mother, and still kept clothes and possessions in his room at South Kingsley Drive; he also kept a love nest in Santa Monica where he took his women. Ann felt lonely and neglected as she watched the ocean.

"Since you're so rich, why do you have to work?" she asked him—a question he didn't deign to answer. By the time their second son, Gordon, was born in December 1933, they were barely speaking to each other. Legend has it that Paul arrived at the hospital to see his wife and newborn child, glanced at the baby, muttered, "Uh-huh, it looks like you," and rapidly departed.

HE had more important things to think about than babies, being obsessively involved by now in one thing and one thing only: the battle for Tide Water Associated. This ailing giant was a seemingly impossible prize for an isolated aggressor like Paul to conquer, and as he pursued it he displayed qualities that account for much of his subsequent success— total concentration, mastery of detail in the complicated deals involved, a love of risk, and a cool ability to exploit any opportunity that worked to his advantage. He was still pursuing his strange solitary game, which only someone with an absolute obsession had any hope of winning.

He knew that to win he had to have the one thing his father had purposely denied him: full financial control of George F. Getty Oil. Not until he had all Sarah's capital in addition to his own could he borrow on the scale he needed. If this had to lead to further battles with "dearest Mama," so be it.

Now it took more than visits to the sea lions to convince her, and she fought a long delaying action. Finally he won by endless argument, and as a Christmas present at the end of 1933, she almost gave him what he wanted. As a negotiator she was quite his equal; in a deal which she specified would terminate "if not accepted by you in writing on or before noon of 30 December" she offered to sell Paul her two-thirds interest in the family company in return for promissory notes for the purchase price of $4.6 million, bearing a fixed income of 3.5 percent a year.

This income from her son was to be her widow's pension, and as a sweetener she offered Paul a timely Christmas present for himself: an additional gift of $850,000 if he accepted. Businesslike as ever, she signed her offer, "Yours very sincerely, Sarah C. Getty."

He had no alternative, for by now his fight for Tide Water was in the open, and he was up against an equally determined enemy: the massive Standard Oil Company of New Jersey, which was already the major shareholder in Tide Water. But once again Paul was lucky. Federal antitrust legislation was making Standard disburse its shares, which it was placing in a brand-new company, the Mission Corporation.

In this multimillion-dollar game of chess, Paul's next move was obviously to purchase as many Mission shares as possible, thereby boosting his holding in Tide Water. But once again he found himself placed in check by his mother.

He was still unable to convince her of the wisdom of having George Getty Oil, Inc., buy Tide Water stock, and since she owned promissory notes from Paul for $4.5 million, she could effectively block the purchase. For as Paul rapidly discovered, no bank would lend him on the scale he wanted once it learned that he was $4.5 million in the red—even to his mother.

So the last round started in this curious contest between "beloved Mama" and her "dearest child." To continue buying into the Mission Corporation, Paul needed Sarah to liquidate his debt. As he reminded her, she had no need of the $140,000 he was paying her each year in interest, since her annual expenses never topped $30,000.

She seems to have agreed, but then, like the smart negotiator she was, she switched the argument. What she was really most concerned about, she said, was not herself but future generations of the Gettys. Paul might be right. Time would tell. But when Papa had left her all his money, he was really leaving it in trust for the grandchildren, and for all the unborn Gettys to come after. She couldn't bear to think that by letting Paul have his way, she might be depriving future generations of their patrimony.

She had clearly discussed this with her lawyers, for her solution to the problem was ingenious. She would set up an irrevocable spendthrift trust to protect the interests of Paul's children against the possible results of his business speculation and would contribute an initial $2.5 million from her own resources. By placing the family capital in a trust, the money would be protected against Paul's supposed spendthrift tendencies, and also against his own possible bankruptcy.

Paul agreed, contributing some overvalued shares he owned in George F. Getty Oil so that the trust could begin at the end of 1934 with a capital of $3.368 million. This was the start of the famous Sarah C. Getty Trust, which would dominate the family finances for many years to come.

Financially the arrangement suited Paul extremely well, since he was appointed principal trustee with absolute power to use the trust's capital according to his judgment for any transaction which involved the family's oil interests, such as acquiring further shares in the Mission Corporation or Tide Water. The trust also suited Sarah, since it satisfied her conscience over her duty to the family fortune and her otherwise unprotected grandchildren.

As far as the beneficiaries of the trust were concerned the terms were simple. To satisfy Sarah's primary concern that her son should meet his duties as a father, it made suitable provision for Ann and for Paul's four children, ten-year-old George Junior, four-year-old Ronald, two-year-old Paul Junior, and one-year-old Gordon. For as long as she remained legally married to Paul, Ann was to receive 10 percent of the trust's income annually, but payments to the children were unequal. During 1934, the $21,000 of the trust's income remaining after Ann had been paid was shared out as follows: Paul Junior and Gordon were each paid $9,000; George II was paid nothing, because he had already benefited from the $300,000 legacy from his grandfather, the late George Getty; and Ronald's portion was limited to $3,000.

This disadvantage was placed on Ronald apparently because his father convinced Sarah that Ronald would be receiving substantial money from the will of his maternal grandfather, Dr. Helmle. The disadvantage would weigh heavily on him in the future, once the trust itself increased dramatically in value. For a further condition was that if the trust earned more than $21,000 a year George, Paul Junior, and Gordon were to share equally in the excess. Ronald was specifically excluded from any further income from the trust beyond his annual $3,000.

A further important clause, which was to cause some trouble in the years ahead, laid down that Paul, as principal trustee, was to have effective control of how all future payments should be made, either in the form of cash dividends, or as further shares within the trust.

As for the future beneficiaries of the trust, his as yet unborn grandchildren, he and Sarah wanted to ensure that they should earn their own livings before inheriting from the trust. It was stated that not until the last of Paul's four boys was dead were the grandchildren as a group to inherit their share of the capital. Although Ronald's inheritance was so strictly limited, there were no such limitations on his children, who would be treated exactly as their cousins.

As it turned out, the founding of the Sarah Getty Trust was an historic moment for the Gettys. For the trust rapidly became a crucial factor in their whole financial future—by becoming the effective guardian of the family's rapidly expanding fortune. What no one, Paul included, seems to have realized at first, was the remorseless way the legendary trust would grow. Not only would it provide its principal trustee with precisely what he needed—a source of capital to use as and when required for his business acquisitions. It was also perfectly adapted to his obsession to amass ever larger sums of money for his family to satisfy his conscience.

By limiting all payments from the trust to share dividends and taking nothing out of it himself, this "spendthrift trust" became the ideal way to accumulate the great fortune he had set his heart on. Proof against taxation, bankruptcy and personal extravagance, the trust named after Jean Paul Getty's mother would help create the greatest fortune in America.

CHAPTER SEVEN

Boom Time

HOWEVER tough the thirties were on America and the world in general, they were unusually kind to Jean Paul Getty. Just as the death of his father in 1930 made him dedicate himself afresh to making money, so the creation of the Sarah C. Getty Trust and his acquisition of full control of the family businesses meant that his campaign to capture the Tide Water Oil Company could start in earnest.

On the face of it Paul's chances of success seemed slim. In 1935 Tide Water had a turnover approaching $100 million, against the $1.5 million of George F. Getty Oil, and by now Tide Water's management, thoroughly aware of the threat Paul represented, was firmly set to block him.

But Paul had the advantages of the small, determined operator: speed, surprise, and the challenge of a personal encounter. And the creation of the Sarah C. Getty Trust had given him the financial weapon he needed. He was banned from using the trust to borrow money, but as its sole trustee was otherwise completely free to use its assets to acquire any oil shares he wanted.

Like some modern takeover tycoon, he wanted Tide Water complete with all its assets—refineries, storage capacity, and the marketing network through which he hoped to sell his own oil products. In taking over Tide Water lay his best hope of acquiring the full-scale oil operation he had set his heart on.

Early in the battle, he shrewdly recruited David Hecht, a smart young corporate lawyer, and with Hecht beside him steadily wheeled and dealed his way toward acquiring the crucial shares he needed. He had his strokes of luck, such as the 1935–36 New Year's Eve party with Randolph Hearst, at which he heard that the Rockefellers were disposing of a 20 percent holding in Mission; with Hecht's help, Paul promptly snapped them up. But for the most part, acquisition was a painstaking, concentrated labor, which only somebody as driven and as dedicated as he could have accomplished.

He worked inexorably; by 1936, when he had built up sufficient equity within the Mission Corporation to give him a 25 percent holding in Tide Water, the financial equivalent of trench warfare started between him and Tide Water's directors. With his single-mindedness this was something Paul was good at, and by the outbreak of war in 1939 he had practically succeeded.

For by then the long-awaited upswing in the oil industry had come. U.S. automobile ownership, and with it gasoline consumption, had in fact begun to rise as early as 1936, despite the Great Depression, so that the Tide Water shares Paul had bought for $2.50 at the bottom of the market in 1930, stood at $17 by 1938.

It was a spectacular advance, and it meant that as well as bringing him so near to controlling Tide Water, Paul's share-buying operations had made him very rich indeed. By 1938, his personal fortune stood at $12 million and, true to his promise to his mother, he had made the Sarah Getty Trust richer still. The trust, which had begun with $3.5 million in 1934, was now worth $18 million, all of which would one day go to members of his family.

THIS money in the Sarah C. Getty Trust was the core of the massive fortune he still needed to create if he was truly to make George eat his words. An important part of Paul's financial strategy was to plow all profits back into the trust itself, thus ensuring that its capital steadily increased, untouched by spending or taxation. This was what Mama had wanted, and since the capital within the trust would benefit his children and his children's children yet unborn, he could argue that the money more than justified him now against any criticism of his way of life.

For the trust itself had become his excuse to live the life he wanted, at a time when he was becoming more opposed than ever to family ties, which he saw as a dreadful obstacle to his success. Even in old age he was still insisting that life as an ordinary husband would have held him back and stopped him from succeeding, since a family would have diverted his attention, squandered his precious time, and sapped his concentration. As he put it in a moment of extreme exasperation, "A lasting relationship with a woman is only possible if you're a business failure."

But if Getty couldn't offer his wives and children his presence or his love, success in business enabled him to give them something he considered more important: large amounts of money for the future. With so much money safely in the trust, he was free to turn his full attention to perfecting his extraordinary existence.

He was still driven by two overwhelming urges—for sexual adventures, preferably abroad, and for acquiring very large amounts of money. To combine successfully these two activities, he needed to devise a way of managing his business interests, which included the day-to-day running of George F. Getty Oil and the battle for Tide Water during his lengthy periods in Europe.

Since he loved anonymity and much of his pleasure in traveling abroad was frankly sexual, the last thing Getty required around him was a staff of executives and aides. These were consigned to the Getty offices in Los Angeles, and he taught himself to operate alone or with a single secretary, storing in his head whatever information he needed. He believed that business wasted too much time on paperwork, committees, and discussions anyhow. Forgetting nothing, and delegating what was inessential, he became a great exponent of the role of capitalist as self-sufficient one-man band, making the most minute decisions with a minimum of red tape and bureaucracy.

Victor Hugo once called Alfred Nobel, the inventor of dynamite, who also loved living in hotels and hated families, "the vagabond billionaire of Europe." Getty, who was much the same, was fast becoming Nobel's successor.

His favored method of replying to a letter was to scribble a reply in the margin and mail it back in the readdressed envelope it came in. He had a particular obsession with saving stationery, particularly expensive manila envelopes, which he always kept and carefully re-used. Any documents he needed stayed in the old-fashioned steamer trunk that accompanied him everywhere. And a crucial item in his business armory was the small black book which never left him, containing the telephone numbers not only of his countless girlfriends, but also of key business contacts around the world through whom he personally conducted all his business.

For the crucial object without which his way of life could not have functioned was the telephone; and as transatlantic telephone service steadily improved throughout the thirties, so did the length of time Paul spent in Europe. It was the telephone that would finally enable him to leave America forever.

As long as the transatlantic lines from Europe to America were open, Getty was fully operational, whatever else he happened to be doing at the time. The eight-hour time gap between Europe and California was in his favor, allowing him to meet a woman, feed her, enjoy her, and be on the telephone again before the Los Angeles offices closed for the evening.

In combining this highly programmed life of pleasure with an otherwise puritanical existence, he was not as hypocritical as he sounds. Promiscuous sex, he would have argued, was nowhere near as bad for a businessman as the marital variety. It took up far less time, cost less, was infinitely less demanding, and actually added to one's financial prowess. As he put it once, "Business success generates a sexual drive, and sexual drive pushes business."

The point was that for Getty, money and success remained the surest proof of virtue; true to the very rigid rules by which he led his life, he was never profligate or rash in any of his personal behavior.

He was compelled to live in good hotels during his periods abroad, but this was principally because only good hotels had reliable telephone switchboards. And even in his favorite hotel, the George V in Paris, he always made a point of bargaining for the the cheapest suite available. He wasted nothing, ate economically, and recorded every cab fare in his diary. He could fornicate, but not be profligate.

Sex helped business, which in turn brought yet more conscience money into the sacred coffers of the Sarah Getty Trust.

UNSURPRISINGLY in these circumstances, his fourth marriage now collapsed like all the others, the only difference being that Ann Rork Getty was a tougher proposition than her predecessors. In this garrulous would-be actress, Paul had more than met his equal in the marriage stakes.

She would marry four times herself; and even first time around she made it clear that she had no intention of enduring her husband's philandering and bullying forever. She was gregarious and popular, and instead of gazing sadly from the beach house at the ocean was soon inviting friends from Hollywood to come and see her. So when Paul did come home, it was often to face a houseful of his wife's guests, who treated him with scant respect. Sometimes he even heard them encouraging Ann behind his back.

"He should give you a Rolls, darling."

"He should dress you in sables instead of mink."

Unable to cope with such behavior, he stayed away more than ever. After one particularly lengthy absence, one of Ann's friends from Hollywood introduced her to the toughest lawyer in town, who opened proceedings in what Getty called "an unusually noisome divorce." "Noisome" was Getty's word for being publicly taken to the cleaners.

Whatever her failings as an actress on the screen, Ann Rork Getty was a star in the witness box, and she made the most of the horror tale of courtship and marriage with J. Paul Getty—her suicide attempts, his behavior on the crater of Vesuvius, and his unorthodox notions of the role of a father and a husband.

As she began by suing for a portion of his fortune, he was lucky that the massive divorce settlements of the present-day state of California hadn't started. As it was she caused him much worry and annoyance before finally agreeing to what she termed "a beautiful settlement" of $2,500 a month, plus $1,000 monthly for each of the two children.

Although he was now the father of four young sons, he showed not the faintest interest in any of them; and with the Los Angeles newspapers feasting on the lurid details of his divorce, he decided to escape to New York before continuing abroad. Thanks to his god, the telephone, his affairs could be conducted just as well from there as from Los Angeles, and with the money he was now amassing, he felt justified in taking one of the smartest addresses in the city.

IT would be wrong to think that Getty's freshly acquired wealth made no difference to his way of life. In fact, a number of important changes in his behavior now occurred. But all of them were governed by two crucial principles: They were not to affect his balance sheets, and they would not deflect him from the great financial game that he was playing. Otherwise he seemed quite anxious to upgrade his life in keeping with his earnings.

In New York he moved to a street that by a strange coincidence had the same name as the Tudor mansion where he would end his days: Sutton Place. But instead of purchasing an apartment on this fashionable New York block beside the East River, he preferred to rent—rent was tax deductible and could be paid by the oil company. Also, the apartment appealed to snobbish elements within his nature, being owned by the wife of Winston Churchill's cousin, the former heiress Amy Phipps, now married to the Honourable Freddie Guest.

Mrs. Guest's eighteenth-century paintings and French furniture also appealed to Paul—enough to make him think about collecting on his own account, which in fact he did, starting to buy with considerable knowledge and success. Businesslike as ever, by reading and by visiting museums he made himself a considerable expert on French eighteenth-century furniture. As he realized, the depression had forced it down in value, and he was able to purchase a number of important pieces at knockdown prices.

This would become the principle behind almost all his subsequent collecting. Whatever it was, anything he bought had to be a bargain, for only with a bargain could he convince himself he wasn't wasting money. This applied to almost everything he bought, from his socks (for which he refused to pay more than $1.50 a pair) to perhaps the biggest single bargain of this period—the Pierre Hotel, on the corner of Fifth Avenue and Sixty-first Street, facing Central Park. When built in 1930, as New York's most exclusive luxury hotel, it had cost more than $6 million. Getty bought it for $2.35 million, and he bought it for the simple reason that it was such a bargain.

ONE realm in which Paul's social aspirations showed around this period was sex. With marital fever once more in the air, it was quite in character for him to start courting Louise "Teddy" Lynch, a buxom twenty-three-year-old nightclub singer. But Miss Lynch was no ordinary nightclub singer. Another Churchill connection, the financier Bernard Baruch, was her uncle; Teddy herself had serious ambitions as an opera singer.

As for Paul, the prestige of having such a chic fiancée must have made him contemplate matrimony again, for he took unusual care to court Teddy's mother, who didn't object to having this four times married, forty-four-year-old as a potential son-in-law. But neither Paul nor Teddy seemed in a hurry to get married after the engagement was announced at the end of 1936.

She was an independent young woman who wanted to perfect her singing, and as long as he would pay for her singing lessons, she seemed perfectly content to treat him rather as an avuncular figure, without making great demands upon his time or his fidelity.

This was exactly what he wanted, and his engagement didn't interfere with his womanizing forays to Europe. While he was pursuing Helga and Trudi and Gretchen in Berlin, Teddy would be taking singing lessons back in London. Despite the trouble over Fini, Paul retained his love of Berlin, which he, like many foreigners in this period, treated as his brothel.

Like many foreign businessmen, Paul also had a fairly uncritical attitude toward the Nazis, frankly admiring the efficiency with which they seemed to run the country. He was not an active Nazi sympathizer, but he might all too easily have become involved with them in ways that could have been uncomfortable for his future, had Teddy not diverted his interest and attention to a slightly safer country. In 1939 she wished to study singing in Italy and, tolerant as ever, Paul accompanied her to Rome. It was a strange episode in both their lives. Intent for once on keeping up appearances, Paul suggested that they stayed in separate hotels; while she sang, he conscientiously visited Rome's ruins and museums.

It was during this period that Paul first became infatuated both with Rome and with fascist Italy. One evening he took Teddy to hear *Rigoletto*, and was excited to see Mussolini in the audience. "The greatest son of Italy since the Emperor Augustus," Paul wrote in his diary that evening.

However much he admired Mussolini, he was becoming highly concerned now about the effect of war on his personal safety, and was anxious to return to America. Teddy was equally anxious to continue singing. Neither would budge an inch, and the result was the curious compromise of Paul's fifth and final marriage.

At midday on November 17, 1939, he and Teddy met before the mayor of Rome in the historic Campidoglio, the Roman Capitol, and were made man and wife. Afterward they lunched quietly at the Ambassador Hotel, then said good-bye. Instead of waiting to consummate the marriage, Paul had to catch the afternoon train to Naples, where he boarded the luxury liner, the *Conte di Savoia* for New York. Teddy remained in Rome.

CHAPTER EIGHT

War and the Neutral Zone

AMERICA'S entry into the war in 1941 had a strange effect on Jean Paul Getty. Although he was nearing fifty, he wrote like a schoolboy in his diary about doing his duty so that "dearest Mama and Papa can be proud of me." But with age he had been growing increasingly fearful for his safety, and what he had seen in Europe had made him obsessed with the power of Nazi Germany.

He volunteered for active service with the U.S. Navy but, as he must have known, was too old to be accepted. Once rejected, he then made an extraordinary compromise between doing his bit and staying as far as possible from danger for the war's duration.

One of the incidental assets of the Mission Corporation, which he now controlled, was the small, half-moribund Spartan Aircraft Company of Tulsa, Oklahoma. Manufacturing aircraft for the war effort was a patriotic occupation, Tulsa was familiar territory, and if anywhere was safe from the German Luftwaffe during the Second World War it had to be Oklahoma.

Even so, when Paul took personal command of Spartan Aircraft, he treated it like some perilous wartime posting, and built himself a four-room bomb-proof concrete bunker by the factory. It was here that he lived and from here that he personally directed Spartan Aircraft from 1942 until the war was over.

He was, in fact, a great success. As much the workaholic as ever, he proved an exceptional factory manager, driving the workforce hard, working late himself on any problem, and getting Spartan to produce an excellent single-engine trainer for the U.S. Army Air Forces. So eager was he for what he felt would be his parents' approbation that he spent almost all his time in Tulsa, and when at the end of 1941 Sarah Getty, finally expired at the age of eighty-nine, his diary entry might have been a young boy's lamentation for his youthful mother:

"Last night, gently and sweetly, my dearest dearest Mummy passed away."

Around the same time, as if in compensation for the loss of his mother, Paul's adventurous wife, Teddy, finally returned from Italy, where she had been interned near Siena. Neither she nor her husband seems to have pined unduly for the other, but they did achieve their long-postponed nuptial night together. Anxious to resume her career as a singer, Teddy was still no clinging vine, although she would have liked a modicum of married life; but when she presented Paul with his fifth son, christened Timothy, in 1946, her husband still opted for duty back in Tulsa rather than married life with Teddy.

Timmy proved an ailing infant. "Poor poor Timmy" was how Paul wrote about him at his birth. And throughout his short life, Timmy suffered dreadfully, at the age of six developing a brain tumor, which required protracted surgery. But although he always said how moved he was by "sad little Timmy," Paul seemed as incapable as ever of coping with personal unhappiness—or married life. Teddy often urged that all three of them should live together as a family, but Paul stayed in Tulsa, relying for relief on waitresses, shopgirls, call girls—anything to save him from the dreaded tentacles of marriage.

By the time the war ended, something had clearly happened to him. Perhaps it was the onset of the male menopause. Some believed he'd burned out young; maybe he no longer felt the urge to make his long-dead father eat his words. Whatever the cause, Paul remained in Tulsa in his precious bunker, and instead of returning to the oil business, organized Spartan Aircraft's switch from making aircraft to building trailers.

It was an odd activity for a financial genius like Paul Getty. But the challenge of producing mobile homes seems to have intrigued him; he took endless trouble working out details of design and marketing, and was proud when production topped 2,000.

After four years in his bunker, he clearly needed something more than trailers to excite him. Lacking it, he was soon muttering about giving up everything to become a beachcomber. He even got as far as selling out a tranche of holdings in his prized Pacific Western—the only time he ever did—and his biographer Robert Lenzner is convinced he would have continued selling had he not found legal obstacles to offloading further shares in the Sarah Getty Trust.

This was fortunate for the Getty family. For it left Paul no alternative to remaining in the oil business; and this in turn meant that in 1948, when he recognized the chance of several million lifetimes, he was poised to seize it.

*

LIKE so much in the Middle East, where little is what it seems, the so-called Neutral Zone between Saudi Arabia and Kuwait is anything but neutral. For centuries the Saudis to the south and the Kuwaitis to the north had argued over the ownership of this apparently useless 2,000-square-mile wedge of desert, lying between its neighbors and the Persian Gulf. The issue was finally settled with a compromise.

Ignoring the nomadic Bedouins, who were the only human beings poor enough to live there, the area was defined as a kind of no-man's-land and called the Neutral Zone. Its two neighbors retained dual sovereignty, each holding an undivided half interest, over the one thing that might one day be of value, the mineral rights. But for many years there were no takers.

Even when the world's greatest oil field, the massive *Burgan* field in Kuwait, was discovered in the 1930s, just a few miles north of the zone's boundaries, the zone itself continued to daunt prospective oilmen with its inhospitable terrain, its scorching climate, and the geopolitical quagmire of its mineral rights.

With the ending of war in Europe, it was clear that the U.S. oil fields would soon find it hard to satisfy America's booming car economy, and interest focused once again on the Persian Gulf as the likeliest alternative. Even the Neutral Zone, with all its problems, began being tentatively discussed among the major oil companies.

Inevitably word of this reached Getty—but unlike most senior executives of major oil companies, he was not a tentative man. He was a realist. "If one is to be anyone in the world's oil business, one must stake one's claim in the Middle East," he said. And since he had decided that he emphatically did want to be someone in the world oil business, he made one of his inspired decisions.

Without having the region surveyed, or placing a foot in the Middle East himself, he decided that he and he alone would have the Saudi concession in the Neutral Zone.

By now he was more concerned for his personal safety than ever, and had decided he would never risk traveling by air. So he had absolutely no intention of venturing to the Neutral Zone himself. Instead he was fortunate to discover the ideal agent within his own organization: Paul Walton, a young geologist who had worked in Saudi Arabia in the 1930s and was currently head of exploration in the Rocky Mountain division of the Pacific Western oil company. Walton knew the Persian Gulf. He knew its people and its problems. He was anxious to return. So Getty invited him to Paris, and briefed him on his mission.

He did so with his customary obsession with detail, spending four full days with Walton in the Hôtel George V until every eventuality was covered: the exact price at which Walton should start bidding for the oil concession; the speed at which he had to move, and the height to which he was prepared to go.

Having prepared to his satisfaction, J. Paul Getty waited.

He was acting entirely on instinct, for at this stage he had not seen so much as a single survey report on the Neutral Zone. But his instinct was as sound as ever. When Walton made his first aerial reconnaissance of the Zone, it was as Getty had suspected. Spread across the desert were a number of domelike mounds identical to similar formations covering Kuwait's Burghan field to the north.

As this made it almost certain that the oil deposits of the field continued through the Neutral Zone, Walton was being ultra-cautious when he reported back that the chances of a major oil find within the Zone were fifty–fifty. (Later he said he would have given higher odds, but he had seen similar perfect sites in Saudi Arabia come up "dry as hell" and didn't wish to overpitch the prospects.)

It was typical of Getty to be so suspicious and secretive that he had forbidden Walton to send back his news by telephone, wireless, or cablegram, all of which might just be liable to interception. Instead he insisted on an anonymous-looking airmail letter, which took nine days to reach Paris from Jiddah. And throughout this period of waiting, Getty, with his somber face and poker player's self-control, continued life entirely as usual, betraying not the faintest sign of what was happening.

But once he had the letter he was jubilant—odds of fifty–fifty are high for the oil business—and he started bidding for the great potential oil bonanza of the Neutral Zone. He was now prepared to stake his entire personal fortune, the funds in the Sarah Getty Trust, and anything further he could raise upon the greatest gamble of his life.

For such a fearful man to make such a bold decision, and for such a miserly one to risk so much, even before solving all the massive problems of transporting, refining, and marketing the oil he hoped to find, is a measure of the unpredictability of Getty's complex nature. It puzzled and astonished even those who knew him best.

But still stranger was the fact that while all this was going on, there was not the least change in the anonymous life he was leading. Now in his late fifties, he continued to direct his multimillion-dollar empire from Room 801 of the Hôtel George V in Paris, where he also slept with his women, washed his socks, played teach-yourself-Arabic records like background music, and every evening dutifully entered his day's expenses in his diary: "taxi 5 francs, bus fare 1 franc, newspaper 10 centimes."

Yet this was the man who was negotiating to pay the king of Saudi Arabia and the sultan of Kuwait, as joint owners of the Neutral Zone, a guaranteed $1 million each a year even if no oil was ever found, an unprecedented royalty of 40 percent on each barrel of oil produced, plus a $20 million down payment for the privilege of wildcatting in an arid desert 2,000 miles away from where he sat.

SUCCESS in the Neutral Zone did not come easily. Paul soon discovered that the Aminoil syndicate, which included one of the major American oil companies, Phillips Petroleum, had got there before him, and had also purchased a concession to the Zone from the Kuwaitis. As Paul's concession was granted by the Saudis, this meant he had to work in tandem with Aminoil employees, which inevitably led to friction, feuds, and terrible misunderstandings.

Nor was it all that easy to strike oil, however convinced Paul might be that it was simply waiting there to be discovered. Not until early 1953 did his Pacific Western technicians finally locate what they were seeking: an oil strike connecting with a virtual underground sea of oil. It was a discovery which, in oil terms, *Fortune* magazine described as "somewhere between colossal and history making." But it was only now that Paul showed the true originality and business flair which would make the Getty fortune stratospheric.

Much of the oil in the Neutral Zone was in the form of cheap so-called garbage oil, a low-grade crude that came from shallow wells and cost little to produce, but for which there was little real demand. Paul realized that provided he could get this oil to America in sufficient quantities, up-to-date oil refineries would have no difficulty processing it for the ever-growing American domestic market. The problem was to get it there, build suitably large refineries, and market it. Solving this problem was to prove the most ambitious undertaking of his life, and required coordination and financing on a massive scale.

Unwilling to give tanker owners the power to hold him hostage in the future, he decided to construct his own tanker fleet, spending more than $200 million on the massive supertankers that would carry his cheap oil from the Neutral Zone not only to America but also to Europe and Japan. (It was typical of Getty that, with the assistance of his well-connected friend the French industrialist and former air-ace, Commandant Paul Louis Weiller, he was able to get these tankers built in French dockyards with a 35 percent French government subsidy—and then receive the Légion d'Honneur for services to France.)

A further $200 million went on a new refinery in Wilmington, Delaware, and $60 million on upgrading the old Avon refinery in California. These were massive undertakings. The Delaware River had to be deepened and port installations built to bring the Getty supertankers up to Wilmington. The number of Tide Water service stations in America was more than doubled to provide outlets for Getty gasoline.

The outlay was vast, but the profits were vaster. The oil from the shallow wells was costing little to produce, so salaries and overhead were minimal. World demand for gasoline and oil continued to increase, and over the next twelve years Pacific Western built fifteen separate wells in the Neutral Zone, producing a major part of American oil imports from the Middle East and making Pacific Western the seventh-largest gasoline producer in the United States.

Since Getty personally controlled the company and he and the Sarah Getty Trust were its major shareholders, the profits immeasurably enriched him and his heirs. And in 1956, to ensure that his contribution to the Getty dynasty would be remembered, he changed the name of his thriving company. Pacific Western would henceforth be known as the Getty Oil Company.

WHAT was so strange about this whole elaborate operation was that Paul continued to direct almost every detail of it all himself. The discovery of a great oil field, the creation of a major tanker fleet, and the building of port facilities and massive refineries in America were all masterminded by this one extraordinary individual, sitting quietly in Room 801 in the Hôtel Georges V in Paris. He would often work throughout the night and not bother overmuch with food. Otherwise this whole amazing enterprise barely changed his private way of life at all.

Provided he was always near a telephone, he could continue his travels, his affairs, his personal interests, while his most ambitious business ventures seemed to remain what they had always been, part of the everlasting game that he was playing with the world for his private satisfaction.

WHEN he met Penelope Kitson in 1953, she was just thirty-one, an elegant, very self-possessed upper-class Englishwoman, with three children and an unsatisfactory marriage. They became intimate friends, and she enjoyed his company, finding him charming, extraordinarily knowledgeable, and possessed of "the sharpest brain of anyone I've ever known."

He made a fuss of her and said he loved her, but from the start something told her that if she ever fell completely in love with him, she'd be at his mercy—so she never did. As an intelligent woman of the world she could see his limitations all too clearly: that he was not a man she ought to marry or permit to dominate her life, and that behind his womanizing lay a total inability to endure the normal bonds, responsibilities, pleasures, problems of a family. As a realist, she did not permit herself the luxury of thinking she could ever change him— not that she really wished to, for she knew that change would inevitably destroy the way of life he had carefully created, which in turn made possible his business ventures. So they stayed lovers, equals, friends, and partners.

The more she got to know him, the more she saw him as a man with extraordinary powers of concentration and strength of will, and realized that his attitude toward women, herself included, was part of something crucial to his nature.

It didn't particularly trouble her that he was sexually obsessive, and that "he simply couldn't keep his hands off any woman who came near him." She says that as she had never had a jealous nature, sexual jealousy wasn't really an issue between them.

But she felt that Getty was a very strange character indeed—dominating, clever, independent, but lacking one crucial ingredient to his nature. "I suppose that one would have to say that part of him had simply never grown up." Part of him remained the selfish, spoiled only child who had been indulged by George and Sarah; hence much of his trouble with his children and his family. "But he was utterly determined over anything he wanted, and would never delegate to anyone, because no one was really up to him."

It suited Penelope to keep her independence, especially as she sensed that at the moment he was more in love with her than she with him, and that once this changed she'd lose him. After her divorce she had a house in Kensington, which he often visited when he came to London, and since she was an accomplished interior decorator, he employed her to decorate the staterooms of the oil tankers he was building.

He excused himself from proposing marriage by saying that a fortune-teller in New Orleans once told him that if he married for a sixth time he would die. (This was probably untrue. He often quoted fortune-tellers to ratify or excuse lines of conduct.)

But he also told her, "Pen, you'll always be my Number One." This time he was not lying; until he died, she remained virtually the only person close to him who was not intimidated by his character, his reputation, or his money—which was why he trusted her.

ONE area where the oddities of Paul Getty's character were particularly evident was in his role as an art collector. With his increased wealth he was starting to take collecting seriously. He had recently bought the so-called ranch house at Malibu, a stone summer house in a prime location overlooking the Pacific Ocean—and he used it as a setting for the valuable French eighteenth-century furniture he'd bought at bargain prices just before the war.

Since then he had picked up further bargains, in particular the Rembrandt portrait of the merchant Marten Looten, which he bought from a frightened Dutch businessman on the eve of war for $65,000, and the superb Ardabil Carpet, which he had personally acquired at the bargain price of $68,000 from the sharpest of international dealers, Lord Duveen, when his lordship was on his deathbed. On an off day at Sotheby's he had also picked up (for $200) a painting known as *The Madonna of Loreto*, which he convinced himself was at least partially painted by Raphael.

In artistic matters his overwhelming motive continued to be to find a bargain—which stopped him from ever becoming a genuine collector. Penelope admits that "Paul was really too mean ever to allow himself to buy a great painting." More to the point, his lack of emotional response made him somewhat like a very clever child who knows a lot but lacks a mature aesthetic response to anything. This was particularly apparent in the small book he put together on his favorite subject, eighteenth-century France. Some of the information was evidently lifted straight from encyclopedias, and much of the book might have been written by a fact-obsessed twelve-year-old—but as a guide to Paul Getty's mind, it is most revealing.

Almost everything within this book relates to money. Various important pieces in his own collection are described, always in terms of market prices, estimated value, and exactly how much Getty spent on them. This can be fascinating. Who but Getty would have worked out the contemporary cost of making a *boule* table and conclude that a French nobleman would have paid slightly more for it in real terms in 1760 than the cost of "a top quality saloon car" in the 1950s? Similarly, he could become absorbed in the minutiae of connoisseurship—for example, the precise pigment used in one or other of his paintings.

What Getty appeared to be unable to do was to trust his emotional response to any work of art, in case his feelings ran away with him; so what he really needed was somebody whose taste he trusted to advise him as he built up his collection. In September 1953, he did meet such a person.

During a trip to Italy with another of his current mistresses, the effusive English art journalist Ethel le Vane, he accidentally met, in a corridor of the Excelsior Hotel in Florence, one of the greatest connoisseurs of Italian painting: Bernard Berenson. Berenson, without realizing who Getty was, invited him to tea at the holy of artistic holies, his Villa I Tatti on the hill of Settignano, close to Florence.

It was a strange occasion. On Getty's side was the profound reverence with which he treated the great connoisseur who possessed in such abundance qualities he was so aware of lacking: artistic judgment, true discrimination, taste, and knowledge. And on Berenson's side was total unawareness that this strange American with the talkative girlfriend was rapidly becoming his country's richest billionaire.

How much in life is timing! Twenty years earlier, Berenson would not have missed anyone as rich as Getty; he and Joe Duveen would have flattered him with their attention, aroused his latent enthusiasm for the pictures they could sell him, and quite probably have ended by helping him create a great collection.

Instead the moment passed. Getty promised to send photographs of some of his marble statuary; and Berenson expressed the hope that they might meet again, but they never did. Berenson was old and disillusioned, not least with himself. Getty was terrified of wasting money or being swindled; not until after he was dead would he give others the pleasure and responsibility of spending just a part of his enormous fortune on appropriate works of art for his collection.

In the meantime, classical sculpture seems to have appealed to him. As a trained geologist, he felt comfortable with marble, and his recent purchase of some pieces of Roman statuary, combined with this autumn visit to Italy, brought some very strange, and, as it turned out, quite far-reaching consequences.

A Roman statue of Hercules, one of the pieces he had bought from the collection of Lord Lansdowne, inspired him to pay a visit to the place where it was supposedly discovered, Hadrian's villa at Tivoli outside Rome. Even though only scanty ruins remain, the villa is a haunted, atmospheric site, and Getty, who was nothing if not suggestible, seems to have been overcome by an awareness of the presence of its onetime owner, the most creative and enigmatic of all the Roman emperors, Hadrian.

The sense of déjà vu is fairly common. But a very rich, self-made man has an additional incentive to believe in reincarnation which can offer an explanation for his otherwise inexplicable success. As E. L. Doctorow has the self-made Henry Ford remark to the self-made Pierpont Morgan in his celebrated novel *Ragtime*, "I explain my genius this way,—some of us have just lived more times than others." Getty, who appears to have felt this very strongly, may also have been influenced by the reason Henry Miller gives for the same belief: "Sex is one of the nine reasons for reincarnation. . . . The other eight are unimportant."

In any case, Getty's visit to Hadrian's villa came at an impressionable moment, when the sudden uprush of his wealth and far-flung enterprises found a sort of echo in what he had already learned of Hadrian's activities. Just as the aging Hadrian had stayed at the villa and continued to initiate enterprises and great events in the farthest corners of the Roman empire, so Getty had been making great things happen in the distant reaches of the Getty empire. Hadrian had been the richest man on earth, and Getty was fast becoming the same. He also liked to think he had a stoical Roman attitude to life, and that he even looked not unlike a Roman emperor. Finally, for the true snob—and snobs came little snobbier than J. Paul Getty—what pedigree could conceivably approach that of a Roman emperor?

The more Getty thought about it—and he seems to have thought about it quite a lot—the more he picked up similarities, echoes, resonances, between the long-dead Emperor Hadrian and himself.

"I would very much like to think that I was a reincarnation of Hadrian's spirit, and I would like to emulate him as closely as I can," he confided to a female friend in London.

CHAPTER NINE

Fatherhood

FOR a man who thought so much of dynasties, Paul Getty was, as has been made clear, a strangely absent father. Had he not been quite so totally immersed in the vast expansion of his fortune, one wonders if he might have found a little time for his four children, who were growing up so far away from him. Probably not. It was not so much that he lacked time as that he clearly saw his children as a threat to the two things that meant most to him: the making of money and the serious pursuit of pleasure.

Nevertheless, very occasionally, he did make contact with them, possibly from curiosity, like a Trappist sniffing at the pleasures of the flesh only to recoil from the temptation. Describing these occasions in his diaries, he always presents himself as such a loving and devoted parent to his children that it is hard to realize that he almost never saw them. Young Ronald is described as "bright and loveable," George is "very mature, with an excellent mind and personality," and young Paul and Gordon are invariably referred to as "my two dear sons."

The most intriguing of Getty's extremely rare adventures into active fatherhood occurred on Christmas Eve, 1939, with war in Europe just declared. It provided the sole occasion in their entire childhood when the four "beloved" sons actually found themselves in one room together.

Paul had just scurried home to Los Angeles from Naples, having left his new bride, Teddy, to face the war alone in Italy. For once he must have felt the need for the consolations of a family; he called up his ex-wife Ann to let him take young Paul and Gordon out to a toy shop, where they saw a penguin dressed as Donald Duck, and where Getty bought them Christmas presents. Fini and Ronald had come to live in Los Angeles just before the war. And so on Christmas Day "all four of my beloved sons"—fifteen-year-old George, ten-year-old Ronald, and Paul and Gordon, seven and six respectively—were brought to the house on South Kingsley Drive to bring Christmas greetings to their eighty-seven year-old grandmother Sarah.

Getty must have arranged this out of filial deference rather than paternal affection, for it sounds as if it was an uncomfortable occasion—the very deaf and lame old lady, the four unknown boys who shared her blood and were so awkward in each others' company, and the mysterious rich father with the downturned mouth, who must have seemed an almost total stranger.

But Getty made it sound like a happy party for a most united family when he wrote in his diary of the "lovely tree in mother's sitting room" and the "heaps" of Christmas presents. "Mother enjoyed it like a youngster," he assures us. He seems to have stayed long enough to greet his offspring and kiss his ancient mother on the cheek before departing like the ghost of Christmas.

As Sarah's health deteriorated after this, and she died two years later, the exercise in Christmas togetherness was not repeated; it remained the only contact between all the boys thoughout their childhood, this despite the fact that they were all living at the time in California, and that on them would ultimately rest the future of the largest fortune in America.

WHAT made Getty such a disquieting and ultimately such a disastrous father was the way in which he almost totally cut himself off from all his sons in their childhood and adolescence, and then, when it suited him, tried to reestablish relationships as if nothing untoward had happened, attempting to groom his sons to perpetuate what he always liked to call "the Getty dynasty."

It couldn't work, for by then the damage had been done. The boys had missed their father when they needed him; none of them really knew him, and each had been damaged in a different way. Almost inevitably, all the boys were jealous and suspicious of one another, so that the "dynasty," instead of helping to support its members, actually produced fearful antagonisms among them. Jealousy, bitterness, and nonstop litigation—all would stem from the problems J. Paul Getty bequeathed his sons when he gave them a phantom billionaire as a father.

The firstborn, George Getty II. should have suffered least. He was far too young to have known his father when he abandoned poor Jeanette in 1927, and she remarried fairly swiftly. Her husband, a well-to-do, kindly Los Angeles stockbroker named Bill Jones, treated young George Getty like a son, sending him to private school in Los Angeles, and then to Princeton, where he planned to study law.

During his childhood George had minimal contact with his father, but Jeanette took him regularly to call on Grandma Getty, who had always had a soft spot for her firstborn grandson. Not only did the child bear the precious name of her own lamented husband, but George Getty, Sr., had left him that $300,000 in his will. Shrewdly invested by his stepfather, this sum of money was increasing, and together with the growing income from the Sarah C. Getty Trust, guaranteed that George would always be comfortably off, quite apart from anything he earned. This situation should have suited George; he had inherited little of his father's drive or business genius, and was made for the undemanding life of an unambitious California attorney of independent means.

It was not to be. Given George's name and position, his fate was sealed from the start. He was destined for the company his grandfather and namesake had founded, and in 1942, when he was just eighteen and in his first year at Princeton, his father claimed him for the role he had to play in life. George was just about to join the U.S. Army, intending to return to Princeton when the war was over, but now for the first time in his life, his father took an interest in him, taking him to visit the old Athens oil field, scene of several of his own successes in his distant youth. Here he made it clear to George that his future lay irrevocably in the oil industry, and that one day he could expect to head the family business.

How could George refuse? But first he had to serve for four years in the army, as an infantry officer, then in the war-crimes prosecution team. Demobilized in 1946, he finally decided that instead of finishing his degree, he would join his father.

George made a conscientious businessman, and as his father's heir apparent, rose with unsurprising swiftness in the management hierarchy of the Getty companies. After serving creditably as his father's representative in the Neutral Zone of Arabia, he returned to California to become vice president of Tide Water Oil at the age of thirty-one. Success was beckoning, and George's life should now have been extremely sweet.

But as a businessman George was already suffering one fatal flaw. In childhood he seems to have picked up from his mother a sense of fear and awe of his absent father, which he never lost. Even as a grown man he never overcame it, and the more responsibility he gained as J. Paul Getty's heir apparent, the more fear of his father served to undermine him. In the end it helped to kill him.

*

BUT George's problems were as nothing when compared with the handicaps his father heaped upon his unfortunate half brother, the "bright and loveable" Ronald. Being half German, Ronald was very much the outcast of the family from the start.

Soon after Getty had obtained his dearly bought divorce from Fini back in 1932, mother and son settled in Switzerland. Fini never remarried, and until the outbreak of the war in 1939, she and Ronald were looked after by Dr. Otto Helmle, who since the divorce had become one of Getty's bitterest opponents.

During this period, Dr. Helmle had other matters on his mind. As a prominent Catholic, he had become secretary of the German Centre Party, precursor of the postwar Christian Democrats and in 1933 had actually refused the post of Minister for Economics in Hitler's first government as chancellor. Later, as his opposition to the Nazis grew, he felt happy in the knowledge that his daughter and grandson were safely in Switzerland where he could easily visit them from Karlsruhe. So as a child, Ronald grew up in Switzerland, speaking German, believing he was Swiss, and more or less oblivious of the existence of his real father.

By 1939, Dr. Helmle had been banned from all political activity along with his friend and fellow party member, Konrad Adenaeur, and was actually imprisoned for a period, losing all his money in the process. (In 1943, he was lucky to escape arrest a second time—for involvement in the plot against the Führer.) At the time of his imprisonment, he sent Fini and his ten-year-old grandson to the safety of Los Angeles, where for the first time Ronald learned about his father.

"Even then," he says, "I didn't know him, as I hardly ever saw him. Occasionally my mother used to take me to visit my Grandmother Sarah, but all I remember about her was that she seemed kind and was in a wheelchair, and was so extremely deaf that communication was impossible. My father was running the aircraft factory in Tulsa at the time so I never saw him. Occasionally a cheque would arrive from him for my birthday; once he sent me a pair of roller skates, and that was about it. I can't say I thought about him very much, although I realised that there was something lacking in my life, particularly when I saw other kids going off to ball games with their fathers and I never did."

It was only gradually that Ronald learned that on top of everything else he missed out on from the absence of a father, he was suffering a more serious handicap. His half brothers, George and Paul and Gordon, were all included in the Sarah C. Getty Trust, and so were destined to become great heirs to the ever-growing fortune of the Gettys. Ronald was not.

What made the situation so unjust was that this glaring inequality was not his fault. Excluding the infant Ronald from the trust had been his father's way of getting even with Dr. Helmle over the divorce, the money that the settlement had cost him, and the fact that the delays had prevented him from marrying Ann Rork before his third son, Paul, was born. And as if to underline the arbitrary nature of the exclusion, while Ronald was excluded from the trust, any children he might have were specifically included.

To be absolutely fair to Getty, back in 1936, when the trust was established for the benefit of his children and unborn grandchildren, the capital involved was relatively small, and since he was smarting over what he saw as Dr. Helmle's victory, he felt that he should therefore have the privilege of providing for his grandson. Neither of them foresaw that Helmle would lose all his money to the Nazis, while Getty would proceed to build the greatest fortune in America.

After the war, Fini and Ronald started to return to Germany or Switzerland each summer, so that, as he says, "Europe was always very much home to me, and Los Angeles a sort of interval in my life. I naturally thought myself more European than American."

Not until 1951, when Ronald was twenty-two and in his final year of business studies at the University of Southern California, did his father see fit to contact him. As with George, he wanted him to take his place in the rapidly expanding Getty business empire. As Ronald puts it, "I was pleased that he asked me to work for him, but I can't say it was a particularly emotional reunion."

A training course followed with Getty Oil, and in 1953 Ronald joined the Getty-owned Tide Water Oil Company's marketing department, where he was so successful that three years later he was running the department with a salary of $40,000 a year.

But at Tide Water he inevitably came into increasing contact with the young vice president, his half-brother George, and a feud began, with jealousy and bitterness on either side. Despite his success, George would always feel insecure before his father; he resented having this half-brother in his company, in case Ronald attracted more than his fair share of his father's affection. Ronald, on the other hand, was becoming increasingly aware of the massive handicap his father had inflicted on him by excluding him, alone of his sons, from the Sarah C. Getty Trust. It was an awareness that would grow like a cancer in the years ahead, until it all but destroyed him.

*

IN comparison with the problems Paul Getty thrust onto George and Ronald, life seemed infinitely easier for Paul and Gordon, his sons by that former child prodigy Ann Rork. As he was increasingly away in Europe and the Middle East during the 1950s, he saw even less of them during their adolescence than he had of George and Ronald, leaving them exposed to the undivided force of their mother's dominating personality.

When her marriage ended with that "noisome"—and profitable—divorce at Reno back in 1936, Ann rapidly embarked upon a marital career in which three further wealthy husbands, interspersed with various lovers, took the unlamented place of Paul Getty. First on the scene was Douglas Wilson, an eminently forgettable millionaire from Memphis, Tennessee, by whom she had one daughter, Paul and Gordon's beautiful but put-upon half-sister, Donna.

Wilson was succeeded by Garret "Joe" McEnerney II, a San Francisco attorney; the breakup of this marriage left Ann—or Mrs. Mack, as she was called—in possession of a comfortable, creeper-hung house at 3788 Clay Street in Presidio Heights, close to the most fashionable part of San Francisco.

During this period, Getty himself was giving the boys nothing but his name and child support. There is a unique entry in his diary in the middle of the war recording just one visit that he paid them. Gordon recited him a poem he had written "on the good qualities of negroes," but instead of saying what he thought of Gordon or his poem, Getty, fact-obsessed as ever, simply recorded that "Paul is eleven years old and weighs 86 pounds, while Gordon is ten and weighs 76 pounds."

"My sons—all of them—are great rewards," he added—so great that he saw neither Paul nor Gordon for the next twelve years. A year after the visit, when twelve-year-old Paul Junior wrote Papa a letter, Getty sent it back unanswered, with the spelling mistakes carefully corrected.

Paul was still bitter over this years later. "I never got over that," he said. "I wanted to be judged as a human being, and I could never get that from him."

Since the boys had virtually no contact with their father, they had no idea of the vast expansion of his fortune. According to Judge William Newsom, a friend and contemporary of both boys at San Francisco's St. Ignatius High School, "They knew they had a rich, even very rich father, but as he had almost no influence upon their lives one didn't hear much about him." Judge Newsom describes life at Clay Street at this time as "financially comfortable, not prodigal, with money no great issue either way. Neither Paul nor Gordon seemed particularly concerned about money or the lack of it—nor did they seem to dwell on expectations."

But if their absent father left a gap in Paul and Gordon's lives, Mrs. Mack seemed more than capable of filling it. Hers was a powerful presence, and she was clearly the dominant influence on both her boys as they grew to manhood in this unconventional one-parent family in the midst of postwar San Francisco.

Now in her middle to late thirties, a sexy, bustling woman with fine eyes and auburn hair, Mrs. Mack was almost everything that Jean Paul Getty wasn't—theatrical, easygoing, and exuberant. Still very much the onetime would-be movie queen, she was a lively woman with, according to her daughter, "a very high IQ." She was consciously artistic, with considerable taste in literature and music. She was clearly a woman of resources, who when short of money could always rustle up a little extra through property speculation in Marin County on her own account. With such a mother, and with no father on the scene to cramp their style, the boys should have had an idyllic adolescence—and in many ways they did.

A natural bohemian, Mrs. Mack believed in freedom, and left the boys largely to their own devices. But she was also a highly social creature, and the gregariousness that had so infuriated Jean Paul Getty made her encourage both her boys to entertain their friends at home. (Being three years younger than Gordon, the boys' half-sister, Donna Wilson, was inevitably overshadowed in this male-dominated household. A very pretty girl, she was also very shy and tended to be overlooked, playing little part in her brothers' lives until considerably later.)

Mrs. Mack was the most hospitable of mothers, and by the boys' middle teens the place on Clay Street had become an open house for Paul's school friends. Part of the attraction was undoubtedly Mrs Mack herself, one of those legendary mothers who enjoy a wide rapport with all her children's friends. Some were probably in love with her, while others recall her as a sort of rakehell aunt. Judge Newsom compares her with Graham Greene's outrageous Aunt Augusta in his comic novel *Travels with My Aunt*, but the usual reaction from old habitués of "3788" is that "Mrs. Mack was Auntie Mame to the life."

Tolerant by disposition, Mrs. Mack raised no objection to the boys and their friends drinking at home as they grew older, on the theory, as Donna put it, that "it was better to have them getting drunk where you knew where they were, than somewhere else where you didn't."

At a time when few other middle-class parents were quite so liberated on the subject, this added greatly to the popularity of the Getty household and of Mrs. Mack herself, who was always partial to a drink and who would "sit down and have a beer with us herself," as one of her sons' friends fondly remembers. Soon the house on Clay Street was referred to as "the 3788 Club"—or simply "3788."

The members of "3788" formed a fascinated entourage around the Gettys. Paul was very much the leader of the pack, which was inevitably called the Getty Gang. Having inherited much of his mother's Irish charm and sociability, he played up to his audience, making them laugh at his stories and his exploits, and dressing the part of the would-be tearaway and playboy.

But there was more to the attractions of 3788 than Ann and alcohol, and the house became something of a cultural beacon in middle-class, postwar San Francisco. Music was of growing importance to the family—particularly to Gordon, whose collection of operatic records was already vast and steadily increasing, as was his knowledge of opera and the greatest operatic singers.

Several of them, including such legendary figures as the soprano Licia Albanese and the lyric tenor Ferruccio Tagliavini, gave recitals at the house when visiting San Francisco, and the boys' love of opera would develop in the years ahead, so that even in their periods of deepest disagreement, they would remain united as members of the esoteric cult of dedicated opera buffs.

As a household, Clay Street seemed a perfect setting for the boys to develop as intelligent and original human beings, and at first glance Paul appeared to get the best of it, living his spoiled, highly social life, aided and abetted by his doting mother. Like her, he drank a lot. (Sometimes he had beer with kippers for breakfast to her dry martinis.) Popular with his friends and attractive to the girls, he seemed to have a charmed life ahead of him.

With Gordon things were rather different. Both boys were handsome, but in very different ways. With his pointed face and lively manner, Paul looked rather like an adolescent satyr, but as Gordon approached his full height of six feet, two inches, he increasingly resembled a large edition of the youthful Schubert. As Donna puts it, "Paul exuded sex, whereas Gordon didn't exude anything very much"; and Paul was inevitably his mother's favorite. According to Bill Newsom, she "thought him the wittiest, cleverest, handsomest boy in California."

Paul's reaction to his mother's spoiling was to make the most of it and cheerfully get on with life. But when Gordon failed to receive the same attention from his mother, he tended to withdraw into himself, building a wall of self-sufficiency that soon became a key part of his character.

By reacting against his mother's easygoing ways, Gordon appeared as something of a puritan; in contrast to his mother and his brother, he never was a drinker. Paul had a succession of glamorous motorcars, including a Cord and a Dodge convertible, which he drove stylishly and rather fast. Gordon chose calmer vehicles: a solid Oldsmobile and a still more solid Buick, which he drove with great deliberation.

But while life on Clay Street seemed particularly relaxed, the absence of a father figure probably affected both boys more than their friends appreciated. In Gordon's case it left him no parental alternative to his mother, and when he found he couldn't cope with Mrs. Mack's shenanigans or drunkenness or lovers, he created a private, separate life away from home. Before going off to college, he actually moved into the easygoing household of his old school friend, Bill Newsom, making a sort of father figure out of Newsom senior. By then Gordon was a clever, inner-directed loner whose true home was music, poetry, and economic theory. These would help to see him through the troubles and distractions of the years ahead.

Unlike the self-sufficient Gordon, who felt no need for organized religion, Paul aged sixteen, underwent a serious conversion thanks to the Jesuits of St. Ignatius. And although at first sight, Paul's life seemed more enviable than Gordon's, he was in fact more vulnerable than his brother. If he modeled himself on anyone it was probably on handsome Edgar Peixoto, a charmingly failed lawyer who was one of his mother's many suitors. "A stylish, most intelligent man whom drink had sadly overtaken" is how one of Paul's friends remembers him. Bill Newsom, recalling Peixoto's conversation and his phenomenal memory for Norman Douglas's most ribald limericks, says that "most of us thought Edgar was a hero." Paul certainly did, but Gordon didn't.

Paul seems to have been afflicted by the opposites of many of his qualities. His wildness had a certain melancholy, and behind the chronic need for friends lay considerable insecurity. Where Gordon loved the certainties of chess and economic theory, Paul was already drawn to the excesses of high Romantic literature. He was a great reader and was soon collecting books, having started with a first edition of *The Great Gatsby*. He relished the fin-de-siècle decadence of Wilde and Corvo, but his prize discovery was that overblown diabolist Aleister Crowley. The self-styled "Prince of Darkness and Great Beast 666," who flourished on a daily intake of heroin that would have floored half a dozen lesser men, Crowley came to be regarded as something of a forerunner of the psychedelic generation of the sixties; for Paul to have fastened upon him now is a hint of how his mind was working and the way his interests would develop.

Paul had finished high school and was about to begin attending the University of San Francisco when the Korean War broke out in 1950. His mother suggested using her influence with a general she knew to stop him being drafted, but he wouldn't let her. Instead he went to Korea, where he made corporal but showed little aptitude for soldiering, serving out his time in an office at the Seoul headquarters. A year later Gordon also broke off his studies in economics at Berkeley to join the artillery; he took a commission, but didn't like the Army any more than Paul did, and spent his service at Fort Ord.

When he returned from Korea, Paul was already in love with pretty Gail Harris, the only child of federal judge George Harris. Unlike Mrs. Mack's family, who were very much newcomers to the city, the Harrises were third-generation San Franciscans, and the judge, a Truman appointee, was a leading figure in the community. But for all Paul's wildness, the judge and his wife, Aileen, became very fond of him, and he in turn was sufficiently in love with Gail to give up drinking. When Paul and Gail decided to get married, the only person not in favor was Mrs. Mack.

Hating to lose her favorite son, she argued forcefully that at twenty-three he was far too young and wild and immature for marriage. But despite her warnings and objections, the Harrises supported the young lovers, who finally married, quietly, in Woodside's Our Lady of the Wayside Chapel in January 1956.

True to form, the bridegroom's father, who was then in England, would have ignored the marriage; prompted by Penelope Kitson, he sent a telegram of congratulation—signed, "your loving Father"—but not a present.

Gordon by now seemed firmly married to poetry, economic theory, and music—above all, music. He possessed a baritone voice to match his size, and he dreamed of studying at the conservatory and one day finding worldwide fame and fortune as an opera singer.

Up to this point in their lives, neither brother had paid the faintest attention to the oil business, to their half-brothers, George and Ronald, or to their unknown father, who was drawing wealth in such unimaginable quantities from beneath the sand in one of the hottest, driest, most uncomfortable spots on earth.

PART TWO

CHAPTER TEN

The Richest Living American

IN October 1957 Getty finally emerged from the capitalist closet in which he had lived in relative obscurity for so long. *Fortune*, after several months' research among America's super-rich, including Rockefellers, Morgans, Hunts, and Fords, publicly proclaimed Jean Paul Getty, an "expatriate businessman living in Paris," the "richest living American."

Photographs taken of him at the time give the impression of a nocturnal creature suddenly flushed out of hiding and exposed to the cruel light of day. The game he had been quietly engaged in since his father died was no longer secret, his wealth was no longer private, and a number of important things began to change for Jean Paul Getty—and for those around him.

The great fortune and the business interests he had been creating could no longer remain the discreet affair that he had been conducting for so long by long-distance telephone from hotel bedrooms, with the records carried in his head or stowed away in shoe boxes. Henceforth it became increasingly like other major fortunes—and although Getty did his best to keep his style of life unchanged, he now, inevitably, became a public figure, subject to all the pressures on the very rich: publicity, begging letters, speculation, envy, fawning ballyhoo. And from now on his features started becoming known as well.

He pretended to regret the loss of his previous "gratifying" anonymity, remembering how reporters covering events at which he was present in the past generally overlooked him. "For all I know," he said, "they took me for a waiter."

But no longer. "After managing to avoid the limelight all my life," he wrote, "to my acute discomfort I became a curiosity, a sort of financial freak overnight." In fact he was vain enough to start relishing the notoriety. But according to his secretary, Barbara Wallace, "it was now that things started going wrong."

*

ANN Rork Getty had been right when she accused her former husband of having had "no interest in his sons until they were old enough
to take their places in his precious dynasty." Indeed, his lack of interest
in his offspring was positively inhuman. How could anyone, one asks,
remain so impervious to his own flesh and blood as to ignore them
totally for years on end, never writing to them, never inquiring if
they were intelligent, halfwitted, handsome, keen on women, keen on
animals, musical, or criminally insane? But Paul Getty never had inquired. He genuinely was not interested in his children, and until they
were old enough to be of use had never bothered with them.

For his son Paul Junior it must have been tempting to respond with
a similar lack of interest. But as he needed to support not only Gail
but his firstborn son, Jean Paul Getty III, born in November 1956, he
decided at around this time to try the family business for a job—
and contacted his half-brother George, who was now vice-president of
Getty-owned Tidewater Oil with headquarters in Los Angeles. (The
company had recently changed its name from Tide Water.)

Apart from a shared father, the two brothers had nothing in common. They didn't know each other and would never come to like each
other. But George did offer Paul a job: pumping gasoline in a Tidewater service station in the crisp white trousers, neat white hat, and shiny
black bow tie of a Tidewater pump attendant.

Soon Gordon, who had nothing very much to do, would join him,
and after a while both brothers were sent for training at Tidewater
headquarters. But there was still virtually no contact with their distant
father until the spring of 1958, when out of the blue he telephoned
Paul to summon him to Paris. Paul was to have a chance to prove
himself at last—in the Getty Oil installation in the Neutral Zone of
Arabia.

Paul answered that as he had a wife and baby son, he would naturally
want to take them with him.

"Fine," said his father. "Bring them to Paris first so I can meet them."

Which explains how Paul and Gail and the baby all arrived for lunch
with the head of the family on an early summer day at the Hôtel
Georges V in Paris. And there something happened that would have
far-reaching consequences for the Getty family. The group around the
table started to get on rather well together.

Gail, who had never met her father-in-law before, had been expecting
"an extremely grumpy man." Instead, he greeted Paul with: "Paul, no
one told me that your wife was pretty." And he proceeded to charm
Gail as only he could charm a pretty woman. The old misanthrope was

equally delighted with his grandson—"a bright, red-haired little rascal" with "a remarkable ability for making his grandpa obey his commands," as he wrote with untypical enthusiasm in that evening's diary.

Even this exercise in family bonding might well have ended there and then, but for events in Paris at the time. A violent demonstration had begun against De Gaulle's Algerian policy, and the barricades were going up uncomfortably close to the Hôtel Georges V. Getty was not a man for violent revolution, and in some alarm he decided to decamp to Brussels with his newfound family. There they stayed for the next few weeks, living in unaccustomed luxury at the Grand Hotel, and going every morning to the newly opened Brussels Exhibition. Here they would breakfast first at the Canadian Pavilion (waffles with maple syrup), then make a trip to the Soviet Pavilion for what Gail still remembers as "the most delicious caviar I've ever tasted." Getty, as a man of habit, started to enjoy himself.

A pleasurable holiday with younger members of his family was something Paul Getty had not experienced before. In Gail he had the perfect daughter-in-law, who found his stories fascinating and would listen to him, more or less entranced, for hours on end. The "red-haired little rascal," seventeen-month-old Jean Paul Getty III, continued as a source of permanent delight; and Paul Junior began to captivate his father as none of his other sons had ever done before. By the time the holiday in Brussels ended, Getty had come to an important decision, not just for Paul and Gail, but for all the Getty family.

Although everything had been arranged for the arrival of Paul and his family in the Neutral Zone, Getty had changed his mind. As he said, life in a trailer in the heat of the Arabian desert was not the thing for a newly married couple with a baby. Gordon was still unmarried, and could easily take his brother's place—which was what occurred a few weeks later, when he was summarily dispatched to the Getty Oil installation in Arabia.

But the truth of the matter was that "Big Paul," as the family sometimes called him, had grown attached to what he called "my little family" and had no intention of losing them if he could help it.

Since Paul had rapidly become his favorite son, it was time for him to have the fatted calf. And as it happened, there was an ideal post within the Getty empire waiting for him. The more the old man thought about it, the more he liked it.

AS part of the expansion of its refinery capacity in Europe, Getty Oil had recently acquired the small Italian Golfo oil company with a refinery at Gaeta outside Naples. The company had an office in Milan, but Getty planned to expand it, change its name to Getty Oil Italiana, and move its headquarters down to Rome. Who better to install as general manager than Paul?

In fact Paul, with his love of travel and books and leisure, was an unsuitable young man to place in charge of anything, particularly as he'd had no experience of management. But none of this counted with his father. Paul was his son, and any son of his should find running a modest operation such as Golfo Oil a picnic.

It was in his newfound grandparental mode that the old tycoon continued to show his "little family" such untypical affection. From Paris he actually drove them to Milan himself—in easy stages and extremely slowly—in his ancient Cadillac; once in Milan, he insisted on installing them in an apartment in Piazza Eleanora Duse in the center of the city, close to the Golfo office. The fateful connection of the next generation of the Getty family with Italy was made.

Not that any of them could possibly have guessed the crucial role that Italy would henceforth play in all their lives, particularly as their first reaction to Milan was by and large unfavorable. The pleasures of Milan take time and patience to discover, and the youthful Gettys hated the climate, didn't like the food, and couldn't understand the language. Also, it was clear that Paul would never make a businessman. But he applied himself, attempted to understand the complications of the oil business, and, when his father told him "Always wear a dark suit," duly purchased one.

It was during this honeymoon period between the father and the reunited son that Paul performed a gesture which touched the old man more deeply than one might have thought.

Twenty-five years earlier, when twenty-one-year-old Ann Rork (as she still was) had given birth to her premature son aboard ship off Genoa, there'd been a muddle over naming him. When the ship had stopped at the next port of call, the infant (small enough to be taken ashore in a hat box) was officially registered by the Italian notary in La Spezia. The proud father had wanted the child named after him— Jean Paul Getty, Jr.—but the notary misheard him and promptly named the child Eugenio instead.

"Eugenio," meaning "healthy offspring" was a popular name in positive-thinking, fascist Italy, but back in America it was less acceptable and inevitably became "Eugene." Paul hated it and never used it; now that he was back in Italy, he took the occasion to change his name officially to the form his father had intended. Eugene Paul was now no more. Jean Paul Getty, Jr., took over.

*

WHILE the renamed Jean Paul Getty, Jr., was basking in the unusual rays of fatherly approval, his siblings were having an altogether tougher time of it. Plump George, although officially singled out as his father's principal heir and successor and appointed independent chairman of the Getty-owned Tidewater Oil Company, was more than ever haunted by his father—and by those letters which began "My Dearest George" and ended with "Your Ever-loving Father." Getty never ceased his eagle-eyed surveillance of every corner of his empire, and his letters criticized in minutest detail the mistakes and failings of his conscientious but cruelly frustrated eldest son.

George was now in his mid-thirties, the father of three lively daughters, and something of a pillar of polite Los Angeles society. But as someone said of him, he would have "made a splendid manager of a small-town, midwest hardware store"; he found command of a major oil company, with a father sniping from the sidelines, something of a nightmare.

Ronald's lot was equally uncomfortable. A journey with his father to the Neutral Zone in 1956 had failed to bring them any closer, and although his fluency in French and German fitted him to be manager of the Getty-owned Veedol Company in Hamburg, where he was a considerable success, relations with his father were as cool as ever. (They were not helped by George's habit of penning unbrotherly notes about him to his father and by Ronald sending similar letters about George's failings in return.)

The truth was that Getty still harbored resentment for the trouble he had had from Dr. Helmle all those years before; and when Ronald married pretty Karin Seibl in Lübeck, Germany, in 1964, the billionaire was to see no reason to break his habit of not acknowledging any of his children's weddings.

Even the sunny Gordon had his troubles when he took Paul's place in the manager's office in the Getty installation in the Neutral Zone. Acting on Big Paul's orders, he refused to pay the customary bribe to a local emir. He also insisted on supporting a female member of his staff who had been discovered having an affair with a local man—an offense for which the penalty was death by stoning. Refusing to accept this, Gordon helped the woman flee the country; when this was discovered, Gordon was placed under house arrest by the Saudis.

The episode reflected well on Gordon as a human being, but it failed to impress his father as a businessman, who felt that the woman had known the rules and should have paid the price. Besides, he was now on good terms with the Saudi king, and wanted to remain so. So Gordon was rapidly recalled and sent to manage what was now the Spartan Trailer Company in Tulsa. When he tired of this, he quietly returned to Berkeley to finish his degree in English.

Getty was clearly not a sympathetic father, but the most unflattering picture of him in this role comes from that summertime of 1958 when he was making so much sentimental mileage out of his "little family" in Milan. His twelve-year-old son Timmy was in a New York hospital, undergoing surgery that was meant to mark the end of a long period of agony. Half blind, and with his forehead disfigured by the removal of a large tumor, he was about to have cosmetic surgery to remove his scars.

While Timmy waited for his operation, he telephoned his father every day, begging him to return to America to be with him. He would also send heart-rending little messages: "I want your love Daddy and I want to see you."

But Getty's heart did not rend easily, and as always, business came before his children; every day he would patiently explain to Timmy that he loved him, too, but that Daddy's work kept him from returning to America just yet.

The operation took place on August 14. Getty was in Switzerland at the time, having accepted a long-standing invitation to visit the industrialist and art collector Baron Thyssen Bornemisza, who was almost as rich as he, and whose great collection far surpassed anything he could ever aspire to.

He was flattered to be invited by such a very grand collector, and even had he been prepared to risk his life in a transatlantic flight to New York, it would have been unthinkable to cancel such a visit. He enjoyed great houses, was predictably impressed by the Thyssen pictures, and had actually returned from the Thyssen villa to his hotel in Lugano when a distraught Teddy finally reached him on the telephone in the early hours of Monday, August 18. Beside herself with grief, she sobbed out the news to him: Timmy, their own beloved son, had not survived the operation.

Teddy needed consolation, and in Paul's dry way he attempted to console her. Normally grief and human feeling failed to reach him, for he had long been able to retreat into the cool inhuman world of business, but his child's death did catch him. Faced with death, he was always vulnerable, and totally alone. When the call to Teddy ended, it was still too early to think of working, and knowing he could not get back to sleep he took out his diary.

"Darling Timmy died two hours ago, my best and bravest son, a truly noble human being," he began, but he could not continue.

"Words are useless," he concluded, and shut tight his diary.

FORTUNATELY he still had Gail and Paul Junior and baby Paul, conveniently installed in the second-floor apartment in the middle of Milan, to take his mind off Timmy's death. And since he was often in the city, running his affairs from a suite in the Hotel Principe e Savoia, he enjoyed seeing them and sometimes took them away from the heat of the city at weekends to chic hotels like the Villa d'Este on Lake Como.

But Paul and Gail and baby Paul apart, there was a further reason for his steadily increasing interest in things Italian. It was not solely the affairs of Golfo Oil that brought him so often to his favorite peninsula, but a married woman of a certain age with one of the most magical houses in that magical country.

He had met her in Paris through his social arbiter and supporter, the rich Commandant Weiler. She was a stately woman *à la* Ingrid Bergman, married to a gloomy Frenchman who, being French, was naturally unfaithful to her. And she, being glamorous and very grand and Russian, was plainly ready for a passionate affair.

Thus began Getty's long and uncomfortable relationship with thirty-six-year-old Mary Teissier. She was elegant, and blond, and a little mad—the last being generally ascribed to her having had a grandfather who was second cousin to Tsar Nicholas II of Russia. Her husband, Lucien, had a house in Versailles, where they spent the summer, but he also owned the Villa San Michele, on the slopes of Fiesole, close to Florence. Some said the villa was designed by Michelangelo. The gardens were exquisite. The rooms were furnished with museum pieces. From the cloistered dining room there was an unrivaled view of Florence below. And Teissier had turned his villa into an exclusive small hotel for the very rich. Whenever Mary Teissier was there, Getty's name began appearing on the guest list.

She had much that appealed to Jean Paul Getty: lineage, style, human warmth, and a considerable knowledge of the world. The fact that she was also jealous, improvident, and congenitally unpunctual, as only a relation of a tsar could be, merely added to her attractions.

It was because of all of this—and because of her status as a married woman with a demanding husband—that the courtship of Mary Teissier took considerably longer than Jean Paul Getty habitually expended on the pursuit and bedding of a simple mistress. Love was mentioned. So was marriage. As he traveled between Milan and Naples, Getty made frequent visits to the Villa San Michele. But 1959 began with Mary Teissier still more or less attached to her gray-faced husband.

NOW that *Fortune* magazine had robbed him of his precious anonymity, Jean Paul Getty's days as a vagabond billionaire were numbered. He still loved living in hotels, where he could eat frugally off the hotel menu, save money by washing his own underwear in the bathroom sink (his excuse being that laundry soap damaged his skin), and guilt-lessly enjoy the women he listed (by name, coloring, and city) in his black address book.

But ever since those few uncomfortable days in Paris, his personal safety and security had begun to worry him. So did reporters and fortune seekers. He clearly needed an established European base from which he could run his empire, enjoy his privacy, and savor his women and his valuable possessions.

At first he thought of France, but the memory of barricades outside the Hôtel Georges V obsessed him. France might well be on the edge of bloody revolution. And, much as he loved it, Italy was little better. One place alone still beckoned him with memories of gentle meadows, gracious country houses, a deferential populace, and a well-fed aristoc-racy: the haven of gentility and peace, with the world's fattest, most secure financial institutions—England.

GETTY was going on sixty-six and his wealth was steadily accruing at an effortless half a million dollars daily, when the most capable member of his entourage, Penelope Kitson, introduced him to George Granville Sutherland-Leveson-Gower, the Fifth Duke of Sutherland.

Although the largest landowner in Scotland, his Grace, who had never been particularly bright, had somehow contrived to be short of money, and was finding it awkward to maintain Sutton Place, the Tudor mansion he had purchased forty years before from the self-made press lord Viscount Northcliffe.

(Before feeling sorry for the duke, one should remember that he also owned a Mayfair mansion next to Claridge's and a somewhat smaller stately home in Surrey, plus Dunrobin Castle, Golspie House, and the curiously named House of Tongue in Sutherland.)

Getty, with that truffle-hound-like nose for a bargain, offered the needy duke some £60,000 for his now unwanted Tudor hideaway—

approximately two hours' income from the Neutral Zone and exactly half what the duke had paid Northcliffe for the place. Sutherland accepted.

Much work and money would be needed to make Sutton Place fit for a self-denying billionaire to live in. And practical Penelope would spend many months selecting curtains, carpets, and furniture and taking charge of builders, plumbers, electricians, and upholsterers on his behalf. Getty also bought a seventy-foot table from the castle his old friend the American press lord William Randolph Hearst had owned in Wales, two grand pianos, and several pictures. "I must not spend any more on pictures," he wrote in his diary.

But by the spring of 1960, Jean Paul Getty would proudly take possession of something he had never really had before: a home.

CHAPTER ELEVEN

La Dolce Vita

ROME is traditionally a dangerous place for romantic foreigners with money, and the city had never seemed more dangerously seductive than at that moment in the autumn of 1958, when Getty Oil Italiana moved its offices from Milan to Rome, and Paul and Gail followed.

They found an apartment in the historic Palazzo Lovatelli in the Piazza Campitelli, one of the smallest and most enchanting squares in the oldest quarter of the city. There was a fountain opposite the great baroque church of Santa Maria in Campitelli, and around the corner were the ruins of the Theater of Marcellus, built by Julius Caesar. After Milan Rome must have seemed like a different country in another century, and the Piazza Campitelli made the perfect setting for a Roman idyll.

Gail was pregnant for the second time, and there was still so little traffic on the streets that she used to hire a horse-drawn open carriage when she went out shopping. In July 1959 she had a daughter, named Aileen after Gail's mother.

Paul had a burgundy-colored MG sports car, which was much admired by the Italians, and sometimes for weekends they would drive to nearby towns like Tivoli and Palestrina. Rome could have hardly seemed more beautiful, but life was not particularly exciting; most of the Gettys' social life consisting of occasional dinners with older couples, usually Americans connected with the oil industry.

Paul enjoyed exploring Rome; he started learning Italian and continued to collect books and records. He was twenty-eight and in that dangerous state of waiting for something wonderful to happen.

But Rome in fact was not as sleepy as it seemed in the Piazza Campitelli. When the Gettys came the great period of the Italian cinema was already drawing to a close, but legendary directors like Visconti, Rossellini, and de Sica were still working in the Rome studios of Cinecittà. The greatest of them all, Fellini, caught the atmosphere of the period with a film which actually appeared that autumn. It was a vivid portrait of the decadence and glitter of Roman society which centered round the Via Veneto. The hero, a journalist played by Marcello Mastroianni, while despising the life he is leading, finds himself unable to escape as he seeks in vain his true identity.

Fellini called his film *La Dolce Vita,* "The Sweet Life." And before long, Paul and Gail would be tasting something of *la dolce vita* for themselves.

DURING that summer, the elder Paul was busily enjoying his love affair with a very different Italy through his continuing romance with the golden-haired, demanding Mme. Teissier. Early in 1959 she left her husband and the Villa San Michele and became his full responsibility.

Her son, Alexis, still believes that something more than simply sex and money was involved. "It was the sense of power that Getty exuded. She was utterly obsessed with him. From the day they met until the day she died there was absolutely no one else."

Getty was in love with Mary Teissier, as he was with all his women, but this didn't mean that he could possibly be faithful to her, and he secretly enjoyed her jealous rages. He certainly provoked them, even at the dinner table, and she was particularly jealous of his friendship with Penelope, which she could neither tolerate nor change nor really understand.

Poor, insecure, unhappy Mary Teissier! Her chronic unpunctuality annoyed him. Her drinking shocked him. And her unpredictable Russian temperament ultimately bored him. But there was something about her—possibly her sense of style and those grand Romanov connections—that always kept a certain hold on him. And during these early days of their affair, she acted as his guide to the upper reaches of the Italian nobility, which for reasons of romantic snobbery held such enduring fascination for him.

In Rome she pulled every string she knew to get him into that most improbable bastion of Roman snobbery, the exclusive Circolo della Caccia, the Rome hunt club. Patterned on a traditional English hunt, the Circolo was dominated by aristocrats jealous of the one thing Getty secretly admired and envied: their titles and their ancestry. And they in turn enjoyed the chance to blackball this parvenu American who possessed the one thing most of *them* admired and envied: vast amounts of money.

Getty would have made a peculiar huntsman, but how he would have loved to have been a member of the most exclusive club in Rome as he entered its discreet headquarters on the Largo Fontana Borghese. His failure to be elected hurt him deeply—and increased his growing discontent with Italy.

As a consolation, when he visited Naples and his new oil refinery at Gaeta, Mary was able to introduce him to what passed for the cream of Neapolitan society, including several dukes and princes. These were no big deal in a country boasting nearly two hundred dukes and practically as many princes, but they made him happy. Then she spoiled things by persuading him to buy an islet called Gaiola in the Bay of Naples. Getty bought it sight unseen when she mentioned that its previous owners had included Tiberius; the Fiat heir, Gianni Agnelli; and the Earl of Warwick. Since she was always short of money, Mary was attracted by the prospect of the $7,000 commission on the deal, but she was smart enough to keep this from her lover. (As she said, he would have wanted it).

The day dawned when Getty came to take possession. Gaiola was beautiful, but had a melancholy atmosphere; and one look at the thirty yards of sea between it and the mainland was enough for Paul. He emphatically refused to step aboard the row boat to take him over; after a hurried meal, he packed his bags and, Mary's lamentations notwithstanding, never ventured there again.

As Penelope remarked, "If you're that rich, what's another island?"

Besides, by now he had bought a more suitable establishment near Rome, from someone with an even more resounding title than the Earl of Warwick: Prince Ladislao Odescalchi.

La Posta Vecchia, one of the prince's former country houses, had been a staging post on the ancient Via Salaria, near the old Etruscan site of Palo, by the sea. Although considerably decayed, as were the Odescalchi, it was an imposing building, with its portico and Roman arches, and when he bought it, Paul had plans of living there for part of every year. The indispensable Penelope supervised the decor, in the comfortable English country-house style that pleased him.

Though Getty loved the house, he had always been concerned about his safety, and all the publicity about his fortune had made him doubly anxious. According to Barbara Wallace, he began worrying about being kidnaped by pirates. In fact, his fear of kidnaping was becoming an obsession.

So La Posta Vecchia never became the center for the grand Italian life he dreamed of. He ordered bars on bedroom windows and maintained the most up-to-date security. He even kept a loaded shotgun in his bedroom. But even so, he rarely stayed for long. In Rome he felt happiest—and safest—in the old familiar Hotel Flora on the Via Veneto.

When he first bought La Posta Vecchia he had consulted his Italian lawyer about adopting Italian nationality—but now it was a subject that he never mentioned. England was increasingly stealing his affections.

Getty had always felt at home in England, and had even come to tolerate the weather. More important, he felt safe there, and the British upper classes were quite different from those dried-up Romans who believed they had a right to teach a Yankee billionaire a lesson.

Even the publicity about his fortune was in his favor. The British aristocracy has always had a deep respect for money—and, as he had discovered in his far-off days at Oxford, it was not too hard to get to know them. More than ever, Paul enjoyed meeting almost anybody with a title.

It was on the suggestion of Commandant Paul Louis Weiller that he now recruited Claus von Bülow to his staff. This Danish lawyer, who had worked for a period in the chambers of the future Lord Chancellor Lord Hailsham, had a reputation as a womanizer and a social figure. (Born Claus Borberg, he had adopted the surname von Bülow from his maternal grandfather, a former Danish minister of justice, after his father, Svend Borberg was imprisoned after the Second World War for collaborating with the Nazis.)

Getty appointed Claus his chief executive, but since the old man hated delegating anything to anyone, he also acted as a sort of social secretary. Here he was invaluable. Claus really did know almost everyone who "mattered"—which was particularly useful now, as Paul embarked on a belated honeymoon with the British upper classes.

Before he purchased Sutton Place from the Duke of Sutherland, he had already met that most relaxed of noblemen, the Duke of Bedford, and was genuinely delighted when invited as a weekend guest to Woburn. He was equally delighted when the Duke of Rutland invited him to Belvoir Castle (which, Claus told him, gentlemen pronounce "Beaver"). But Getty's desire to establish his credentials as a fellow owner of a stately home brought trouble.

It was Claus's idea to combine the coming-of-age of Jeanette Constable-Maxwell, the daughter of a kinsman of the Duke of Norfolk, with a gala party for refurbished Sutton Place in June 1960. Paul had met Jeanette and her father, Captain Ian Constable-Maxwell, through the Duke of Rutland, and it seemed generous of this famously ungenerous American to be offering his house for the occasion.

But at some stage things got out of hand, and what began as a twenty-first birthday party rapidly became the monster bash of the London season. To the last moment, Claus was busily suggesting even more distinguished guests. So was Commandant Weiller, and by the night of June 2 the list had swollen to 1,200. It included royal dukes like the Gloucesters, humdrum dukes like the Rutlands and the Bedfords, and ship-owning Greeks like Onassis and Niarchos, plus Mr. and Mrs. Douglas Fairbanks, the Duchess of Roxburgh, and Duncan and Diana Sandys (who came in lieu of Mrs. Sandys's father, Sir Winston Churchill, whose partygoing days were over).

Apart from the Rutlands and her immediate family, young Miss Constable-Maxwell knew almost no one. Nor did Getty, who had not seen fit to ask any members of his family.

Worse still, what had been carefully planned as the acme of the social season finally became an outright free-for-all. After much advance publicity, the freelance partygoing classes were alerted, and just before midnight, gate-crashers started to arrive in droves. By the standards of the sixties, the result was fairly harmless. No one was seriously hurt; the Cellini salt-cellars were *not* stolen, as had been thought at first; and, although a photographer was thrown in the swimming pool, damages were estimated at a mere £20,000.

The only lasting damage was to Getty's reputation, which never quite recovered. For although he gained sympathy for what had happened, there was also an impression that the whole affair had been excessive and distinctly vulgar—somewhat on a level with the previous year's Battersea Park party thrown by American impresario Mike Todd, but not such fun.

Certainly the party did little to establish Getty as an honorary member of the British upper classes, nor did it herald an era of feudal extravagance for the latest lord of Sutton Place. On the contrary, while it may have seemed that he had now ascended to the dizziest reaches of high living, he was in fact as firmly rooted in economy as ever.

It was the same old puritanical response to self-indulgence. Deep down Getty must have known that neither George nor Sarah would have wasted money on a party such as this, still less upon a house as opulent as Sutton Place. Once more he was forced to justify himself before those ghostly keepers of his conscience—which meant that from the moment he took possession, everything about his life at Sutton Place became a challenge to save money and avoid unnecessary expense. Indeed, Sutton Place called forth the highest flights from Getty in his long career as virtuoso in the subtle arts of saving money.

It was typical of him to have discovered a young woman lawyer to help him with this sovereign task. Robina Lund, the twenty-five-year-old daughter of Sir Thomas Lund, the president of the Law Society, had recently qualified as a solicitor when Getty met her and her parents. Despite rumors to the contrary, she insists that—not for Getty's want of trying—she never did become his mistress, but remained his friend, admirer, legal counselor, and "honorary daughter." She was certainly a shrewd adviser, and she helped him achieve the magical fiscal situation of being legally resident in Britain while regarded by the tax authorities as domiciled in his native but now never visited United States.

In addition to this memorable achievement, she also helped him make another massive saving which presumably assuaged whatever guilt he felt at living in unseemly splendor. This had to do with the actual ownership of Sutton Place. Although Getty had made the original deal with Sutherland, the house was actually purchased, not by him, but by a subsidiary of Getty Oil called Sutton Place Properties, of which Robina Lund was a director. Sutton Place was then designated Getty Oil's official European headquarters.

Thus, in effect, Paul could live at Sutton Place for free, with his home charged to the company, which in turn could charge the cost against its tax as part of its operating expenses. Nor were the minor costs of daily living overlooked. Getty was always careful to explain to anybody interested that at Sutton Place a dry martini was actually costing him a quarter of the price he would be paying at the Ritz. He was also very much aware that his few servants and the gardeners cost approximately a third of what he would have paid in California. Ordinary guests tended to get ordinary fare, like simple cottage pie, and office costs were kept in check by reusing envelopes wherever possible, recycling rubber bands, and frugality in the use of printed writing paper. In the dining room, small electric fires were used to save on central heating.

Having spent his life avoiding giving anything to anyone, Getty saw no reason now to change his style, and it was only right that his deep obsession with economy finally brought its own poetic retribution.

As he had learned when staying as a guest in the stately homes of his beloved British aristocracy, there has always been an unstated but effective rule that just as guests are expected to put their own postage stamps on letters, so they are naturally expected to insist on paying for their personal telephone calls. But after a while he realized that this was not happening at Sutton Place, and that some of his guests were making expensive calls to Australia and the States.

It seems that this upset him deeply, partly from meanness, but also because he felt that, since he was American and rich, he was being taken for a ride, his guests treating him as they'd not have dreamt of treating, say, the Duke of Westminster.

This was the origin of Getty's greatest social blunder: the installation of his famous pay phone for his guests at Sutton Place. The action was quite logical, but that was not the point. He should have realized that as a billionaire, and an American one at that, he could simply not afford to seem as stingy as an English duke.

ONE of the interesting might-have-beens in the Getty saga is what would have happened had that lunch party at the Hôtel Georges V not occurred, Paul going as planned to the Neutral Zone, with Gordon being made manager of Golfo Oil instead.

Gordon, with his passion for music, would have loved Milan and its opera house. Being unmarried and susceptible, he would probably have married an Italian. And then, when Paul and Gail returned to California—as they undoubtedly would have, given the heat and horrible discomfort of the Neutral Zone—Gordon and not Paul might well have started the Italian branch of the Getty family, with a very different outcome for the future.

Instead, by 1962, having left his father over the trouble in the Neutral Zone, Gordon was safely back in San Francisco. He was standing in a bar called La Rocca's Corner when he met tall, auburn-haired Ann Gilbert, daughter of a walnut farmer from Wheatland in the Sacramento Valley. He was twenty-eight and she was twenty-three. They fell in love. In 1964 they married. And over the next six years they produced four sons, Peter, Andrew, John, and William. Thus, while his brother Paul was busily creating Roman Gettys, Gordon's boys grew up as true Americans.

Even in his Clay Street days, Gordon had always been in search of the simple pleasures of a settled home. In total contrast to his father, he was naturally uxorious, and his marriage proved that rarity among the Gettys—a stable and happy relationship.

One of the reasons was probably that Gordon and Ann were largely complementary. Ann had a strong puritanical element, having been brought up according to the precepts of fundamentalist Baptist Christianity, but she was also worldly, very practical, and thoroughly determined to enjoy the good life after enduring the opposite for so long on a walnut farm in the Sacramento Valley.

In many ways Gordon remained harder to fathom than his wife. Perhaps as a defense against his father, he continued to appear a sort of absent-minded professor. "I am not entirely of this century," he admitted on one occasion, and Penelope's verdict on him was more or less typical of how most of his father's friends at Sutton Place regarded him. "Gordon," she said, "is potty but in a highly intelligent way."

But Gordon's pottiness was deceptive. He was to prove extremely down-to-earth where his family was concerned, and he was determined that his sons should never suffer what he himself had endured in childhood. He was also the most indulgent and generous of husbands, so much so that Ann was often said to wear the trousers.

But beneath his undoubted kindness and the protective camouflage of the mad professor, Gordon could be extremely sharp, and surprisingly persistent where his interests and those of his immediate family were concerned—as his father now discovered.

For as well as producing further male heirs to the enormous fortune in the Sarah C. Getty Trust, Gordon's marriage had a more immediate—and, for his father, less agreeable—result. As a married man with a young wife who herself saw little point in needless self-denial, Gordon soon discovered he was short of money—which struck him, as it struck his wife, as utterly absurd.

He had a father known to be his nation's richest citizen; dollars were gushing ceaselessly into the trust specifically established by his grandmother for her grandchildren's benefit; yet he and his wife were currently living in a small motel and wondering where their next few thousand dollars were to come from.

It is often claimed that Ann was the cause of what ensued, but Gordon's friend Judge Newsom firmly insists that it was he, not Ann, who encouraged Gordon to commence the lawsuit to compel his father to disgorge at least a little of the money locked away in Grandma Getty's trust. The outcome was predictable: uproar from stately Sutton Place.

Although the amiable Gordon tried to describe his lawsuit as a "friendly" legal action simply intended to clarify an obscure financial situation, it was the equivalent of placing ground glass in the old man's coffee, or barbed wire in his double bed. Worse—for by questioning the legality of the Sarah C. Getty Trust, Gordon was not just threatening the future of the Getty fortune. He was getting at his father at the crucial point where the older man would always be acutely vulnerable.

For years the trust had been at the center of the weird emotional and financial game Paul Getty had been playing as he built his fortune. By existing to receive the accumulated conscience money he had been paying to his parents' memory, the trust had also become a wonderfully tax-efficient method of protecting and enlarging the fortune itself.

"Whatever they say about J. Paul Getty," says Judge Newsom, "he was pretty good at one thing—accruing and preserving capital." And the way he did it was to use the trust to hold his accumulated capital and thus avoid taxation. (It has been claimed almost certainly correctly that for many years Getty never paid more than $500 a year in tax.) With age, building up the corpus of the trust had become his absolute obsession.

Since he controlled the trust, he was able to ensure that it never paid a cash dividend to the beneficiaries—that is, himself and his children. Since a cash dividend constituted income, it would have been subject to taxation. Instead Getty always paid a stock dividend, which increased the beneficiary's holding in the trust, but was not considered income and so remained untaxable.

For a miserly man like Getty this was a perfect method to create a private golden mountain. His surplus wealth would make it grow. The tax authorities couldn't touch it. And nobody threatened it—until Gordon went to law to ask for some of the money that Grandma Getty had clearly intended him to have.

One can see how deeply threatened Paul Getty must have been. For the real danger to his whole magnificent creation was not the payment of a relatively small cash dividend to keep Gordon happy. It was more complicated—and more dangerous—than that. As one of the income beneficiaries of the trust, Gordon was entitled to 6.666 percent of his father's income from the trust—and he was claiming retrospectively that, in order to pay him this, his father should have paid himself dividends in cash, not stock, ever since the trust was founded back in 1936.

If Gordon could establish this in court, the Sarah C. Getty Trust would fall apart, as the tax-free basis of its dividends unraveled.

Gordon and his legal adviser, Bill Newsom, were as aware of this as Getty himself, and were counting on the threat to make the old man see a little sense and find a way of disbursing some badly needed income to the income beneficiaries. But Paul Getty was not a man to submit to threats, and particularly not threats that concerned something as important as his mother's trust and came from someone as unimportant as his youngest son.

The result was a bitter, complicated legal battle, which dragged on, with intermissions and explosions, for the next seven years, at the end of which, by a judgment of the California Supreme Court, Gordon lost.

This was largely because his father had engaged the most powerful legal hotshot of the day, the formidable trial lawyer Moses Lasky. Also, if Bill Newsom is correct, at the last moment the judge himself recoiled from the enormity of submitting the great Sarah C. Getty Trust to the potentially lethal machinations of the IRS.

After his father's death, when he himself became one of the trust's greatest beneficiaries, Gordon would have reason to be grateful for this judgment. Meanwhile, during the seven years the case lasted, it produced much tension in the family, and a number of surprises that were going to affect the Gettys' future.

In the first place, during the legal process Gordon had been able to persuade his father to pay out certain sums of money from the trust to him and his brothers Paul Junior and George. Despite this, George had dutifully sided with his father, to the point of writing outraged letters to Gordon along the lines of "How could you do this to our own dear father?" Already little love was lost between the two half-brothers, and this trouble over the trust widened the rift, which continued to the following generation.

But the strange thing was that—such is the perversity of human nature—in spite of George's loyalty, it was Gordon, not George, who ended up in favor with their father.

Ann played a part in this. "See here, Mr. Getty"—as she always called her father-in-law—"let's have an end to this," she is supposed to have said when things were getting particularly hard for Gordon. And the billionaire who never said no to a woman is said to have agreed to give a grudging semblance of forgiveness to her husband.

More to the point, perhaps, the way in which Gordon had maintained his case impressed him. Of all his sons it was the vague and unworldly Gordon who had shown the courage and determination to oppose him. This was an important omen for the future, and Getty almost certainly respected Gordon for it.

He still insisted that he couldn't understand Gordon's economic theories, still less his music, but they started seeing more of each other. He got on well with Ann and liked the children. Then, as a sign of his father's ultimate acceptance, Gordon was appointed a trustee of the museum and—ultimate accolade—in 1972 was reinstated as a trustee of the very body he had tried so hard to break—the vast, ever-growing and still unassailable Sarah C. Getty Trust.

CHAPTER TWELVE

New Beginnings

MEANWHILE in Rome, life was looking up for Jean Paul's favorite family, who had now moved on from Piazza Campitelli to a house on the Via Appia. By 1962 they were six in number, two more children, Mark and Ariadne, having been born in 1960 and 1962 respectively.

With the children born so close together, they formed a tight-knit family; the eldest, red-haired Paul, particularly adored his father. He remained his grandfather's favorite too, and was a bright, unusually affectionate small boy.

But Paul and Gail were very much innocents abroad and the unreality of Rome started to affect them. It's hard to describe the atmosphere of Rome in the early sixties. It was still very much a pagan city. Today's traffic and pollution hadn't taken over, and something about the city's beauty and antiquity gave the sense that life in Rome was richer, sexier, and more instantly enjoyable than life in any other city in the world. Like most things in the Eternal City this was largely illusory, but the fact remains that Rome at this period seemed extraordinarily exciting— particularly for young, good-looking foreigners with money.

Apart from Rome itself there was another reason for the feeling in the air. Attracted by the reputation of the Italian movie industry, and the weakness of the Italian lira, in the spring of 1962 20th Century–Fox had just begun production of one of the most expensive, crisis-ridden film epics of all time: *Cleopatra*. Further productions followed, including Clint Eastwood's Italian-made spaghetti Westerns, all of which brought actors, writers, U.S. dollars, and a touch of glamour to the nightlife of the city. Paul and Gail found their social life improving.

An American friend remembers them from the summer of 1962. "There were parties almost every night. It seemed that none of us had any worries, and Paul and Gail appeared the most carefree of all. Paul was elegant and slim and very bright, and Gail seemed particularly pretty with her short hair and great vitality. They made the perfect couple, and I remember thinking how enviable they were—and how lovely it would be to be so rich and married with four nice children. Looking back, they both seemed just a shade too perfect."

Which, of course, they were—but they did enjoy themselves. They could afford sufficient help to look after the children, and they made a host of friends, including the writer William Styron and the film director John Huston. Paul spent a lot of time with Mario Lanza working out a way to bring American baseball to Italy, while Gail loved dancing at clubs like Lollobrigida's on the Appia Antica, or the famous Ottanta Quattro on the Via Margutta.

Gradually they found that they were leading almost separate lives, and differences in their characters began to show. Gail was gregarious, loved parties, and had a great deal of energy. Paul was different. Part of him wished to be a glamorous playboy, but, as Gail says, "he didn't realise how glamorous he was, and anyhow was much too shy to do anything very much about it." His other side was extremely serious and hankered after books and learning.

Life in Rome had done nothing to resolve the two sides of his character. Paul had begun to hate his work with Getty Oil Italiana, he was responsible for a large young family in a foreign city, and he had the feeling that something in his life was seriously adrift. He told Gail that what he really wanted was to be an oceanographer.

As this seemed impossible, he became discontented. He was drinking and became increasingly reclusive. Often when he and Gail had planned to go out, he would change his mind at the last minute and decide to stay at home reading. Whenever possible he avoided driving. He had always been an introvert at heart, and was showing signs of opting out of the life around him. This left Gail to enjoy the dancing and the parties on her own.

As she admits, "I really wasn't the maltreated wife, St. Gail, who stayed at home while Paul was out swinging around. To be honest it was rather the reverse."

One of the qualities the *dolce vita* of Fellini's film failed to encompass was monogamy, and it was probably impossible for the marriage to have lasted in the midst of so much worldly glamour. So-called open marriages rarely do, particularly if there are differences of personality between the partners. Inevitably Gail fell in love with someone else. And just as inevitably—being the character she was—she decided that she had to go.

*

LANG Jeffries was almost entirely Paul's antithesis—and Paul, who knew and liked him, was surprised as well as rather shocked when Gail confessed she was in love with him and wished to live with him.

A rugged, all-American former actor from Los Angeles, Jeffries had been married to the film star Rhonda Fleming. He was a great sportsman—golfer, yachtsman, tennis player—and he had come to Rome to make low-budget Italian television epics, which, as Gail says, "he didn't take too seriously." Young Paul and Aileen inevitably resented him, but Mark and Ariadne came to like him, for, if nothing else, Lang was dependable.

Paul was genuinely upset that Gail wished to leave him, but they had a pact that they would never lie to each other. Paul had had love affairs himself, so he couldn't argue when Gail said she was in love. Still fond of each other, they made the sort of pact affectionate couples often do when their marriage dies on them.

Gail would have the children and set up house with Lang in a new apartment. Paul would also move. (In fact, Gail found a flat for him.) And as she was breaking up the marriage, she felt she had no financial claim on him, so there was no question of alimony. Nor, at this point was there any talk of remarriage. Paul begged her not to think of getting a divorce, and she agreed. They would all remain in Rome and stay friends; Paul, of course, would see the children as and when he wanted.

It seemed the best solution—if a very Roman one. "We were absurdly civilised," says Gail. "It might have been better if we'd not been."

Now Paul, left to himself, decided to enjoy life, and despite his shyness and his love of privacy he seems to have had great success with women.

Von Bülow loyally describes him now as "incredibly handsome and sexy," and probably overstates the number of his Roman conquests when he says that "he slept with more beautiful women than his father." (Perhaps the claim depends on how one interprets the word "beautiful.")

On the other hand, there may be something in the implication that Paul was covertly competing with the old man's exploits as a womanizer. Sex was very much a game for him, and friends from this period now insist that his love affairs were always tactful and discreet—as a friend said, "not blatant and exhibitionist like so many visiting Americans with their women." The Getty name would prove a great advantage when it came to stars like Bardot, who was in Rome making *le Repos du Guerrier* (English title: *Love on a Pillow*) in 1962.

At this period, Paul was drifting. He found even less pleasure than before in his work for Getty Oil Italiana, and had little of the self-control his father derived from the need to make a lot of money. Paul knew quite well that, work or not, he would finally inherit his due portion of the trust, and so he was currently marching to an old Italian tune. It was entitled "dolce far niente"

In Rome there had always been an accepted role for rich young men like Paul to play. Nothing vicious or particularly depraved; the young *signore* desires to enjoy himself before shouldering life's burdens, which come soon enough. He wishes to relax, drive slowly around the city, meet interesting people and be gracious in return, collect books, eat well, drive down to Positano or up to Santa Margherita, lie in the sun with someone pretty, drink, get laid, and then next day begin again. Dolce far niente.

Happiness. Like everyone in Rome Paul simply wanted to be happy. So did Gail, but in Paul's case the search for happiness would lead him to the love that would all but ruin his life.

TALITHA—pronounced "Tah-lee-tah"—Pol was as pretty as she sounded, with doll-like face, an eager, sexy nature, and a sense of happiness that spread to those around her. She was that perilous rarity, an enchantress, and only in retrospect does one see the danger enchant-resses can bring to others—and ultimately to themselves. For those who fall beneath their spell expect too much, indulge them to excess, then blame them when the spell is broken.

Although she lived in London, Talitha was Dutch. Her father, Willem Pol, a handsome painter, had married pretty Adine Mees, from a well-to-do Amsterdam family, in 1936. Three years later, they found them-selves in Java on a painting expedition as war began in Europe, and the German invasion of their homeland kept them in Indonesia.

In September 1940, when Talitha was born, the Pols were still in Java, and rather than bring her back to Europe, they moved on to Bali, where they were captured and interned when the Japanese arrived in 1943. The conditions of their captivity were appalling. Willem was parted from his wife and baby daughter, and although they were re-united after the Japanese surrender, Adine never fully recovered from her sufferings. She died in 1948.

When Willem remarried, three years later, it was to Poppet John, the daughter of Augustus John, a celebrated English painter of an older generation. They bought a simple terrace house on Chilworth

Street in Paddington, but spent their holidays in a cottage in what was then the sleepy village of Ramatuelle, near St. Tropez in the south of France.

Having no children of her own, Poppet acted as a mother to Talitha, who particularly needed affection after the horrors of the prison camp. Talitha grew to love the South of France, and she and Poppet and her father were extremely close.

Like many spoiled pretty girls, Talitha longed to be a film star. She was actually in Rome in 1963 as an extra in a five-second crowd scene in the all-providing *Cleopatra*. On this brief visit she did not meet Paul, and afterward, apart from carnal propositions from various producers, her career in films seemed over. Not that this worried her unduly. With her looks and her family connections, she could enjoy a lively social life in London, then marry.

For an enchantress like Talitha this shouldn't have been difficult. As a friend of hers remembers, "She had a penchant for attracting clever older men, but actually preferred the company of younger smarter ones." Some of them were very fashionable indeed. Lord Lambton knew her, Lord Kennet thought her "an absolute knockout," and Lord Christopher Thynne fell in love with her. But the last also remembers "how difficult Talitha was to keep as a girl-friend because she was a most tremendous flirt, or rather an overflirt, and I never knew where I was with her." Nor, it seems, did any of her lovers.

For she was not as carefree as she seemed; she still bore the mental scars from her childhood in the prison-camp. Lord Christopher tells of how he once jokingly made the sign of the evil eye at her by pointing two outstretched fingers at her face, and how she cowered. When he asked her why, she told him that his gesture reminded her of how the camp guards used to push their fingers into the children's eyes to hurt them.

Much of her flirting served as cover for her insecurity. What she needed was someone young and rich and handsome to look after her—someone exactly like the now unattached Paul Getty. All that was needed was a catalyst to make this happen.

IN gothic tales there is often a doom carrier who emerges from the shadows, plays his fateful part, and then departs on his separate unhappy destiny. For Talitha and Paul, this role was played by Claus von Bülow.

When Getty died in 1976, von Bülow was to leave England for America and the heiress Sunny Von Auersberg, who had inherited a

$700 million fortune from her father, the American utilities multimillionaire, George Crawford. There is an eerie symmetry in the way von Bülow, who would one day find himself accused of trying to murder his glamorous rich wife, was already pointing Paul and Talitha to an equally harrowing disaster.

Von Bülow was living in a grand apartment in Belgravia, and naturally knew Talitha. Shortly after New Year's, 1965, he invited her to dinner.

Like many at the time, Talitha was fascinated by Rudolf Nureyev, who had just fled Russia and was starting his career in London with the Royal Ballet. She had already met him at Lee Radziwill's house in Henley-on-Thames. Von Bülow told her he was coming and promised to place her next to him at dinner.

But the temperamental dancer never came, and von Bülow sat Talitha next to Paul instead. Paul was in England visiting his father, and had not expected to encounter anyone so pretty and amusing in London.

Next morning at the house at Chilworth Street, Talitha complained of a cold, and told her father she would sleep late. Willem, having heard her returning in the small hours, guessed her trouble was probably a hangover, and left her to sleep it off.

But later that morning, Poppet Pol returned from a shopping expedition to discover a young man on the doorstep with a bulky cardboard box of flowers. He asked where Talitha Pol lived, and when she asked him who he was he introduced himself.

He was invited in and, having charmed Talitha's parents, Paul invited her to Sutton Place to meet his father. Surprisingly, she failed to impress him, for the ancient amorist possessed a prudish side and disapproved of modern girls in miniskirts. But if Talitha and old Paul failed to hit it off, this did not keep her from sensing the attractions of his son. When Lord Christopher saw her a few days later he knew at once his hopes were dashed. Soon afterward, Talitha and Paul flew to Rome together.

This was the last the Pols would see of them till early summer, when they came to stay at Ramatuelle. Willem found Paul "more likeable" than ever—easy to talk to, erudite, and still a little shy.

At this point there was still no talk of marriage. But everywhere Paul went with Talitha people remarked on what a handsome, happy pair they made together.

ARRANGIARSI—a particularly Italian word for a particular Roman specialty. It means, literally, "to arrange oneself."

In the spring of 1966, life was arranging itself around the Roman Gettys with the deceptive ease that is another specialty of the city. The sun was shining, Gail had settled down with Lang in a large flat in a modern quarter of the city, and Paul and Talitha were living happily together in a penthouse apartment of some luxury next to the Carlo Pontis in Piazza Aracoeli.

At the very center of ancient Rome the venerable church of the Aracoeli, the altar of heaven, derived its name from the altar that the Emperor Augustus supposedly erected in a temple on the site after seeing a vision of a virgin and a child.

Thus, as well as being in a highly fashionable location, Talitha and Paul were living in one of the most historic parts of ancient Rome. They were also near the city's famous "Wedding Cake," the great white marble monument to the first king of united Italy, Victor Emmanuel, and close at hand was the balcony from which the elder Getty's onetime hero, Mussolini, harangued the Roman multitudes in Piazza Venezia.

But that was in the past. For the present, now that everyone seemed happy with the current dispensation, it was time to sort the situation out as fairly and as fast as possible.

Despite their earlier agreement, Paul and Gail had finally divorced, but since the parting was so amicable and Gail got nothing, they decided to invite their mutual friend Bill Newsom to help arrange the details of the children's settlement. Everybody liked and trusted Bill and he knew the law. Invite him over.

So William Newsom arrived in Rome. He had always been extremely fond of Paul—but he was also wary of him. He responded to Paul's charm, his cleverness, his wit, all of which were reminscent of his mother, Ann—although he also remembered something of Paul's wild side.

Here in Rome, Paul was happily in love—and Paul in happy mood was the most irresistible of mortals. (When the black mood descended, things were different.) So Bill Newsom found it relatively easy to arrange the details of a settlement for the children.

As Gail was not requesting alimony for herself, Paul readily agreed to pay approximately a third of his after-tax income as child support. In 1965 this meant a third of $54,000, plus medical and educational expenses. It was also agreed that above $54,000 there should be a sliding scale, so that if Paul's income rose above $1 million, 5 percent of it should be paid annually into trusts of which Paul, Gail, and Bill Newsom would be trustees.

An additional clause was inserted in the settlement. In order to protect the children from fortune hunters while they were still young, it was decreed that any child who married before the age of twenty-two would lose his or her share of the trust.

It all seemed generous and straightforward—not that this would keep the agreement from causing trouble in the future. Like everyone that summer, Paul simply wanted everybody to be happy. Bill Newsom felt the same, and as he boarded his San Francisco–bound plane at Fiumicino, he was hopeful for the future of his friends.

It seemed that everything was working out, and the perfect weather, continuing through August and September, made this a celebratory Italian summer for the Gettys. Wishing to have somewhere far from Rome where they could take the children, Gail and Lang discovered a Tuscan house called La Fuserna in the tiny village of Orgia, south of Siena. The house was absurdly cheap but needed renovating, while the village was still miraculously unspoiled, the countryside spectacular; everyone who stayed there loved it. For the children this would become their favorite home—the place where they would spend their holidays, play with the children in the village, and hunt for mushrooms in the nearby woods in autumn.

Even old Paul appeared in his nearest to a sunny mood when he arrived at the Hotel Flora in Rome with Mary Tessier.

He once wrote of the Emperor Hadrian that "the great traveller had come to a time of life when the inconveniences of travel made him loath to take long journeys." Now in his early seventies, he felt the same. He was increasingly scared of travel, and coming to Italy at all had been an emotional ordeal. Since he wouldn't fly, and wouldn't risk the Channel ferries, his answer was to board the *Queen Elizabeth* at Southampton at the start of its transtlantic voyage, then disembark at Cherbourg. Even he had to admit that a transatlantic liner was unlikely to be shipwrecked in the English Channel.

But once in Rome, he felt safe in the haven of his beloved Hotel Flora, and began his tour of the sights that he had always loved. Again, as he strolled through the Roman Forum, he had that strange sensation of déjà vu, of having seen everything centuries before. The sense of returning to the past was at its most intense when he visited his favorite building: the great rotunda of the Roman Pantheon, which was rebuilt in its present form by the Emperor Hadrian around the year 120 A.D. Convinced that he was the emperor reincarnate, Getty seemed to take a personal pride in it and its survival, and on seeing the building yet again he explained to Mary something that only he could possibly have thought of.

Had it ever struck her, he inquired, that the Pantheon was so well built that during the whole time of its existence it had never needed fire insurance? "Just think of how much money that had saved," he added. "Had it been kept insured since the day it was built 2000 years ago, the total insurance premiums with compound interest would add up to more money than there is in the world today."

It was a somber thought, and grounds for self-congratulation. But at the same time, as he looked at the building, Getty realized that Hadrian had missed a splendid opportunity to immortalize his name. The emperor had been too modest in giving credit for the building to its original founder, the consul Marcus Agrippa, whose name he placed in massive letters on the pediment.

This was a grave mistake, which Getty would not repeat when he came to build another Roman villa to perpetuate his own memory. He had been considering doing this for some time, and not until 1968 would the work begin. But he had now decided to create a museum near the ranch house at Malibu; it would house his furniture collection, items of marble statuary, and the pictures he was buying.

There had already been discussions concerning the form of the museum, but against some contradictory advice, Getty had decided on exactly what he wanted. Some years before, on a trip to Naples, he had visited the site of the fabled villa of the Roman multimillionaire Calpurnius Piso, which had been buried in volcanic ash when Vesuvius erupted and destroyed Pompeii and Herculaneum.

Detail-obsessed as ever, Getty had taken the trouble to find out all about the villa. It had been excavated in the 1760s for the King of Naples by a German archaeologist, whose report Getty had studied, together with the plans of the villa, the treasures with which it had been crammed, and the mass of records on papyrus preserved in the volcanic dust, which had given the place its name—the Villa dei Papiri.

He had been most impressed by it, and once he had convinced himself that in a former life he had been the Emperor Hadrian, the Villa dei Papiri took on a particular significance. Hadrian had been a friend of Piso's and had often visited his villa—which meant that Getty himself must have been there.

It had once been part of Hadrian's imperial power to order the construction of temples and great public buildings in the farthest reaches of his empire. Desiring to "emulate his spirit," Getty would now repeat these earlier activities, recreating this villa, which he knew so well, in a distant spot he also knew: facing the Pacific on the shore at Malibu.

The museum could be made identical to Calpurnius's villa—with the same decorations on the walls, the same plants and shrubs, even copies of the original bronze statues in the gardens. Since he was now as rich as any Roman emperor, Getty could make sure that his replica was filled with even more prestigious treasures than Piso's. And he could correct the error he—Getty-Hadrian—had made when he built the Pantheon. His name, and his alone, would be recorded in the villa he would build in California.

WHILE Getty was still in Rome, the sense of family occasion was completed with the arrival of Ann and Gordon from America. As paterfamilias, Getty was becoming positively benign; he accompanied Gordon to an unusual family occasion—the recording, in the Naples opera house, of a full-scale opera that Paul Jr. was backing to the tune of $20,000.

The budget did not stretch to one of the Verdi operas Gordon would have liked, so his brother had chosen one of Mozart's lesser-known operas, *Il Rè Pastore*, "The Shepherd King." Set in the sunlit world of classical mythology, it is the story of a lost inheritance and the rediscovery of a king disguised as a shepherd boy. As the old man and his two sons heard the ravishing Lucia Popp sing the lead part in one of the happiest of Mozart's operas, the music may for once have matched the mood with which they faced the future.

CHAPTER THIRTEEN

Roman Weddings

IN December 1966, as if to underline the part that Rome was playing in the fortunes of the Gettys, Paul and Talitha married in the very place where Gail had wed Lang Jeffries a few months earlier, and where Jean Paul Getty had married Teddy Lynch in 1939: the city hall, the Campidoglio, crowning the Roman Capitol. The central point of ancient Rome itself, it was a spectacular setting for a wedding, with its views across the ruined Roman Forum and the nearby Palace of the Senators of Rome. The ancient bronze equestrian statue of the Emperor Marcus Aurelius still rode the plinth designed for him by Michelangelo, and the antique statues of Castor and Pollux, guardians of Rome, flanked the steps descending to the city. The wedding photographs show Talitha in a mink-trimmed bridal miniskirt, holding a lily and looking like the sixties flower child she was. She stands between two smiling adults, Paul and Penelope.

Paul, at thirty-four, was better-looking than he'd ever been, and his smile gives just a hint of the shy charm people still remember. Penelope in her beautifully tailored coat was standing proxy for the bridegroom's father, who was too busy making money to attend. (According to one story, he told a visiting oil tycoon that he didn't know about the wedding.)

Not that Getty Senior would be greatly missed at the ceremony or at the ensuing bridal lunch at the Casa Valadier restaurant, in the Borghese Gardens. Still less was he missed at the big, all-night reception held in the apartment of a sculptor friend. It was a memorable affair, one of several "parties of the year."

Next morning the bridal pair rose early and departed for an extended honeymoon in Marrakesh. For various reasons that city appealed to them.

*

OF course the old man had known all about the wedding, but he disapproved of everything to do with it. For by now he had fallen out of love with handsome Paul—which, combined with escalating troubles at the Naples refinery, placed a further strain upon his love affair with Italy.

Behind Getty's changed attitude toward his once-favorite son lay rumors he had been hearing concerning Paul and Talitha. Both, it seemed, had recently become hippies, and had joined the counterculture of the sixties with extremely worrying dedication.

By being in Europe, Paul had in fact originally missed out on the hippie phenomenon when it started in his native San Francisco. But it might have been devised with him in mind; and now, like the man in Molière who suddenly discovers he had always spoken prose, Paul discovered he had always been one of nature's hippies. The Eastern-born Talitha encouraged him, and flower power, self-fulfillment, and the drug-hazed lure of the magnetic East had entered both their lives with a vengeance.

A sort of gentrified hippiedom was the perfect way of life for a couple like Paul and Talitha. With its cult of nonviolent anarchy and self-expression, and its rejection of Western materialism, the hippie movement was particularly adapted to the easy rich with nothing very much to do. Almost overnight nobody in Rome had been cooler and more hip than Paul and Talitha, but not even charming Paul could manage to combine the hippie ethic with the oil industry. Nothing seemed more soul-destroying than the activity from which his family derived its money, nothing more crucifying than to have to work in a dark suit in the offices of Getty Oil Italiana. So the offices of Getty Oil Italiana rarely saw him any longer.

Nor did Gail and the children see much more of him, although they were all still living in Rome at the time. One afternoon the family had been enjoying an English film at the Fiammetta Cinema, and noticed a bearded man enter wearing long hair and small John Lennon glasses. Only young Paul had recognized him as his father.

Soon after this, Paul and Talitha had gone to Thailand, where they had conducted their first serious experiments with drugs. Back in England someone at Sutton Place made sure that the old man saw a magazine with pictures of his son, bearded, longhaired, and dressed in what the caption called "a tie-dyed green velvet outfit that would have made any hippie green with envy."

Big Paul was not impressed, for unlike his son he was emphatically not a natural hippie, and although the Emperor Hadrian had worn a beard from the age of thirty-two, Getty had always had a powerful dislike of facial hair.

Also at Sutton Place, there was no dearth of information over what was happening in Rome, and in particular over the affairs of Getty Oil Italiana. Angry words were shouted down the telephone. "Any idiot can be a businessman," said Paul—which was rather like the Prince of Wales informing Her Majesty that any fool could be a monarch.

It was shortly after this that his father's latest mistress, the notorious Duchess of Argyll, had calmly announced at lunch at Sutton Place that she had heard that Paul Getty, Jr., was on heroin. Getty had been deeply—indeed painfully—shocked. He had a genuine horror of drug addiction, and he now broke off relations with his son until he promised to desist. Paul Junior wouldn't promise, and it wasn't long before he tendered his resignation as general manager of Getty Oil Italiana. His father, as head of the company, accepted.

This left Paul without a job—but not without his income, currently approaching $100,000, courtesy of Grandma Getty.

It was early summer. The tourists were already in the city, and the penthouse flat was airless in the Roman evenings. Now that Paul was jobless, were the newlyweds feeling a touch of that Roman sickness known as accidia—the boredom that afflicted monks and courtesans?

"Carpe diem," says an inscription that recurs on the city's monuments and public buildings: "Seize the day."

They did.

LE Palais da Zahir—mixed French and Arabic for "The Pleasure Palace"—had belonged to a French property developer called M. Aigret, who had bought it twenty years before as a speculation and couldn't sell it. In the picturesque ancient quarter of Marrakesh known as Sidi Mimoun, it had been standing empty ever since.

The enterprising Bill Willis—a fashionable, high-camp American interior decorator—had shown it to Paul and Talitha while they were there on honeymoon, and they fell in love with it and bought it for $10,000. Since then Bill had been restoring it for them with typical panache, repairing ancient woodwork and mosaics, finding them decorative objects, furniture, and carpets in profusion, and having tiles specially baked in Fez to replace the antique tiles that were missing.

Paul had known handsome Bill when he still owned the small antique shop at the top of the Spanish Steps in Rome. Bill had always had an instinct for the very rich, which is a prerequisite for success in his profession, and he was most successful. (Since the 1960s he has done over villas for Alain Delon, Yves St. Laurent, and the sister of the King of Morocco.)

When the Palais da Zahir was finished, John Richardson (distinguished biographer of Picasso) found it sinister, but most other visitors thought it fun and loved it.

It had a blue front door to guard against the evil eye, four separate courtyards (in one of which Talitha planted roses), spectacular views of the Atlas Mountains from the roof, and an air of timeless beauty and decay, which was part of the charm of old Marrakesh before they built the ring road and the modern airport.

Tout lasse, *tout casse*, *tout passe*, and nowhere more seductively than here in Marrakesh, "the most southerly town of civilised history," as Sacheverell Sitwell once described it.

Since the wartime days when Allied statesmen like Churchill and Eisenhower came here to enjoy the climate and the scenery, the town had become fashionable as a staging post on the hippie trail to the East. With Paul and Talitha in residence, da Zahir was becoming part of the trail itself.

"The house was a dream, like so much round Talitha and Paul," says a visitor remembering that summer. "It was always *en grande fête*, always a perpetual party with fascinating and amusing people and something wonderful occurring. It might be jugglers and fortune-tellers or musicians. One evening a Moroccan general turned up just like that with his private troupe of dancers. Thanks to Talitha, the food was quite delicious—when it came."

As hosts Talitha and Paul were not wildly rich, certainly not in the hyperwealthy class of millionaire American expatriates like Peggy Guggenheim or Barbara Hutton. But they possessed the Getty name, with its promise of imminent riches which was somehow more exciting than the ponderous reality of total wealth.

Even then this somehow marked them out from all their guests. Not that their guests were poor themselves, or boring. *Au contraire*, they included literary figures like Gore Vidal, serious celebrities like Mick Jagger, and cosmopolites as socially impressive as Prince Dado Ruspoli.

But as a son of one of the the richest human beings in the world, Paul was starting to project a touch of the revered apartness once exhibited by minor European royalty. Two centuries earlier, he might have been a dauphin to a Bourbon king. Now he and Talitha were becoming members of a lonely superclass with rules and tastes and mores of its own.

*

THE unsuspecting Pols arrived at da Zahir on a two-week holiday late that autumn.

Finding the gardens lit by camphor flares, huge fires of olive logs blazing at each end of high-beamed rooms, jasmine and woodsmoke flavoring the air, and delicious meals consumed at night on priceless rugs beneath the stars, they formed predictable first impressions: "Arabian Nights, no less," they murmured to each other.

But from the start they also felt uneasy about Talitha and Paul, who frequently seemed moody. Also, they worried about the number of freeloading guests whose presence could infuriate their son-in-law, so much so that the Pols heard him shout to Talitha to kick them out. When this happened Talitha became moody.

Then it rained—heavily—and despite the tasteful work of Mr. Willis, the roof leaked. And finally it dawned upon the Pols that there were reasons other than rain and guests for Paul and Talitha's moodiness. As Poppet put it, she and Willem realized that the diet at da Zahir was not confined to orange juice, char-broiled lamb, and onion tart.

The local cakes from Mr. Very Good the Baker had curious ingredients, as had the homemade jam with the lingering aftertaste which everyone apparently enjoyed. In Poppet the hashish produced heightened colors and made everything move in slow motion. Willem said he would have prefered two double scotches. She soon discovered to her cost that drugs could induce extreme loquacity, as well as drowsiness, in others.

One night at dinner she was seated next to a nice young man with long blond hair who fell asleep between courses, resting his head upon her shoulder. When he awoke, he started begging her to let him take her with him on a trip, explaining that, although LSD was wonderful, you needed somebody beside you until you grew used to it.

Despite the presence of so many charming people, the drug scene at da Zahir failed to captivate the Pols, and when they left for France soon afterward, they were uneasy for the future of the Getty marriage. Their unease lifted somewhat when a child was born to Talitha in Rome on May 30, 1968, but the baby boy's names worried them: Tara Gabriel Galaxy Gramaphone Getty. "Rich Kid with Daft Name," as the newspaper in Paul's native San Francisco put it.

AFTER the baby's birth Talitha and Paul were off on their travels again—"Come East, young lovers, the journey not the arrival matters"—taking with them baby Tara G. G. G. plus scatty English nanny.

They were bound for Indonesia and Bali, to rediscover people and places Talitha remembered from her shattered childhood.

But the Pols' old house in Bali had been destroyed. The nanny's culinary skills stretched no further than scrambled eggs, and while Tara was developing a lifetime aversion to that dish, Paul and Talitha were forming a taste for something more exotic. What Paul wanted more than ever now was happiness—along with love and peace and the heightened self-awareness only drugs could bring. So did Talitha. But her letters to the Pols began to hint that she was not entirely happy. Heroin was giving her a sense of mounting persecution and unease— and spots on her face, which also worried her. By now both she and Paul were totally addicted.

When the Pols visited their daughter and son-in-law in Rome they were shocked at the change in both of them. Even Poppet knew enough to realize that the ingredients of Mr. Very Good's cookies were not the cause.

The enchantress's spell was broken. So was her marriage. Privately Talitha told her father that she couldn't cope and was frightened and wanted to return to London. For Tara's sake she felt she must escape from drugs and hippiedom and Italy.

Soon after this a friend of Talitha's, passing through Rome, called at the apartment in Piazza Aracoeli on the off chance of seeing her. Not realizing that Talitha was back in London, and finding the house wide open, she entered and walked up the stairs to look for her. No one was about, but, hearing music from the top of the house, she went to investigate. Instead of Talitha, she discovered Paul recumbent on cushions on the floor, smoking opium. Lost in another world, he did not notice her.

WITH the marriage breaking up, neither spouse was being faithful, and there was now another woman on the scene—Victoria Holdsworth, a former model and the ex-wife of Lionel Brooke, the last white rajah of Sarawak. Victoria was young and very beautiful; since she'd been brought to Marrakesh for a holiday, Paul had been seeing her a lot, so she dates the beginning of their long and intermittent love affair to this period. But although Paul was infatuated with Victoria and grew to depend on her, he also stayed deeply and possessively in love with Talitha.

One of the benefits of wealth is that you can always shelve your problems, keep your lover, buy an unhappy wife a house in another country, and thus solve everything and nothing. Thus too a sort of compromise was reached. Paul would go to London with Talitha; there they would buy a house together so that she could live with Tara, start her life afresh, and undergo a cure for heroin addiction. Paul meanwhile would continue living in Rome with Victoria, but also visit Talitha and Tara in London as often as he could. Talitha promised she would visit Paul in Rome with Tara. In this way life could cheerfully continue. No one would be hurt. Everybody would be happy.

IN its day, Queen's House on Chelsea's Cheyne Walk must have been one of the loveliest houses in London. Built beside the Thames in 1707 and sometimes erroneously attributed to both Christopher Wren and John Vanbrugh, it had been modernized by Edwin Lutyens in the 1930s, and was still one of the most desirable residences in this most desirable quarter of the city when Talitha and Paul first saw it.

(Its new owner, hoping to exorcise its ghosts, has returned it to its original name, Tudor House, but throughout this period it was known as Queen's House.)

It possessed a forty-foot-long drawing room with original eighteenth-century paneling and splendid views across the river, a fine old garden once part of the original Chelsea Manor, magnificent gates by an anonymous Surrey ironmaster, and one of the prettiest dining rooms in London.

For Paul its immediate attraction was that for several years in the 1860s it had been home to one of his heroes, the poet and Pre-Raphaelite painter Dante Gabriel Rossetti. The Pre-Raphaelite Brotherhood, which Rossetti founded with the painters Millais and Holman Hunt, held a special place in the hearts and minds of the hippie generation of the sixties, who had seen them as Victorian precursors of much that they believed in—romantic idealism, a carefree and nonjudgmental attitude toward sex, and, in Rossetti's case, the strong element of drug-induced hallucination they detected in his painting.

Queen's House was one of the shrines of the Brotherhood, for it was here that Rossetti came to live in 1862, after the mysterious death a few months earlier of his favorite model, whose features haunt many of his paintings: his auburn-haired, drug-addicted wife, Lizzie Siddal, who had consumed an overdose of laudanum in his presence.

Rossetti's story fascinated Paul. Whatever the reasons behind Lizzie's death, it had clearly marked the painter like a sudden stroke of high romantic doom. He was at the height of his powers as a painter, but from the moment he entered Queen's House, Rossetti's guilt and grief for his dead wife started to obsess him. Already addicted to chloral, one of the Victorians' preferred recreational drugs, he relied on it increasingly to calm his nerves and alleviate his sadness, drinking it in quite alarming quantities despite attempts by friends like the poet Algernon Charles Swinburne and the novelist George Meredith to stop him. Under the influence of drugs he became increasingly reclusive, his health gave way, and he died at the age of fifty-four in 1882.

Paul, excited by the strong associations between Queen's House and the Pre-Raphaelites, was not troubled by the gloomy nature of the story or by any parallels it might hold for him. On the contrary, feeling so much in common with the Pre-Raphaelites and having purchased the house, he was anxious to restore it as much as possible to what it must have been in the years when the painter lived there.

By a strange coincidence Poppet and Willem Pol also knew the house, but in a very different guise from the gloomy haunt of Rossetti in his "chloralized years" of the 1860s.

Lutyens's modernizations had banished the murk and cobwebs of the past, and the house had been owned in the 1930s by the queen's stockbroker, urbane Hugo Pitman, who was a friend of Ian Fleming and a patron of Augustus John. Poppet could remember visiting the house on several occasions as a child and seeing her father's pictures hanging on the walls. She even remembered meeting Queen Elizabeth (the present Queen Mother) there. Pitman was always rumored to have been in love with her, and Poppet's memories of drinking champagne in Queen's House with a real queen made the house seem very special.

Because of this she was shocked to see decorators putting dark paint onto eighteenth-century paneling, hanging somber-colored curtains, and installing modern central heating. The Queen's House she remembered was a place of gaiety and light, with open fires in the rooms, and she felt unhappy as the house took on an atmosphere of curious ill-omen such as it must have had when Rossetti lived there.

Once Talitha and Tara were in residence, however, none of this seemed to matter any longer. Talitha loved the house and her return to London soon became a great success, as her social life there began again. She was not as deeply addicted to heroin as Paul; alcohol had been a greater problem. She had had little difficulty giving up the drug for periods, and by the summer of 1970 she seemed completely cured of heroin and hippiedom and Rome. She also seemed cured of Paul, and had even gotten on friendly terms with his father. The old man was still refusing to speak to his son, but occasionally took Talitha out to dinner.

Inevitably she found herself a new young lover, and she had become friendly with her old hero Nureyev. (She was said to have been the only woman he was ever physically in love with.) Soon the trips to Rome with Tara tailed off. By the spring of 1971 she plucked up courage to inform her husband that she wanted a divorce.

It is a measure of his lack of contact with reality that Paul was genuinely shocked. He insisted he was still in love with Talitha, and the prospect of losing her made her doubly precious. So he begged her to return to Rome at once to talk things over. At first she was reluctant, but her lawyers told her it would strengthen her position over a divorce if she could show that she had tried for a reconciliation. On the morning of July 9 she duly caught the morning plane to Rome.

That evening she visited Paul in their old apartment, but the meeting ended badly and she returned to spend the night at the Dutch embassy in Rome (conveniently, her aunt Lot Boon was married to the Dutch ambassador), promising to return to continue the discussion next evening.

On her second night in Rome, Talitha returned to Piazza Aracoeli at around nine-thirty. The atmosphere was calmer than the night before, for Paul had made it clear that he definitely wanted her back and was even prepared to change his way of life if necessary. He would give up both his drugs and his mistress if she promised to return to him.

If anyone knows for sure what happened then, it's Paul. Somehow he persuaded Talitha to stay, and finally she fell asleep in the terrace room on the roof of the apartment, with its views of the Roman Capitol where she had married Paul just five years earlier.

Sometime after ten o'clock next morning Paul awoke. Talitha did not.

CHAPTER FOURTEEN

Casualties

JEAN Paul Getty himself had been in Rome shortly before Talitha's visit, and invited Gail and the children for a few days' holiday at La Posta Vecchia. She and her family still enjoyed the old man's favor, and she particularly recalls a luncheon at the house in honor of his rival Dr. Armand Hammer, head of Occidental Oil, who was also visiting the city.

Even now old Paul took an old man's pleasure in provoking jealousy among his women. Placing Gail beside him, he had whispered, "Just watch this!", knowing that the presence at table of his latest mistress, the voluptuous Mrs. Rosabella Burch, would inevitably upset the insecure Mary Teissier. But in fact Rosabella provided a more engrossing spectacle by flirting outrageously throughout the meal with the aged but patently entranced Dr. Hammer.

During this short stay in Rome, Getty had still refused to contact Paul and returned to England at the end of June without seeing him. However, he insisted that Gail and the children should stay on for a few days longer if they wished. They did, and because of this had just got back to Orgia when Gail received a call from her distraught ex-husband late in the afternoon of July 11. He told her what had happened: Talitha had been taken to Rome's Villa del Rosario Clinic in deepest coma. There they had tried to rescusitate her—unsuccessfully—and shortly after midday she had died without regaining consciousness.

Paul sounded so desperate that Gail decided to drive to Rome at once to be with him. She found him overwhelmed with grief and terrible remorse. He couldn't face returning to Piazza Aracoeli, so she suggested that he go to La Posta Vecchia instead. He agreed, and as he seemed inconsolable, she stayed with him.

Everyone mourned Talitha, not least Gail and the children. As she says, "Talitha played no part in the breakup of our marriage, and we'd grown extremely fond of her." The funeral was held in Amsterdam,

119

where Talitha was buried in a simple grave beside her mother. Those present included Paul, the Pols, a few close members of the family, and Talitha's old admirer Lord Lambton, who had flown in from London with three of her old women friends.

The Pols were numbed with grief, Willem in particular. Shortly afterward he had a heart attack, from which he never fully recovered. But it was Paul who appeared most riven at the funeral. With Talitha gone, he realized he loved her more than ever. Stricken with remorse and guilt, he could not forgive himself for what had happened and for having been incapable of saving her.

But what exactly *had* occurred that night in Piazza Aracoeli? Since Paul himself refused to say, the sequence of events was never clarified and the facts behind Talitha's death remain a mystery.

According to the death certificate signed by doctors at the clinic, death was due to cardiac arrest; high levels of alcohol and barbiturates were discovered in Talitha's blood. As she was known to be a heavy drinker who sometimes took barbiturates to offset the effect of alcohol, there is no firm reason to doubt the facts recorded on the certificate. Barbiturates and alcohol taken together in large quantities can be a lethal combination and could certainly have accounted for her death.

But as a heroin addict, Paul was in a vulnerable position and could not risk saying anything himself about the circumstances of Talitha's death. Possession of narcotics was an indictable offense in Italy, often carrying a penalty of imprisonment, and things would almost certainly have turned extremely nasty for him if the police had initiated an official inquiry and his addiction had been revealed.

To avoid this and stay safely out of Rome until the situation cleared, he opted for a period in Bangkok, which he had loved when he visited it with Talitha in happier times. In Thailand drugs were available if he needed them, and he would have peace and quiet to recover from her death and decide about the future. To keep him company Gail persuaded one of his oldest Roman friends, the Runyonesque ex-restaurateur Jerry Cierchio (famous proprietor of Jerry's Club on the Via Veneto) to go with him. If anyone could keep Paul from brooding, it was Jerry, and during their two-month absence, Paul did his best to come to terms with what had happened.

But once he was back in Italy, it was clear that he would never recover from Talitha's death. Paul was obsessed with it. Sometimes his grief became unbearable, making him rely on drugs more heavily than ever—which fueled his anxieties and sense of guilt, until they formed a vicious circle.

The children were affected too, and Gail had to cope on her own with them as well as with two-and-a-half-year-old Tara. When the child's future was discussed, she had said at once, "Tara's place is with his family here in Rome."

Simultaneously she had had to deal with Paul, who relied upon her more than ever for advice, and whose state of mind was not improved by growing rumors that the true cause of Talitha's death had not been barbiturates but an overdose of heroin taken in his presence.

There was no evidence to support this, and it was unlikely that, having finally gotten off heroin herself, and then made Paul's addiction such an issue over their separation, Talitha would suddenly have succumbed to the drug on her second night in Rome. It was equally unlikely that, had she really died from heroin, the doctors at the clinic would have missed the evidence.

It has been asserted that an autopsy conducted eight months after Talitha's death revealed traces of heroin in the body. If this is true it still does not prove that heroin was the cause of death. The combination of alcohol and barbiturate, would still have been a more likely cause. Also in a former heroin addict like Talitha, traces of the drug could have been deposited a considerable period before she died.

IT would have taken a braver man than Paul to have stayed in Rome, faced the Italian drug squad, and tried to clear his name before an official Italian inquiry. In the first place, he would have had to face simultaneous trial by the Italian media, with world press and television eager for the story. Every item from his private life would have been sensationalized, along with details of his most intimate relationships— with Talitha, with Victoria, and with Gail and the children. Innocent friends would have been involved.

But the real danger was that any inquiry would inevitably expose details of his own addiction. Irrespective of what had happened to Talitha, this would soon have led to a court case with the likelihood of prison at the end of it.

The judge issued a request for Paul "to come here voluntarily and give what help he can to the inquiry." Hardly surprisingly, he got no answer, and although for a time Paul was dreading extradition back to Italy, his fears proved groundless. It would have been unusual for the Italians to ask for extradition of a witness in a case involving foreigners whose own government was not demanding action.

So the inquiry into Talitha's death was inconclusive and the file stayed open, but Paul could never return to Italy. His children being still in Rome, their already slender contacts with their father all but ended.

More serious, perhaps, by evading the inquiry, Paul deprived himself of any chance of explaining—or publicly expiating—his wife's demise. The most unlikely accusations—that she had taken a massive overdose of heroin, that Paul had actually provided it, even that he had helped inject her—were never answered, and whatever actually took place on that July night in the apartment in Piazza Aracoeli would remain unknown.

WITH all this hanging over him Paul returned to the riverside house where a century earlier his hero Dante Gabriel Rossetti came to brood on the death of beautiful Lizzie Siddal. This was the house where Talitha had also lived until recently, and which Paul had so carefully restored to the state it was in when Rossetti lived there. Now it seemed he had succeeded all too well, and thanks to an eerie trick of fate, he found himself reliving the whole grim saga of Rossetti's downfall.

This was probably an important factor in Paul's subsequent behavior. Heroin addicts are often imitative, finding security and satisfaction in mirroring the lifestyle of another addict. In Paul's case he might have almost been Rossetti, and there was a disturbing symmetry in the way he seemed to duplicate the latter's actions. This very house had seen Rossetti become increasingly reclusive, haunted by remorse, and reliant on ever greater quantities of alcohol and chloral, until his health was virtually destroyed. Paul's behavior was identical, except that he had more effective soporifics now than chloral.

But the cause of his misery was so similar to Rossetti's that the words employed by Hall Caine, Rossetti's first biographer, to describe his plight could have applied to some extent to him: "Above all it was my impression that Rossetti had never ceased to reproach himself for his wife's death as an event that had been due in some degree to failure of duty on his part or perhaps to something graver."

FOR somebody like Paul, England, unlike both Italy and the United States, possessed one great advantage: its official policy toward narcotics. In England, addiction was regarded as a medical rather than a social problem, and addicts who registered with a doctor could legally receive their drugs by prescription. In theory the dose should steadily diminish, as the aim of the "treatment" was principally therapeutic.

Thus, for Paul, London was something of a haven, and he discovered a doctor who was happy to call on him at Queen's House in his Bentley. With Paul in residence, the house became as idiosyncratic as it had been with Rossetti. Rossetti had kept a menagerie which (included his famous pet wombat) in the garden, but Paul had a number of stuffed animals in the house itself. In his bedroom was a more puzzling memento, a wooden model of a flying boat. This was in fact a model of the legendary *Spruce Goose*, the huge wooden flying boat obsessively constructed by another son of an oil tycoon who made himself a notorious recluse: Howard Hughes. Paul did the same now as he shut himself away and made the house a shrine to Talitha's memory and a ghetto for his own oblivion. Everything to do with Talitha was lovingly preserved, including her clothes and letters and her photographs and her portrait painted by her father.

On the face of it, Paul's was a deeply tragic situation—he was bereaved, addicted, cut off from those he loved and from his beloved Italy. But one can also see the dreadful consolation that it offered someone of his increasingly reclusive temperament, and why it kept its hold on him so long. Here, in the very house where a romantic poet had destroyed himself with drugs while mourning his beautiful dead wife, he could do the same, joining a hazardous tradition of narcotic self-destruction. He and the ghost of Dante Gabriel Rossetti could come together in their grief around the memory of the beautiful departed.

Paul's days must have dragged interminably, and at times his depressions were appalling, but he was strong and single-minded and he felt that this was what his fate intended. He was punishing himself for what had happened. Believing himself valueless, he could find little of value in his own surroundings. Thus, for all his wealth, his world became a tiny segment of a very private hell. He played his opera records, watched interminable TV, drank much, ate little, and when life became unbearable, he always had what seemed to be the perfect antidote. At times he tried to kick the habit, but kicking is something wealthy addicts always find a problem. On the few occasions when he couldn't find money for drugs, the Getty name was good for credit.

Although Paul was often lonely, he was not alone. Victoria helped to keep him company, and he soon built up a very private group of friends. Gradually, some members of the sixties counterculture who had been his guests in Marrakesh joined his circle. These were people he could trust and who understood his situation. Mick Jagger and his wife, Bianca, lived just a few doors away in Cheyne Walk and often saw him. So did Marianne Faithfull and the hopelessly addicted gallery owner Robert Fraser. But as far as his future was concerned, his most important visitor was another neighbor: a knowledgeable Old Etonian who had a small antique shop around the corner and had been a friend of Talitha's.

During the sixties, Christopher Gibbs was a well-known figure in Chelsea. Handsome, stylish, and extremely well connected—his father was a banker and his uncle had been governor of Rhodesia—he was a most unusual character. Having attended university in France and studied archaeology in Jerusalem, he became something of a trend-setter for the sixties with his parties and the Arabic furniture and carpets he dealt in. His flat, a short stroll along Cheyne Walk from Paul's house, had been used as the setting for one of the theme films of the sixties, Antonioni's *Blowup*. But his most famous role was probably his friendship with the young Mick Jagger. It was Gibbs who discovered Stargroves, the Jaggers' splendid Victorian country house in Berkshire, and helped them furnish it. Gibbs was often with them in Marrakesh, where he introduced them to his friends the Gettys.

At the time Paul had lent him £1,200 for a small house in the Atlas Mountains. Gibbs still owned it, and was grateful. Now that Paul needed company and friends that he could trust, he was anxious to repay the debt. Besides, he genuinely liked Paul, and like most of his friends felt desperately sorry for him.

DURING this period, one member of the family appeared entirely immune to what was going on: the aging patriarch of Sutton Place. At seventy-eight Big Paul was still as firmly in command of Getty Oil as ever, and richer than he'd ever been. With Neutral Zone production at its peak in 1971, his personal fortune climbed to $290 million, with the Sarah Getty Trust ahead of it at $850 million.

Getty himself had single-handedly fought off a number of attacks upon his empire, and had saved his tanker fleet despite declining American demand, so that when the Arab-Israeli Yom Kippur War began in 1973, Getty Oil would be well placed to profit from the worldwide oil shortage.

Typically, when told about Talitha's death, he showed no flicker of emotion. He seemed to have the same non-response to Paul. "No Getty can be a drug addict," he said firmly, and although his son was living barely thirty miles away in London, he adamantly refused to see him. From time to time, Paul would try to reach him on the telephone, begging Penelope to use her influence. She always got the same reply: "When he stops taking drugs we'll talk, but not till then." Twelve days after Talitha's death, echoing the way his own father had treated him, Getty struck Paul from his will, leaving him $500.

Behind the show of strength, the lord of Sutton Place was vulnerable. He had never been as big a man as he had wanted, and he now looked rather small, with shoulders hunched, and liver spots mottling his cheeks. Suddenly, despite his money and the women around him, he seemed very much alone.

His policy of abandoning his sons in infancy and then recalling them to take their places in the business when they came of age simply hadn't worked. There was no closeness or affection, nor had there been much understanding, between him and his sons. He still resented them, still angrily attacked them when he felt that they were threatening his own unique position.

Timmy apart—and he had loved Timmy only after the boy was dead—the one exception, for a while, had been his precious Paul. Gail still says how sad it is that Paul never realized until too late how much his father loved him. Possibly Getty did, but when his son fell from grace, this simply made the old man's heart set harder.

"The only way we can preserve what we have created is through our children," he had written recently, like the old Victorian he really was at heart. Had he thought about this earlier, he might have been more careful in the way he had treated these four beings on whom so much depended.

In many ways the unkindest cut of all had been the one he dealt his half-German second son, tall unhappy Ronald. Had Ronald possessed a little of the charm of his half-brother Paul, things might have been different. But Ronald wasn't easy. He had a stubborn streak that had made Getty say occasionally, "Ronnie's the son that's most like me," but the truth was that the older Ronald got, the more he reminded Getty of his German grandfather, his old enemy Dr. Helmle. And the vendetta with Dr. Helmle was at the root of all the trouble.

Ronald's exclusion from the Sarah Getty Trust had been a cruel injustice, which always made him feel an outcast, rejected by the other members of the family. During the ups and downs of their relationship, Getty had sometimes given Ronald his faithful promise to rectify the situation, and include him in the trust. But he never had. Perhaps he was concerned that by adding to the number of beneficiaries, he would have made the trust vulnerable to his eternal enemies, the tax authorities. Perhaps when it came down to it he simply didn't want to include Ronald and was still seeking his revenge on long-dead Dr. Helmle by victimizing his grandson.

One effect this had was to make Ronald feel that he had no future in the family business, and in 1964, shortly after his marriage, he left Germany and his position in the Getty-owned Veedol company and returned to California. He was intent on making large amounts of money on his own account to prove his independence and show what he thought of his father. Unfortunately he chose Hollywood, and swiftly showed that, for all his alleged similarities to his father, he lacked Big Paul's obsessional capacity to learn every detail of whatever business he embarked on.

He had inherited nearly $2 million from his grandmother Getty, who had always thought that he was badly treated, and he allied himself with two Hollywood producers, to make a number of low-budget films like *Flare Up* starring Raquel Welch, *Zeppelin* and *Sheilah*. But although still shown on TV, these films failed to make his reputation or his fortune.

"I'll have the money, and they'll have the know-how," said Ronald, referring to his co-producers.

"And by the end they'll still have the know-how *and* they'll have your money," said his father.

GORDON was completely different, and recently, despite their lawsuit and their differences in character—which were considerable—Getty had come to feel a grudging admiration for his absentminded son.

Gordon had courage and was clever—probably too clever; that was his trouble. Gordon had tried his economic theories on his father, who, by and large, couldn't understand them. Nor could he appreciate Gordon's music. Occasionally at Sutton Place the great voice would go booming down the corridors.

"Gordon practicing," Getty would say, almost benevolently.

But he rarely failed to add that Gordon wasn't practical. Sometimes Gordon could surprise Getty, for some of his wild ideas actually worked—as when he suggested that the heating system in the Pierre Hotel could double up for air-conditioning in summer, thus saving the several million dollars it would have cost to upgrade the whole system in the hotel. Gordon was also an admirable family man, and he had followed his father's example by producing only sons. Big Paul was proud of them.

To show that the lawsuit was forgiven, he bestowed on Gordon the highest accolade in the Getty firmament: the all-powerful position of trustee of the Sarah Getty Trust. But try as he might, he could never see Gordon taking a more active role in the Getty empire.

In contrast, George, the eldest son and heir-apparent, as president of Tidewater was deeply conscious of family tradition.

Like most bad parents, Getty was always inconsistent with his sons, favoring one over another and thus creating jealousy just as he did among his women. George was the most jealous of them all. Trying to curry favor with his father, he was a great teller of tales against his siblings, first against Ronald, then against Gordon during his lawsuit; he even said that Gordon was not a Getty but the child of Ann Rork's third husband, Joe McEnerney, which was ridiculous.

But George had truly suffered. His father had always had an instinct for the weaknesses of others, and rarely spotted them without attacking. He'd been unforgiving when Tidewater's oil-exploration bids—particularly those in Pakistan and the Sahara—had failed one by one, and he shut down the company's exploration section without consulting George. Similarly, he had personally sold off part of Tidewater's unprofitable marketing network in the western United States. He went over George's head, making a $300 million deal with John Houchin of Phillips Petroleum at the Hotel Flora on Houchin's most recent visit to Rome.

George had been incensed. "My father's the president in charge of success and I'm the president in charge of failure," he lamented—a fairly accurate assessment of the situation.

George's personal life had also deteriorated since he broke with his wife, Gloria (née Gordon), in 1967. In the divorce proceedings Gloria claimed that George had been distant, cold, aloof, unfeeling—all the things that George's father's wives had said about *him*.

For a period George had thought himself in love with Lord Beaverbrook's granddaughter Lady Jean Campbell. She had met him at dinner at Sutton Place and found him "very strange, very unrelaxed, and always referring to his father during conversation as 'Mr. Getty.' " She thought this odd, and tried persuading George to call Getty "Father" or even "Dad," but it was always "Mr. Getty." "I realised then that George was scared stiff, absolutely terrified of Mr. Getty and of what Mr. Getty thought of him."

In 1971 George was remarried—not to Lady Jean, who preferred Norman Mailer, but to Jacqueline Riordan, a San Franciscan who had inherited $30 million from her previous husband, an Irish-American financier who had made a fortune from a dubious pension scheme in Switzerland and who perished when a mudslide engulfed him in his bedroom. (Jacqueline somehow managed to escape.)

The old man had been fond of Gloria, who'd been a good wife to George and mother to his three daughters, and felt saddened by the divorce. But he couldn't help approving of a new wife who had so much money. "It's not so much a marriage as a merger," he began to say, with satisfaction. But once the merger was effected, Jacqueline soon became its senior partner, using her power unmercifully against poor George when she had reached the same conclusion as Lady Jean about his attitude toward his father.

George, in fact, was secretly becoming frightened of almost everything by now—his enemies, his wife, his ex-wife, the Tidewater executives, life itself. To counter this he did his best to earn respect from those around him as a prominent social figure, fund-raising for the Los Angeles Philharmonic, sitting on the board of the Bank of America, even breeding horses just as the Queen of England did—in short, turning himself into the sort of character he could respect. It didn't work. Papa was always there to rule his life, and making no attempt at all to hide the fact that he despised him.

Not surprisingly, by now George was drinking—more or less secretly, but to excess. By the beginning of 1973, he was taking sedatives and speed and probably injecting something inadvisable. On the night of 6 June he had had another bitter row with Jacqueline, once again over "Mr. Getty." Their rows were almost always over Mr. Getty.

At the end of the argument he flipped, all the frustrations, hatreds, impotence and rage surfacing in one great wave of anger, and he panicked. He locked himself in the bedroom of their valuable house in beautiful Bel Air and started shouting. He drank. He swallowed a lot of Nembutal. He tried to stab himself with a barbecue fork, but failed to pierce his stomach. Then he fell into a coma.

Finally friends broke down the door and got him out and called an ambulance, but there was a muddle now about the hospital. No one could permit Tidewater's president to be taken, in what was thought to be a drunken stupor, to the emergency room of the nearby UCLA hospital. So they took George to a more discreet hospital instead, which took twenty minutes longer.

To save his name they may have lost his life. For George wasn't drunk, but suffering from a potent overdose of all the drugs he'd swallowed. Unfortunately, nobody knew he had taken any drugs. By the time they reached the hospital, George, beloved eldest son and heir-apparent to the richest and coldest man in America, was dead.

"His father killed him," said his widow when journalists came to see her.

IN London it was early evening when the news of George's death reached Barbara Wallace, who telephoned Penelope. Penelope knew that Getty was having dinner with the Duchess of Argyll at her house in Mayfair. But one of her daughters said, "You must go to him and break the news to him. He'll need you."

So she did.

When she told him George was dead, Getty was transfixed with grief, pole-axed, stricken, unable to weep or speak, such was his anguish. This was one of those extremely rare occasions when the structure of his life—his fortune, his ambition, his constant activities, his women, and his powers of concentration—all were useless, blown away, leaving the lonely child who had grieved for his dog Jip, for his dear Papa and darling Mama, and for Timmy, "bravest and best of all my sons." Now George had joined them in the lineup of this old man's misery.

On the way back to Sutton Place, he wouldn't speak to anyone, and next morning he still refused to talk of George. But he had a portrait photograph of him hung in the hall of Sutton Place with purple around it, purple being the imperial color of the emperors of Rome and also of mourning.

Shortly afterward he agreed to speak to journalists, one of whom repeated the widow's original remark.

"She says his father killed him. Have you any comment, Mr. Getty?"

"None," he answered.

CHAPTER FIFTEEN

Kidnap and Ransom

THE area between Corso Vittorio Emmanuele and the Tiber includes many of Rome's great Renaissance palaces, for this was where papal families like the Borgias, Farneses, and Riarios once resided. And these narrow streets have seen more mayhem in their time than any other quarter of the city. At night they still seem faintly sinister, but by the small hours there is rarely any sign of life, apart from the Roman cats and the occasional night watchman on his rounds. So no one could have missed the young Paul Getty III as he walked down the Via della Mascherone toward the masklike fountain of a girl spouting water from her mouth, after which the little street is named.

He was a redhaired, beanpole of a boy and after a night out he often wandered home like this to the apartment he was sharing with two young painters in Trastevere on the far side of the river. Today it would seem a stupid thing to do, but Rome was a safer city then, and when an elderly white Fiat drew up beside him with a squeal of brakes, he was not particularly alarmed.

"Excuse me, *signore*. Are you Paul Getty?" called the driver.

"Yes," he said, "I am."

At which two men jumped out, grabbed him, and, despite his struggles, forced him into the back of the car, which swiftly drove away. As the clocks of Rome were striking three on the morning of July 10, 1973, the next disaster to afflict the Getty family had started.

SINCE the death of Talitha, and Paul's flight to London, Gail's chief preoccupation had been to hold her family together; although her marriage to Lang Jeffries had ended two years earlier, she felt she was succeeding. She turned thirty-seven that April.

She and the children all loved Italy. They went to the house at Orgia for weekends and holidays, and in Rome were now inhabiting a modern apartment in the middle-class area of Parioli. In those days living was so cheap for foreigners with dollars that she could live comfortably, but she was far from rich, and child support from Paul in London tended to be erratic. She drove an Opel station wagon, had many local friends, most of them Italian, and lived an essentially private life centered on her children.

Wishing them to enjoy a European education, she sent them, not to the American School in Rome, but to solid old St. George's on the Via Salaria, which still claimed in its prospectus "to provide a sound, all-round British style education for English-speaking children between the ages of eight and eighteen."

But like much in Rome in the early seventies, St. George's was affected by the new-wave culture hitting Italy. The three younger children made the most of their time there, but Paul rebelled. He was more seriously affected by the divorce and by Talitha's death than the others, and proved harder to control without a father.

By 1973, when he was just sixteen, he had effectively given up on regular education. Paul had never gotten along with Lang, resenting his presence in his father's place. Now, being highly independent, he had set his heart on painting and on educating himself by reading what he wanted. He was serious enough about this for Gail to agree to let him share the Trastevere studio with two older friends of the family, Marcello Crisi and Philip Woollam.

As she says, "Paul was doing his *vie bohème* thing, and in Paris no one would have noticed." But Rome was different. With the dolce vita dead and gone, Rome in the early seventies had lapsed back into something like an old provincial city, where the cult of the family was still very much intact, so that leaving a sixteen-year-old like Paul to his own devices could later on be made to seem distinctly shocking.

Paul kept in close touch with all his family in Rome. As he had little money, he was smart enough to get his local trattoria to accept his paintings occasionally in return for meals, but most days still saw Gail driving over to the flat with food for him and his flatmates. When she didn't, he usually came home to eat and see his siblings. They were devoted to him, so that although Paul was living on his own, the Getty Family Italiana managed to remain most united.

Young Paul was a strange mixture. Gail described him as "extraordinarily precocious, more like a boy of twenty than sixteen." After the divorce, his reaction against Lang had made him increasingly idolize his father and the hippie lifestyle he embodied. Aged eleven, Paul had been invited for a fortnight to Marrakesh, which naturally struck him as the most glamorous place on earth. He became very fond of Talitha, and her death when he was fourteen came as something of a blow, as did his father's flight to London.

Gail recalls that "around that time, Paul became very quiet, very locked-in"; it was because of this that she had encouraged him to paint and to mix with others. He still spent his summer holidays with the family at La Fuserna, and had grown to love the people and the romantic countryside south of Siena. Mark, his younger brother, was devoted to him and tells of how they once got lost exploring the woods above the house. When darkness fell and they had failed to return, Gail was beside herself with worry, but it was Paul in his role as elder brother who kept his nerve and brought the two home in safety.

One friend of Paul's who came to stay in Tuscany each summer was Adam Alvarez, son of the writer Al Alvarez. Adam remembers Paul as "surprisingly straightforward and nothing like the wild character the press created after the kidnap. But his life was complicated by what had happened in his family. He missed his father and he often seemed unhappy."

Back in Rome he changed, for in Rome the Getty name could give him what he undoubtedly enjoyed, the status of a minor celebrity. Someone in the press had called him the Golden Hippie, and he had earned some easy money modeling nude for a magazine. The nickname was repeated when the police grabbed him on the fringe of a student demonstration and made him spend a night in prison—which brought less agreeable publicity. This seems to have put him on the side of the oppressed, for he was soon taking a powerful line against the rich, rather as his father used to. "The rich are the real poor of the earth. Their malnutrition is of the spirit. One should pity them," he said— which sounded better in Italian. The remark was picked up in the foreign press and duly found its way to Sutton Place, where his grandfather read the piece but made no comment.

However, the old man was unlikely to forget the previous summer when Paul had come to visit him in brightly colored jeans and sneakers. Grandpapa didn't approve of jeans or sneakers, and the visit hadn't been repeated.

It was in early 1973 that Paul began dating Martine Zacher, a pretty German divorcée with a year-old baby daughter. She was a very liberated woman, eight years his senior, who acted in a small alternative theater. He became fond of her, but saw no reason to be faithful. Since becoming known as the Golden Hippie, he was surprised at how many women made themselves available.

Thus in Rome Paul had enjoyed an enviable existence—going to discotheques, (where in fact nothing very much occurred), chasing women, smoking hash, and playing at being a dedicated artist. Since he was very young his mother felt that, given time, he would finally grow up and leave all this behind him. Far from condemning him, she believed that, as she put it, "rebelling against convention can be a sign of originality, and an indication that someone might be special."

According to Bill Newsom, Paul was behaving as he did because he "worshipped his father and was trying to outdo him as a hippie," this despite the fact that he rarely saw his father and had had little contact with him since the flight to London. ("We communicate by occasional postcards and mysterious telegrams," said Young Paul in an interview with *Rolling Stone*.)

ON the night of the kidnaping, Mark was away in San Francisco with his maternal grandparents, and Aileen was off with friends, leaving Gail with Ariadne and Tara at La Fuserna. But that Sunday morning, something made her feel uneasy and she decided, on the spur of the moment, to drive back to Rome. When she rang Paul, one of his flat-mates told her he had not returned.

This worried her, but there was no further news of him until that evening when the phone rang and someone with a southern Italian accent asked politely if she were the Signora Getty.

When she said yes, he answered, like someone from the cleaners telling her her clothes were ready, "We have your son, Paul Getty."

"What do you mean?" she said impatiently. "He's here in Rome."

"No, Signora. He is with us. We are kidnappers and have him captive. He is safe, but we will require much money to release him."

She stammered that she had no money.

"Then please prepare to ask for it from your father-in-law. He has all the money in the world."

It was then she understood her caller wasn't joking.

"Where is my son?" she asked angrily.

"I tell you he is with us. He is in good health and he'll stay that way as long as you do as you are told and arrange about the money. But don't go to the police. Just wait to hear from us."

With which the man hung up—and Gail collapsed.

When she recovered, it was as if her world had suddenly collapsed as well. She had never felt thoroughly frightened before, but she now experienced real terror, blanking out all other feelings and leaving her weak and shaking. All her thoughts of Paul were suddenly of the vulnerable child she remembered, with his private weaknesses and fears. He was a shy, extremely loving child, and she could not stop thinking how frightened he must be and how easy it would be for his kidnapers to hurt him.

She had always felt at ease with people, particularly Italians, and she loved Italy. But Italy was suddenly a foreign land. "I felt utterly alone, and I had to find out what in God's name I should do."

Her first reaction was to call her parents in America, who did their best to reassure her and said she must certainly contact the police, which she did, telephoning the Carabinieri station in the nearby Piazza Euclide. Then she called her ex-husband Paul in London.

They had recently been drawing closer to each other. Paul was on his own but seemed more in charge of his life than at any time since Talitha's death. Gail had spent part of May with him at Cheyne Walk, and since then few days had passed without them speaking to each other on the telephone.

So when she broke the news of what had happened, they shared the sense of shock and horror for their child. Both were in tears, and since Paul seemed even more upset than she, Gail found herself trying to console him. It was only when she said he must contact his father to raise money for the ransom that he seemed to move away.

"I can't," he said. "We never speak to one another."

"Then I'll have to speak to him myself," she said. But before she could, the Carabinieri had arrived.

The Arma dei Carabinieri prides itself on being a tough, hardheaded *corps d'élite* that helps hold Italy together in spite of the most corrupt governing class in Europe. What the carabinieri lack in imagination, they make up for in cynicism and knowledge of the world—and they are rarely oversympathetic to what they see as rich, self-indulgent foreigners living in their midst.

Three local officers were commanded by one Colonnello Gallo— Colonel Cockerel—"who looked and behaved exactly like a rooster." They were soon joined by officers from Carabinieri headquarters, who grilled her for the the next five hours, chiefly about her and her son's private lives. She repeated the words of the telephone call verbatim, but they made little attempt to hide their doubts about the kidnaping— and about young Paul himself.

"We know your son, Signora. He is probably with a girl or with his hippie friends. He will almost certainly turn up."

THE Carabinieri left at around eleven P.M. and it was agreed that because of the Getty name, and the danger to the other children, the press was not to be informed. But someone did inform them, and it wasn't Gail. Within twenty minutes, the Italian press was on the phone, followed by ABC New York, NBC Chicago, and finally CBS from London.

By then there was no point in denying the kidnaping and next morning it was the front-page story of Rome's daily paper, *Il Messagero*. The story followed the line the officers had taken during Gail's interrogation.

Under a banner headline—"Joke or Kidnap"—most of the article concentrated on the character and lifestyle of the "Golden Hippie," and suggested that quite probably Paul, "famous for his wild hippie lifestyle," had gone off with a girlfriend or some of his wilder acquaintances. There was no reference to Gail's conversation with the kidnapers or to a demand for ransom. As far as *Il Messagero* was concerned, Paul had simply "disappeared."

But the article changed the situation. In the first place, it would take some time for the element of doubt over the kidnaping to go away—and endless complications would ensue until it did. More serious still, since the Getty name was always news, the chance of dealing with the kidnapers quietly, behind the scenes, was gone from the start.

Gail's flat in Parioli instantly came under siege from journalists and television crews desperate for a story, making her effectively a prisoner with Aileen, Ariadne, and Tara. For, as well as being trapped by the media, she also had to stay within reach of the telephone and wait for the kidnapers to call.

ALTHOUGH it is often seen as the Italian crime par excellence, kidnaping was rare in Italy until the early seventies when Luciano Liggio, the Milan-based *capo dei capi* of the Sicilian Mafia, developed it as a means of raising capital for the Mafia's rapidly developing international drug cartel. It was then that the crime began to flourish, and the Sicilians had many imitators. The smartest were probably the students in the Red Brigades, who kidnaped and murdered ex-premier Aldo Moro in 1978 with terrible efficiency, and the crudest were undoubtedly the Calabrians from the south of Italy.

The Calabrian Mafia, the *N'drangheta*, was an ancient, loosely linked federation of families from this poorest part of Italy, who for centuries had been making money from protection rackets on the local peasantry. Recently some of the younger, more ambitious members had been contemplating kidnaping as a quicker source of profit.

Paul's captors were a gang of petty criminals from Calabria with tenuous connections to the n'drangheta. Gail believes that someone in the trattoria where Paul sold his pictures fingered him to them. Until now there'd always been an unspoken rule among mafiosi against harming or involving foreigners, but Paul was so vulnerable—and, as everybody knew, his grandfather was so extremely rich—that the kidnaping must have seemed a foolproof source of easy money.

The planning apparently took some months. There was no problem trailing Paul, as he had absolutely no awareness of his danger. Seizing him was just as easy; and once his captors had him in their car, they held a chloroform-soaked pad across his face, then drove him through the night, still gagged and blindfolded and more or less unconscious, till they reached the desolate countryside they knew well, in the toe of Italy.

Here they kept him captive, much as they kept their animals—generally in cattle huts or shelters in the woods. To begin with they were not so much cruel to him as callous, as southerners tend to be with animals. He was chained by the ankle, but since his captors all wore masks, they removed his blindfold except when they were on the move.

For one so young Paul did his best to keep his dignity. When he complained about the dirt, they took him to wash in nearby streams. He had nothing to read, but they gave him a radio—on which he heard reports about the "mystery" of his kidnaping. They fed him cold spaghetti and canned tuna fish and water. They told him that as long as he did what he was told he would not be hurt, and his ordeal would soon be over.

At this stage his captors seemed highly confident—and were clearly counting on a speedy deal to make their fortunes. Since the boy's grandfather was so rich, they were certain there would be no problem finding the money for the ransom.

"CI sentiremo—"You'll be hearing from us"—were the kidnaper's final words to Gail before hanging up, and she stayed like a lover by the telephone waiting for the call to come. But kidnaping is a form of torture, and they let her stew. For ten long days and sleepless nights she had no hint of whether Paul was alive or dead or what had happened to him.

Not that she sat by her telephone in silence. She was plagued throughout the day by telephone calls—supportive calls, abusive calls, and even obscene calls, none of which made life easier. She had still been unable to make contact with Big Paul at Sutton Place, as he was never available and never rang her back. Nor did she hear from Ann and Gordon in America. Thinking herself totally abandoned by the Gettys and left to face this disaster on her own, she had never felt so lonely in her life; as day dragged after day, with the promised call from the kidnapers never coming, she became convinced that something unspeakable had happened. At night she could not sleep because of the nightmares that pursued her. Did the silence mean the kidnapers had killed Paul? What if they never rang? What if she simply never saw her son again?

But finally they did communicate with her—not by telephone, but through the mail, in a colorful, artistically done collage of letters cut from magazines, briefly setting out the ransom demand. The kidnapers were asking for 10 billion lire, roughly $17 million—a considerable sum even by Getty standards, which could come from one source only, the eighty-one-year-old family patriarch back in Sutton Place.

Shortly after this, Gail received a second letter, this one from Paul himself. It had been posted in Rome, and her heart missed a beat when she recognized his writing on the envelope. The letter started by telling her what she knew already, that he had been kidnaped, but gave no clue as to his whereabouts or the identity of his captors. He simply wrote that he was safe and well, and added a fresh warning against going to the police. Clearly writing at the kidnapers' behest, he concluded by begging her to speak as soon as possible to his grandfather about the ransom. If his captors failed to receive the money swiftly and in full, he would be "badly treated."

The letter's ending made her blood run cold: "Pay up, I beg you, pay up as soon as possible if you wish me well. If you delay it is very dangerous for me. I love you. Paul."

PAUL Junior still could not talk to his father about the ransom, and although Gail continued ringing Sutton Place, Getty was never available. This puzzled her. Big Paul had always been extremely charming to her in the past, but now it was clear that he wished to have no contact with her.

By now he had, in fact, made his attitude to paying ransom money all too clear in a statement issued to the press. J. Paul Getty was standing firm on what he claimed to be a matter of principle. As he put it in his statement, "I have fourteen grandchildren, and if I pay a penny of ransom, I'll have fourteen kidnapped grandchildren."

As a public statement meant to warn off other potential kidnapers, this was fair enough. There was presumably a chance, however minimal, that payment of a ransom for one child might encourage somebody to kidnap another, and the statement also squared with the law in Italy, where the payment of a ransom to kidnapers is theoretically illegal.

But all of this was in theory. In Italy it has always proved impossible to forbid the payment of ransom money to release a loved one, and the reality was that Getty's eldest grandson and his namesake, Jean Paul Getty III, was actually in the hands of criminals and at that very moment in danger of his life.

As everybody knew, his grandfather—and he alone—could pay virtually any ransom demand and barely notice. So could he seriously intend to leave his grandson in captivity? What if the boy became sick or was tortured? Would he still stick firmly by his principles and high-mindedly refuse to save him?

Getty made it clear he would, and that his reasons for inaction had less to do with principle than with his personal feelings on the matter. In the first place there was his disapproval of his so-called hippie grandson. He had heard enough about Paul to believe that he was like Paul Junior, and he wanted nothing to do with either until they changed their ways.

He also blamed the boy for getting kidnaped in the first place, and thereby involving him, his grandfather, with the dreaded Mafia. For the truth was that the old man had been terrified of kidnaping even before Paul disappeared. This was why he had never stayed for long at La Posta Vecchia (where he had kept the loaded shotgun in his bedroom) and at Sutton Place was already taking serious advice from his personal security expert, Colonel Léon Turrou.

For several years, Turrou, a Frenchman and former CIA agent, had studied kidnaping prevention; he had written a book on the classic case of the 1930s, the kidnaping of the Lindbergh baby in America. A scared old billionaire like Jean Paul Getty was an ideal client, and by now the colonel had put him in a state of semi-siege at Sutton Place, with armed guards in the house, lethal German shepherds in the grounds, and the latest in surveillance technology almost everywhere. Impressive locks and a bulletproof steel plate were fitted to his bedroom door, and armed guards with unsmiling faces drove before and after his Cadillac on the few occasions when he ventured out.

Paul's kidnaping made things that much worse, and so terrified was the old man that he grew afraid to answer the telephone, firmly refusing to use it to discuss anything remotely connected with the kidnaping just in case the Mafia got through to him. As Gail put it, "he seemed to think that they might come up and grab him through the telephone."

Perhaps he did think so, but his fear of the telephone probably had a more plausible explanation. In Paris eight months earlier, the Israeli secret service, the Mossad, had actually used the telephone to assassinate Mahmoud Hamshari, the PLO representative in France. A small Semtex device with an electronic sensor had been planted in Hamshari's apartment, and when the Israelis reached him on the telephone, they transmitted a signal down the line to activate the bomb, which killed him.

At the time the case made a stir among intelligence professionals; as one of them, Turrou would certainly have known about it, and it was just the sort of tale to have captured Getty's imagination. Certainly, throughout the period of his grandson's kidnaping he took exceptional precautions with anyone he spoke to on the telephone, and in any discussion related to the crime would generally get Penelope to speak on his behalf.

Not that Getty ever talked about the subject if he could help it. As he had shown when Timmy died, he couldn't cope with unhappiness or grief, nor would he permit anyone to question his decisions. As Penelope put it, "with the kidnapping it was quite frightening to see how totally the shutters descended on the subject."

THREE weeks had passed since Paul's disappearance, yet nothing had been done to further his release. Apart from the two letters there had been no more contact with the kidnapers either. The Carabinieri had drawn a total blank on their identity; J. Paul Getty, Sr., was standing absolutely firm against paying them a cent; and J. Paul Getty, Jr., was insisting there was nothing he could do.

In Rome everything continued to devolve on Gail who was living through a more and more appalling nightmare. Time dragged interminably; as she says, "in a kidnap situation, every hour is twice as long as an ordinary hour." Apart from a few friends there was no one she could turn to. The only members of the family who came near her were old Willem and Poppet Pol who had flown to Rome from the south of France on hearing of the kidnaping, and had now returned to Ramatuelle with five-year-old Tara. Gail was sad to see Tara go, but she was also grateful, as it would have been hard to cope with a five-year-old while doing her best to keep Aileen and Ariadne happy.

Gail was feeling anything but calm herself. She was powerless and desperately anxious, yet she knew she had to keep her wits about her to deal with the kidnapers when and if they did decide to call. All she could do was go on sitting by that telephone until they rang—which they finally did when least expected, late in the evening of July 30.

She recognized the voice of the man who had telephoned originally, and this time he introduced himself. To identify himself in future, he would supply a code name she could easily remember: "Cinquanta," "Fifty."

As before, he sounded oddly respectful, using the third person singular and calling her Signora; but when she broke the news that no money was forthcoming for the ransom, he exploded—first with anger and then with disbelief. He could not believe that anyone as rich as Getty utterly refused to pay, and accused her of a trick. She tried explaining the old man's reasons—naturally, without success. As an Italian, Cinquanta simply couldn't comprehend anyone behaving like Jean Paul Getty.

"Who is this so-called grandfather?" he shouted. "How can he leave his own flesh and blood in the plight that your poor son is in? Here is the richest man in America, and you tell me he refuses to find just ten *miliardi* [ten billion] for his grandson's safety. Signora, you take me for a fool. What you say is just not possible."

Gail could hardly say that she agreed with him, but she did her best to calm him down, saying that she needed time, and begging him to be as kind as possible to Paul. He said he would, but told her to contact the rest of the family to get the money.

MOST families draw closer in a crisis and support each other during a disaster, but not the Gettys. With his limitless money and his close connections with Italy, the old man could certainly have had the boy released quite swiftly had he wished. Gail believes that "had Big Paul dealt with the kidnap as he dealt with a business deal in his prime, Paul would have been free within twenty-four hours."

Not only was Big Paul refusing to do so, but by cutting himself off from Gail completely and retreating into his fortress at Sutton Place, he effectively paralyzed the rest of the family as well, since none of them wanted to offend him. As he was not on speaking terms with Paul Junior, and Gordon and Ronald were both in America, one of the richest families in the world was rendered incapable of helping a grandson of sixteen who was in peril of his life.

Nor was any support forthcoming for Gail herself at a time when she was sick with anxiety, harassed by the press, and trying desperately to keep the rest of her family afloat while she dealt with the kidnapers. By now she had started to receive countless letters of support and sympathy from unknown people around the world, but not a word from any member of the family.

It was then that she saw the Getty family as it was: remote, unreachable, closed off from human contact. This emptiness went back to Big Paul himself, who had always used his money as a substitute for human feeling. Gail felt that being a Getty was like becoming part of a mathematical progression; as the family empire grew more complex and remote, those within it found it impossible to maintain normal relationships with anyone outside. Like Big Paul, they too became frightened, always needing to protect themselves and their precious money from outsiders.

It was only now that she realized how different they all were from her parents and her own supportive family, and that something human had been lost as the great financial empire had expanded. How lifeless and devoid of love it had become. And Big Paul was the most loveless and lifeless of them all.

AUGUST started with a heat wave. Italy had gone on holiday, and those responsible for finding Paul seemed to have gone on holiday as well. Possibly this was because of the heat, but nothing at all was happening. Officially it was the task of the Carabinieri to deal with the crime and rescue Paul, but as they were having not the faintest glimmer of success they had fallen back on the easier option of claiming that the kidnaping was a hoax.

According to their theory, Paul and his so-called hippie friends had simply staged the whole affair to extract money from the family. There was not a shred of evidence to support this; it was inconceivable that Paul would torture his mother in this way, and his subsequent sufferings totally disproved it.

But as a theory it was a convenient way for incompetent policemen to save face. Face, *figura*, is particularly important for the Carabinieri as for most Italians, and they could claim, as claim they did, that the reason they were getting nowhere was not because of their incompetence, but because there had been no kidnaping in the first place.

The hoax idea was also attractive to the general public. Romans love rumors, particularly cynical ones about the rich, and even more they love rumors about rich foreigners. So the story gathered credence in the press, and was soon reported back to Britain, where it inevitably reached the patriarch of Sutton Place. Given his attitude toward the ransom—and toward his grandson—it clearly suited him to believe it, too. "D'you think the boy and his mother cooked this up together for the money?" he is said to have asked his personal assistant, Norris Bramlett.

The reaction at Cheyne Walk was not dissimilar. As usual in the face of unhappiness and worry, Paul Junior had become more reclusive, resorting increasingly to drink and drugs, so that Gail was finding it more and more difficult to get through to him by telephone. Now the suggestion that his son was simply indulging in a massive practical joke ended his anxiety, and gave him and the family a perfect alibi. Not only did it excuse them for doing nothing; it also reassured them with the thought that, far from being kidnaped, that rascal Paul was hiding somewhere with his friends in perfect safety.

But as he was actually still chained up like an animal in a hovel in the wilds of Calabria with a group of increasingly edgy criminals trying to extort a ransom for his life, the situation was in fact becoming more and more dangerous. Apart from antagonizing Paul's captors still further, the hoax rumor meant that if they were to get their money, they would need to do something to prove beyond the shadow of a doubt that the kidnaping was genuine.

By the fourth week, there was still no movement, and Gail was desperate. Since her angry conversation with Cinquanta, she had heard no more from him. This endless waiting was the chief component of her misery. Throughout the day she was still waiting by the telephone for news, and when none came she began imagining all the horrors which might have befallen Paul: an accident, illness, violence from his captors; anything was possible. The greatest torture was the total lack of information.

By the second week of that stifling August, she could bear it no longer. She had to get news from Paul, and it was then that her lawyer, Giovanni Jacovoni, suggested she should make a direct appeal to the kidnapers on Italian television.

Gail was wary of doing this, as her experiences with the Italian media were far from happy. In the first few days after the kidnaping she had tried being helpful to reporters, but when there was nothing to report, they became hungry for fresh stories and turned on her instead, criticizing her attitude toward her son, her performance as a mother, and her situation as a member of the richest family on earth. "They felt that somebody must be to blame for what had happened, and since there was no one else around, they picked on me."

It was bad enough being blamed for being a Getty; she was also the victim of the cultural differences between Anglo-Saxons and Italians. Gail was a great believer in maintaining the stiffest of stiff upper lips in public, if only out of pride and to avoid upsetting everyone in the family (especially her parents and Mark, who was still with them back in San Francisco). "I was damned if I was going to show my grief publicly, and share it with a couple of million newspaper readers."

Above: Jean Paul Getty was eighty-three and had had three face-lifts, the last of which had failed, making him look inordinately old. (*Camera Press*)

Right: Getty with his mistress, Mary Teissier. 'She was utterly obsessed with him. From the day they met until the day he died there was absolutely no one else.' (*Hulton Deutsch*)

Left: Gail Harris marries Paul II, 'quietly' in Woodside, California in 1956.

Right: Paul II at his Roman wedding with his second wife Talitha Pol, December 1966. Penelope Kitson is on the left with Talitha centre, 'looking like the sixties flower child she was'.

Left: Getty's eldest son and heir, George Getty II. 'The more responsibility he gained as Paul Getty's heir apparent, the more his fear of his father seemed to undermine him.' (*PA News*)

Right: Paul and Talitha on the roof of their flat in old Rome shortly after their wedding in 1966. It was here she died five years later. (*Camera Press*)

Above: The bronze statue of the Roman emperor Marcus Aurelius 'still rode the plinth designed for him by Michelangelo' at the wedding of Gail Getty and her second husband, Larry Jeffries, in Rome in 1966.

Left: Gail Getty shortly after her marriage to Paul II.

Above: Getty's second son Ronald, left, with his sister-in-law Gail, his half-brother, Paul II, and the family patriarch, J. Paul Getty himself.

Right: On the hippie trail. Paul II and his wife Talitha beneath a Viet Cong flag at a peace demonstration in Rome in 1969. (*Hulton Deutsch*)

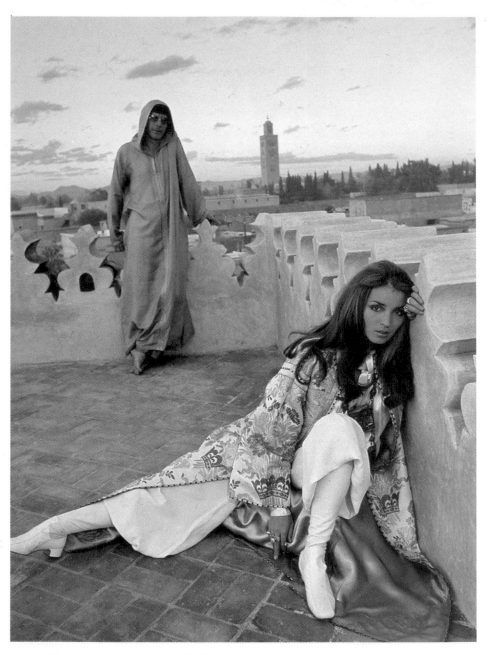

Above: Paul II and his wife Talitha go Arab on the roof of their house,
Le Palais da Zahir (the Pleasure Palace) in Marrakesh. (*Patrick
Lichfield/Camera Press*)

Opposite page: Talitha Getty and Nureyev. Her obsession with the dancer led
her to meet Paul II – and after her marriage she was said to have been the only
woman Nureyev was physically in love with. (*PA News*)

Left: The red MG which played an important part in the life of Paul II. This was the car which he enjoyed during his time in Rome and later sold to his half-sister Donna.

Right: Paul and Gail's three children in Rome in the sixties – Aileen (left), Mark and Paul III.

Left: Gail Getty meets the Italian press after the disappearance of her son Paul Getty III to announce his kidnap by the Calabrian Mafia. (*Hulton Deutsch*)

Paul III shortly after
his kidnap in 1973.
His lost right ear
was later rebuilt with
cartilage taken from
one of his ribs.
(*Camera Press*)

Eighteen-year-old
Paul III on honey-
moon shortly after
his release, and
marriage to
Martine Zacher.
(*Camera Press*)

Paul II with Bianca Jagger (left) and Penelope Kitson (right) at the London memorial service to his father in 1976. This was to be his last appearance in public for nearly ten years. (*Hulton Deutsch*)

Aileen Getty with her first husband, Elizabeth Taylor's son Christopher Wilding. (*PA News*)

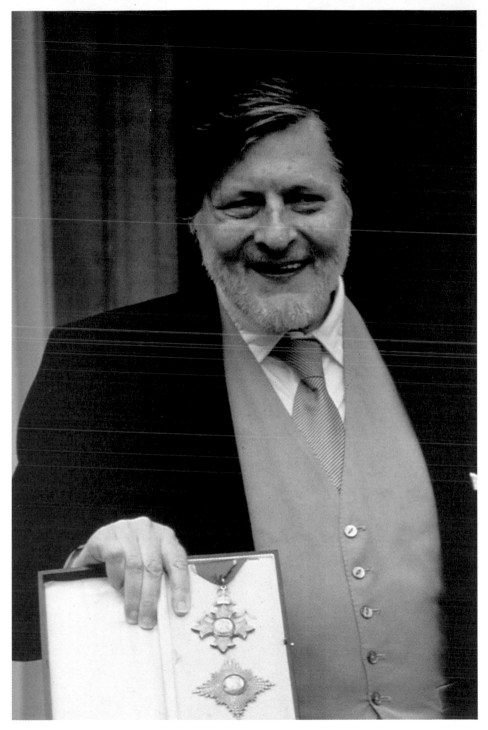

Paul II receives an honorary knighthood from the Queen. 'The Cabinet wishes to express its warm appreciation of, and profound gratitude for, your magnificent generosity.' (*Hulton Deutsch*)

The family peacemaker. Paul and Gordon's boyhood friend, Judge William Newsom.

Composer's triumph. Gordon Getty rehearsing with the Russian National Orchestra in Moscow before a performance of his work in 1994.

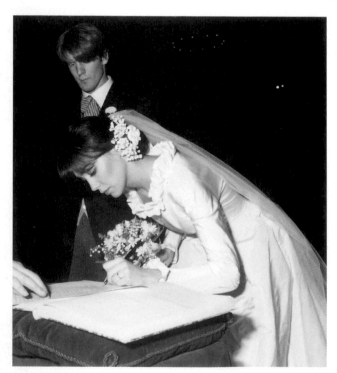

The Gettys are united with the Italian nobility. Paul II's son Mark marries Domitilla Lante della Rovere Harding, a descendant of the family of Pope Julius II, in Rome.

Gordon's wife Ann. 'I think it is possible to be very rich and happy and I suppose very poor and happy. But it's easier to be very rich and happy.'

California boys. Ann and Gordon's four sons (from left to right), Peter, Bill, Andrew and John. (*Thomas J. Gibbons*)

Next generation. Paul and Talitha's son Tara Gabriel Galaxy Gramaphone Getty, Paul III's stepdaughter, Anna, and Ronald Getty's daughter, Cecily.

Wormsley. 'The creation of a billionaire's Shangri-La in the Chilterns might all too easily have ended as a nightmare or a joke.' (*Mark Fiennes*)

Victoria Holdsworth and Paul II, shortly before their marriage in London in 1994, greeting Gordon Getty.

Gettys in Moscow. Gordon and Ann *en route* to the concert of Gordon's music by the Russian National Orchestra in 1994.

Christopher Gibbs, art dealer extraordinary and close friend of Paul Getty II, who saw how his friend's enormous fortune could be used to restore his self-respect and then achieve his remarkable salvation. (*Mrs Paul Getty*)

Right: 'Entering the family at last'. Ronald Getty leads the guests at the sixtieth birthday party for his brother Paul at Wormsley, September 1993. Judge William Newsom is on his left.

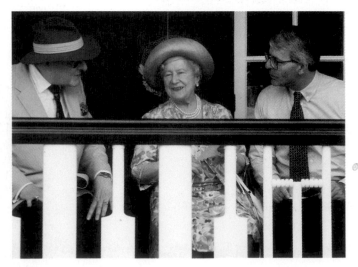

Left: Paul II watches cricket at Wormsley. 'On his left sat a self-confessed "cricket fanatic" (the Prime Minister, John Major), and on his right and enjoying every minute of the game was Queen Elizabeth the Queen Mother.' (*Brian Smith*)

But this was not what the Italian media wanted. When disaster hits an Italian family, there has to be a sorrowing mother, a *mater dolorosa* with eyes turned hopelessly to heaven and body racked with anguish. When Gail failed to oblige, the media treated her with deep suspicion.

Because of this, she insisted on making her television appeal to Paul's kidnapers on her own, directly to the camera; but the producer, anxious for some real-life drama, brought a reporter with him when he arrived for the recording. Gail objected, but the producer was insistent. Only when he promised her extremely sympathetic questions did she agree. But a few minutes into the interview the reporter paused, stared her full in the face, then asked her in a voice of doom, "Signora, do you think your son is dead?"

For the second time since Paul had disappeared Gail fainted. She had been refusing to accept this possibility for so long that when someone actually suggested it, something snapped within her. By suppressing so much strain and worry over the last few weeks she had brought herself to breaking point, and needed several days in bed to recover.

But the interview brought results from the kidnapers. Soon after it was broadcast, Cinquanta called again to reassure her that Paul was certainly alive and well.

"How do I know you're telling me the truth?" she answered. The kidnaper thought before replying, then told her to ask him certain questions to which only Paul could know the answer. He would call her back with the replies, and if they were right she'd know Paul had to be alive.

So she began asking questions such as "What is the picture on the left of the door in Aileen's bedroom?" and "What is the name of our next-door neighbor's cat?" When Cinquanta called her back that afternoon with the correct answers it was virtually the first crumb of reassurance she had had since Paul's letter.

This was the start of more regular conversations between her and Cinquanta, and to a point Gail felt they came to understand each other. She had read somewhere that in kidnapings the negotiators always try to establish a human relationship with someone among the kidnapers. She also had a vague idea of picking up some crucial piece of information from these conversations, but she never did. The most she ever learned about Cinquanta was that he had a wife and children, and on one occasion she asked him how as an Italian he could be involved in such a cruel crime against a family.

"Signora, it's a job like any other," he answered. And although he continued bringing her Paul's answers to her questions, he never actually forgot his "job" for long. He kept telling her how urgent it was to start negotiations. Some of his friends were becoming unpleasantly impatient. He also kept repeating something that she couldn't bear to hear: Paul was facing danger if the Getty family continued to regard the kidnaping as a hoax and refused to take it seriously.

It was now five weeks since Paul had disappeared. Gail was increasingly frightened that the kidnapers were about to harm him. She told her father so when she telephoned him in San Francisco, and since Judge Harris was one of the few people Getty respected and would talk to on the subject, the judge was at last able to convince him that something must be done.

Getty still insisted he would never pay a ransom, but he did agree to send somebody to Rome to offer Gail professional support and deal with the situation. The man he chose was a former spy who worked for Getty Oil, J. Fletcher Chace.

Chace has been described as "one of the good ol' boys from the good ol' CIA." Since retiring he had worked as security adviser to the Getty installations in the Neutral Zone. At six foot four, with very bright blue eyes and craggy profile, he was a handsome man, and Getty, who was impressed by clean-cut men of action, thought him the ideal character to deal with the case. And when Chace arrived in Rome on August 12, Gail was relieved to have this assured professional to help her. But as far as Young Paul was concerned, Fletcher Chace was probably the worst emissary the old man could have chosen.

By now the situation in Rome had actually become extremely simple. From the moment Paul was kidnaped there had been two alternatives if he was going to return alive: Either the police would catch the kidnappers, or the Gettys would have to pay a large sum of money as a ransom. After more than a month of trying, it was clear that the Carabinieri couldn't solve the case had Paul been held by Donald Duck—which left the family to face the second option. However distasteful it might be, the only point remaining was to negotiate a price and get the boy released as soon and as painlessly as possible. Anything else was quite irrelevant, and would serve only to extend the agony.

Since the elder Getty utterly refused to pay a ransom, the agony had to be prolonged until he would, and handsome Fletcher Chace prolonged it with a vengeance.

Like many ex-spies, Chace was a great conspiracy theorist. He was also highly confident of his abilities. One of his first priorities was to make contact with the kidnapers in person, so Gail readily agreed to let him take the call when next Cinquanta telephoned. But Chace spoke no Italian, and his rusty Spanish first baffled Cinquanta, then annoyed him, and finally convinced him that, for all his warnings, the Getty family still refused to take the kidnaping seriously.

Chace was in fact a natural victim for the double-dealing and deceit that were building up around the whole affair. As a former spy he might have realized that the woman he met in his hotel and started sleeping with was actually on the payroll of the Carabinieri; her task, apart from making Fletcher feel at home, was to feed him the views of those she worked for and find out what he knew himself.

Chace actually knew very little. There had been numerous reports of false sightings of Paul—several coming from people Gail knew quite well—and as Chace insisted on following up each one personally, doing so took time. One plausible young man claimed to know where Paul was hiding, and took Chace to the monastery town of Monte Cassino, pocketed the $3,000 the agent offered him, and promptly disappeared.

So, far from bringing matters to a head, Chace's arrival on the scene served to complicate a situation that was already getting out of hand, and to postpone yet further any chance of serious negotiations. Indeed, by the end of August a distraught and highly frustrated Fletcher Chace was falling back on the Carabinieri's theory of a hoax. Baffled, bad-tempered, and thoroughly bewildered, Chace believed he was at the center of a considerable conspiracy himself—and he reported all the details back to Sutton Place, where they strengthened the old man's resolution not to pay a penny.

It was now early September, and to deal with this supposed conspiracy, Chace thought the time had come to baffle the opposition and the Italian press by taking Gail and the children out of circulation. It was actually extremely dangerous to break off contact with a group of jumpy and potentially lethal kidnapers at a time like this, but Chace was adamant, and insisted on flying Gail and the children back to London, where for ten days he kept them in conditions of maximum security in a carefully prepared safe house at Kingston upon Thames.

It was the sort of cloak-and-dagger operation he enjoyed, but its connection with a kidnaped boy in Calabria was none too clear. Nor did it give Gail the chance that she was counting on for meaningful discussion either with her former husband or with Big Paul himself at nearby Sutton Place. Paul Junior had been growing even more reclusive; when Gail saw him at Cheyne Walk, he refused to talk about the kidnaping.

So did his father, who was so frightened of the Mafia by now that he insisted any contact with Gail had to be through Chace. Chace made even his go-between work an undercover operation, meeting her at secret rendezvous in the park, but although he promised to convey to

Getty her frantic pleas to do something for his grandson, there was never any answer. Big Paul was sticking by his principles and was now thoroughly imbued with Chace's version of events and with his tales of the undercover world. After ten days Gail and her family had had enough and returned to Rome. Chace remained for several days at Sutton Place to reassure his employer.

By mid-September it was clear that the situation was a disaster and that none of the people meant to deal with it could cope. But two things did make Gail's life a little happier. The first was that she managed to move to a new apartment in the heart of old Rome, in a livelier area than anonymous Parioli. The new flat practically overlooked the old Campo dei Fiori market; both the girls loved it, and she felt less of a prisoner than she had in Parioli.

It was now, too, that a member of the Getty family did arrive to keep her company—her thirteen-year-old son Mark. He had been pining for his family, and in the end, despite their determined efforts to keep him safely in San Francisco, his grandparents had to let him go. In her new flat and with Mark beside her, Gail began to feel a little stronger.

This was as well, for relations with Cinquanta and the kidnapers were worsening dramatically. Cinquanta had already warned her that, baffled by the silence in the press, members of the gang were planning something drastic that would prove they still meant business.

From the way he spoke Gail knew he wasn't bluffing—any more than he was taken in by her excuses for failing with the ransom—and he suddenly produced a fresh demand: "Signora, you must come to talk to us yourself. We will deal with this together. You will be able to see your son, and I will guarantee your safety."

Gail asked for time to think this over. He replied that he would telephone next day for her decision.

All her instincts told her she should go. Of course she knew the dangers, but by now she was long past caring. For she also knew that she was doing Paul no good in Rome, and that if things were left to Chace and the Carabinieri the kidnaping could go on for ever. If she met Paul's captors face to face, there was at least a hope of bringing the situation to a head and diverting their anger from her son. She was also naturally excited by the chance of seeing him again.

So when Cinquanta telephoned she said she'd come. He seemed relieved and gave precise instructions. She was to drive a car of a certain make with a bumper sticker and a white suitcase on the roof rack. She should travel so many kilometers down the autostrada to a point south of Naples, where a man would be waiting by the roadside at a certain time. He would throw gravel at her windshield to signal her to stop. Someone from the gang would then take over and bring her to the place where Paul was hidden. Once again Cinquanta guaranteed her safety. Gail said she understood, and once again agreed to come.

But afterward pressure rapidly built up against the whole idea. When she told Judge Harris, he was alarmed for her safety and pointed out some of the risks she would be taking. "What would happen to the other children if they killed you—as they might—and what good would that do Paul?" Chace, now back in Rome, was even more opposed to the idea, and firmly barred her from going. With so much opposition, Gail changed her mind.

She now believes that this was "a terrible mistake. For had I gone, it could have brought everybody to their senses and got things moving. Besides I would have been with Paul, and might have stopped them doing what they did."

Instead, her last-minute cancellation of the meeting made relations with the kidnapers that much worse. She had no way of telling them she'd changed her mind, and they were furious when she failed to come. Even the normally polite Cinquanta was enraged when he telephoned her later, accusing her of playing tricks like all the others. At one point they were screaming at each other over the telephone, and the call concluded with Cinquanta saying he had done his best, that harder men would now take over, and that whatever happened wasn't his responsibility.

As Gail soon discovered, Cinquanta wasn't bluffing, and Paul's sufferings now began in earnest as his captors took their anger out on him. They began by confiscating his radio, which had been his one link with the world outside. Fresh chains were fastened on his legs. A small bird he had made a pet of was killed before his eyes and he was told that, because his grandfather wouldn't pay to save him, the time had come to do the same to him. His captors kept him bound and gagged for several hours, then played Russian roulette against his forehead with a .45 revolver.

Paul never knew if the gun was loaded. After it failed to go off several times he was blindfolded, bound more tightly than ever, and left like this until next morning.

Around this time a fresh event occurred which added to his misery. As Cinquanta had hinted, some of the original kidnapers sold out their stake in Paul just as they might have sold a piece of real estate or a share in a casino. The new purchasers, who ranked higher in the N'drangheta were particularly anxious to raise capital to develop the narcotics business on their own account. They were colder and more ruthless men than their predecessors, and they were looking for a quick return on their investment.

PAUL'S captors were unusually affable that morning, which instantly aroused his suspicions. October had come; with the colder weather they had been giving him cheap Italian brandy to keep him warm, but never before in the morning. When he said it was too early to start drinking, they told him to take it—it would do him good. Then they told him that his hair had grown too long and needed cutting.

He tried to argue with them. He liked his hair long, and didn't want it cut, but they said it was dirty and insisted. He might have struggled but there were four or five of them, and he had grown weak with captivity and could see that they meant business. So he sat quietly as one of the men sheared his long red hair clumsily with a small blunt scissors. It was the first time he had had a haircut from a barber with a mask, and the man took particular care to clear the hair from each side of his head. When he finished, he dabbed alcohol behind Paul's ears.

It was then Paul guessed what they intended.

Again he might have struggled, but again he knew there was no point. If he attempted to resist, they would only hurt him, and they would end up doing as they wanted anyway.

So when they offered him more brandy he drank it. And when they gave him a rolled-up handkerchief to bite on, he placed it in his mouth and started biting. And while he was biting he felt somebody behind him grab his right ear between a roughened thumb and finger and hold it tight.

Then came the searing pain as with one swift stroke of a cutthroat razor, the whole right ear was severed from his newly shorn head.

ON October 21 Cinquanta informed Gail of what had happened, but he refused to elaborate. At first she refused to believe him, but he insisted it was true and said he would send her photographs to prove it.

Like any mother, she felt sick with horror at the thought of the mutilation of her child. Despite so many warnings, she had never quite believed that Cinquanta and his friends would harm Paul. Now that they had, she tried to keep herself from thinking about it all the time.

But it was hard to stop brooding over the savagery of such men and the fear and suffering they had cold-bloodedly inflicted on her child.

With this latest touch of horror she began to wonder how much longer this interminable kidnaping would continue—and how much longer she and, more important, Paul could take it.

As a result of a call to the police, Polaroid snapshots of Paul were discovered in a garbage can at a certain spot in Rome. They had been taken recently outside a cave; when Gail saw them she was horrified, for they showed an emaciated Paul, with an unhealed wound where his ear had been.

Shortly afterward Cinquanta rang again. He asked if she believed him now, and said he had warned her this would happen. He added that the ear was in the mail. Gail was too numbed to argue with him then, but later, when the ear failed to arrive, and he called to ask if she had received it, there were furious exchanges. Cinquanta insisted that the authorities must have the ear, and Gail attempted to express something of her rage and horror at what had happened.

By now the disappearance of the ear itself was creating yet another mystery, more misunderstandings, and further excuses for inaction. The kidnapers had sealed it in a plastic container filled with preserving fluid, which in turn had been placed inside a padded bag and mailed from the main post office of Reggio Calabria to the editorial offices of *Il Messagero* on October 20.

If nothing else the arrival of this gruesome package should have ended all talk of hoaxes and added a sense of urgency to the negotiations. It would have done so anywhere except Italy—but, as Gore Vidal happened to observe around this time, "there is no such thing as a mail service in Rome." Officially a postal strike was in progress, and Paul's ear, along with countless other parcels for the city, moldered in a warehouse till the strike was over.

Finally, on November 10—three weeks after the mutilation—the package was delivered to the offices of *Il Messagero* on the Via del Corso, and the secretary who opened the parcel fainted.

By now Gail, having lost all faith in the Carabinieri, had enlisted the support of their rivals, the Italian Polizia. Carlo, the head of the Polizia Statale Squadra Mobile—the Rome Flying Squad—now took on the case and proved an energetic and effective officer. He had helped Gail come to terms with what had happened, and prepared her for the grisly task of identifying the ear, if it ever did arrive. At his suggestion she studied photographs of Paul to check upon its shape and appearance.

So when Carlo told her it had arrived, and asked her to come to police headquarters to identify it, she was more self-possessed than the secretary at *Il Messagero* had been. She ignored the press photographers waiting for her outside the building, and was quite certain when confronted with the ear. Yes, she recognized it by the freckles and the shape. It certainly belonged to Paul.

Four months had passed since Paul was taken, but even now his agony was far from over.

There had been some small advances. Through Judge Harris, who was a prominent San Francisco Catholic, the Vatican had become involved, and Gail had met the Pope's "gorilla," massive Archbishop Casimir Marcinkus of Chicago. Marcinkus had been very charming and said he might be able to assist her: "I know some important people who I'm sure could help you. If you like I'll talk to them about your son." The archbishop later became notorious for his connections with the corrupt financier Michele Sindona, and Roberto Calvi, the head of the Banco Ambrosiano, who ended up hanging under Blackfriars Bridge in London. So it was probably just as well that Chace refused to let her take advantage of those underworld connections.

The American government was also showing signs of some concern, since Gail had sent a personal message to President Richard M. Nixon. Thomas Biamonte, a highly competent ex-FBI lawyer of Calabrian extraction who worked in the U.S. embassy in Rome, was assigned to the case; speaking the local dialect of Calabria, he had made useful contact with the kidnapers on his own account. Largely as a result, they had dropped their demands from 10 billion lire, or $17.4 million, to a more realistic 2 billion, approximately $3.2 million. But having lowered their price, they had also made very clear that they were sticking to it.

Back in Sutton Place, the octogenarian grandfather was also holding out. Hoax or no hoax, ear or no ear, principles were principles, and he still refused to pay a penny.

AS winter started in the uplands of Calabria and the injured boy was dragged to yet another hiding place, his captors issued one more ultimatum. They were showing signs of losing patience once again, and said that if there was no deal soon, a second ear would be on its way to *Il Messagero*, to be followed by yet further portions of the kidnaped boy's anatomy if it failed to get results.

Paul himself was in a wretched state by now. The pain of the rough-and-ready amputation had continued, and an infection set in. Cold and malnourishment coupled with nervous shock from the operation left him weakened and dispirited. Since childhood he had suffered from weak lungs, and what started as a bad cold rapidly became pneumonia. His captors, anxious not to lose $3.2 million began injecting him with such massive doses of penicillin that he became allergic to them. When he couldn't take any more antibiotics and his condition continued to deteriorate, they panicked.

As a last resort Cinquanta telephoned to Gail to ask her for advice. "Signora. You must tell me. What can we do for him?" he wailed, unable to disguise his anxiety for Paul's condition and knowing that he and his colleagues could lose everything if the boy's illness worsened.

This was the point when Gail knew for certain that if the kidnaping lasted any longer, Paul would die. Nothing on earth was worth that— not Big Paul's precious principles and his fears for his other grandchildren, nor the fortune of the Gettys, nor the problems over raising so much money.

So she decided that the episode had to end. If no one else would end it, she would. If no one else could save her son, she would save him. She told Cinquanta to keep Paul as warm as possible and get ready to release him. The ransom would be paid.

GAIL'S determination effectively transformed the situation. Suddenly her single-mindedness became contagious. She spoke to her father, who argued so forcibly on the telephone to Sutton Place that Big Paul finally gave in and agreed that somehow the money would be found. But even now, the old man was typically insisting that he would pay only $2.2 million, which according to his accountants was the *tax-deductible* portion of the ransom; the boy's father had to foot the rest.

This caused problems: Gail could no longer make meaningful contact with Paul Junior, who was making little sense to anyone. But he did finally agree to his father's terms. Since he didn't have the $1 million that was his share of the ransom, Big Paul would lend him it, at 4 percent interest computed annually. But Gail had been led to understand that, as a precondition of payment, Paul Junior was insisting that she immediately surrender custody of all her children.

Gail thought she could bear anything by now, but this was the cruelest blow of all. She had endured five months of hell to save her son, and at the moment when she almost had him back, it seemed she had to lose him—and the rest of her children.

But there was nothing to be done, and her feelings were no longer terribly important. All that mattered was the money, and to get Paul released as soon as possible. So she wearily agreed, even getting as far as making arrangements to take the children to the airport—only to discover there had been yet another misunderstanding and Paul was denying ever having asked for custody.

This was typical of the atmosphere of drama and distrust that hovered round the crime to the very end. But Jean Paul Getty had agreed in principle. That was what counted, even though he would contribute only $2.2 million, and stuck to his demand that Paul Junior should pay the rest in regular installments from his trust income.

Until the very last moment, Gail dreaded that some other hitch might occur. Then on December 6, Chace received authorization to withdraw the massive sum of 2 billion lire in used 50,000-lire and 100,000-lire notes, all of which had been microfilmed. The notes filled three large carryalls which Chace actually took to the U.S. embassy on the Via Veneto for safe keeping.

Even now there was a muddle, caused by fog and snow on the autostrada north of Naples, which was in the grip of its worst winter for nearly fifty years. On the first trip with the money, Chace failed to make contact with the kidnapers. Tempers frayed, and Gail was afraid of yet more dramas that could still prolong the five-month agony. But on December 12, Chace picked up the three bags from the U.S. Embassy for the second time and drove 250 miles south of Rome to the rendezvous Cinquanta had arranged. Four kilometers south of the turnoff to the town of Lagonegro he spotted a man standing by the road, pistol in hand and balaclava helmet obscuring his face. Chace stopped the car, deposited the three bags by the road, and returned to Rome. He had been shadowed all the way by members of the Squadra Mobile disguised as workmen in a van, who had photographed the man in the balaclava.

Although the kidnaping was so nearly over, Gail still had to face the cruelest wait of all. Next day she heard nothing, nothing the day after, and she became convinced that, having gotten the money, the kidnapers must have killed her son. From their point of view it would have made a sort of sense to have taken the ransom and destroyed the evidence, Paul included.

By the evening of the fourteenth she was on the edge of despair, convinced by now that this had happened. Five months of misery had ended with a silent telephone.

But at 10:30 at night the telephone did ring. It was Cinquanta. He was very formal. He could have been someone in a bank as he confirmed that the money had been paid and that his colleagues were keeping their part of the bargain and releasing Paul within the next few hours. The boy would be left on a hillside close to where Chace had left the money. Cinquanta gave a precise description of the spot, adding that Gail should come there on her own to fetch him.

"Please keep him warm," she said, mindful of the freezing weather.

"I'll make sure he has a blanket," said Cinquanta. These were the last words he spoke to Gail, and she never heard his voice again.

All thought of sleep was over for the night. The police had been tapping Gail's telephone and passed the gist of the conversation on to the Squadra Mobile, who soon arrived at her apartment. She rang Chace, who came at once. By midnight, she and the ex-CIA man were in the back of a car from the Squadra Mobile with Carlo at the wheel.

For most of the way it was snowing heavily; dawn was breaking when they reached the hillside. The countryside was white, and in the early light there was no sign of Paul. They called his name to no avail. Gail whistled as she and the children used to whistle to each other at Orgia. Paul would have recognized the call at once, but there was still no answer.

"You must be prepared," said Chace. "They may have killed him." The men from the Squadra Mobile went on searching the hillside without discovering any sign of him. Then they heard one of the men shouting. He had found something at last—an old blanket, and a blindfold. They must have belonged to Paul, and they were the first evidence that he was still alive. But where was he?

"You know your son," Carlo said to Gail. "What would he have done?"

"Headed for home," she said.

So the Squadra Mobile drove slowly up the autostrada, searching for him, with Gail and Chace in the back of a squad car. They saw nothing, but over the car radio they picked up a report from the police. An unidentified male had been found in the vicinity, and taken to the headquarters of the Carabinieri at Lagonegro.

At first, no one at the headquarters would admit that Paul was even there—and when someone did finally admit it, Gail was told she could not see him because he was being interrogated.

A possible reason for this apparent hostility lay in the fact that she was with members of the Squadra Mobile, who have always been at daggers drawn with the Carabinieri—and the Carabinieri were determined to retain the credit for "rescuing" Paul Getty.

But Gail had endured too much by now to bother with such niceties. "I want my son," she said. "Let me see my son." And the sight of this angry and exhausted woman calling for her child made the officials relent; finally they brought him to her.

He was so thin and ill that she scarcely recognized him as he came shuffling in, wearing clothes the Carabinieri had bought him. He was filthy, he could barely walk, and a bloodstained bandage around his head covered the wound where his ear had been.

Now that the moment they had longed for had arrived, Gail and Paul were both too overcome to speak. They clung to one another and it was only when she held him in her arms that she knew for certain the long ordeal was over. All that mattered was to get Paul safely back to Rome, and before the Carabinieri could object, she and Chace half dragged him to the waiting car outside and started home. All she remembers of the journey is that "Paul and I were both like zombies, and so tense with emotion that we could still barely speak to one another."

By the time they reached Naples, news of Paul's release was on the radio, and at Rome reporters were waiting for them by the toll booths as they left the autostrada. People were waiting in the street to watch as they drove by. Some of them cheered and waved, but Gail could feel nothing but a sense of total unreality and relief that the horror of the last five months was over. As yet she had no inkling of the damage that those months had done to Paul—and her, and all the family.

A friend had already booked both of them into a clinic in Parioli, where they spent the next three days recovering before going off on holiday to Austria. On their arrival at the clinic, the doctors had examined Paul and the results seemed reassuring. He was young and strong. Physically he'd soon recover, and with modern plastic surgery, even his ear could be rebuilt.

"And the psychological effects?" Gail asked.

Time alone would tell, the doctor answered.

That afternoon, Gail remembered the date: December 15, Big Paul's birthday. He was eighty-one, and she suggested that it might be tactful if Paul telephoned his grandfather to thank him for what he'd done and wish him a very happy birthday.

At Sutton Place, the old man was in his study when the call came through and one of his women came to tell him who was on the line.

"It's your grandson, Paul. Do you wish to speak to him?" she asked.

"No," Getty answered.

CHAPTER SIXTEEN

The Dynasty

BEHIND the stern façade that Jean Paul Getty managed to maintain throughout the kidnaping, things were beginning to go wrong at Sutton Place.

This had nothing at all to do with Getty's commercial interests, which had never looked brighter. The worldwide oil shortage following the Yom Kippur War of October 1973 had sent the price of oil from $3 to $12 a barrel on the international market, and shares in Getty Oil were rising steadily. During 1975, the old man would increase the company's cash dividend from $1.30 to $2.50 a share, thus incidentally awarding himself a record income for the year of $25,800,000. By then he and the Sarah C. Getty Trust between them would be worth a staggering $2.4 billion.

But this flow of wealth could not prevent an ill-defined but most disturbing feeling that had started to affect him. It was something he had not experienced before, and was as painful as it was unexpected. At the age of eighty-two one of the richest men in the world was experiencing a sense of failure.

The feeling had started in 1972, not long after his eightieth birthday party, held at the Dorchester Hotel and arranged by the Duchess of Argyll. At the party everything had still been wonderful. When Getty's friend the Duke of Bedford had proposed the toast—"May the many witty and lovely ladies around him grow even wittier and lovelier"— everyone applauded. President Nixon had sent his daughter, Tricia, especially to represent him; and at midnight the President himself had telephoned from Washington with birthday greetings to his loyal supporter and generous contributor, his good friend, J. Paul Getty.

But a few months later the unthinkable occurred: His confidante and friend Penelope Kitson left him. When she had told him she intended to get married once again, to businessman Patrick de Laszlo, he had done everything he could to stop her, including using the ultimate Getty sanction: cutting her from his precious will. He was upset to find this made no difference, but let himself be mollified when the marriage failed some months later, and Penelope returned to see him.

"I won't say I'm sorry, dear" was all he said—and he quietly reinstated her in his will and in her cottage on the estate. But Penelope's show of independence had upset him, as had reactions to something else that meant a lot to him: the official opening of his museum at Malibu at the beginning of 1974.

Getty's architect, the amiable Englishman Stephen Garrett, had always had his doubts about the whole idea of re-creating this Roman villa by the shores of the Pacific, and had tried to warn his patron. But Getty wouldn't listen, and had continued to follow every detail of the construction from 6,000 miles away. When it was opened, Getty's precious dream-child was greeted with almost unanimous derision by the press. "Vulgar," "tasteless," and "straight out of Disneyland" were among the reactions, and the *Economist* was particularly snooty. Art historians, it said, would be hard put to decide whether J. Paul Getty's folly was "merely incongruous or genuinely ludicrous."

As usual when faced by something that he didn't like, the old man narrowed his already very narrow lips and said nothing. But coming right on top of widespread criticism of his behavior over the kidnaping, these reactions to his museum genuinely shook him. Later he would write that young Paul's release was "the finest and most wonderful birthday present of my life." Few believed him.

Faced with a similar situation, poorer men had mortgaged homes, borrowed what they could from friends, even gone into bankruptcy in their attempts to find money for a grandchild's ransom. And it did not entirely escape public notice that while Getty had at first refused to find the money on the grounds of his so-called principles, he had finally overlooked those principles when he had to; people also noticed that by delaying payment of the ransom for as long as possible, he had actually forced the kidnapers to drop the asking price from $17 million to $3.2 million—a saving of some $13.8 million.

As a businessman Getty was certainly aware of savings. And to achieve those economies his once-favorite grandson had been forced to suffer a five-month nightmare with the Mafia. Getty presumably felt the price worth paying.

But now he must have had his doubts. For the kidnaping proved a genuine disaster to the whole family as well as to Getty himself. The boy's own sufferings had barely started, and in different ways the damage would continue spreading, bringing yet further misery and grief for years to come.

This was not evident at once. After the release, Gail and young Paul spent two months quietly recuperating in the Austrian mountains, along with Aileen, Mark, and Ariadne. The mountains calmed their fears and restored their spirits, and they were soon enjoying life again. Years later Aileen would remember this holiday as the last time she had been carefree and completely happy. The rest of the family felt much the same, and they returned from Austria believing that the nightmare of the kidnaping was over and forgotten.

It was a good sign that the crime had made curiously little difference to their feelings for Italy, and once Gail was safely back in her house at Orgia she shrugged off suggestions from her friends that she might possibly be in need of therapy.

Young Paul had been reunited with Martine by now, and it was only when he returned to Rome to be with her, leaving Gail alone at last, that she realized how right her friends had been. "For suddenly and without warning, I quietly fell apart." She was hit by nightmares from the period of the kidnaping; these were followed by uncontrollable fits of weeping. She took to bed in the depths of black depression. Then, slowly, painfully, she pulled herself together.

At this stage, Paul appeared less affected than his mother. This was partly the effect of youth and partly because he had the strong-willed Martine to depend on. For the first time in his life, he found himself enjoying a settled relationship with a girlfriend; and that summer, when Martine discovered she was pregnant, he acted in accordance with the bourgeois principles he had previously rejected—and proposed.

It was a happy wedding, held before the mayor of Sovicille, the seat of the local commune, with virtually the whole of Orgia attending. Conscious of her condition, Martine wore a simple dress, and it was Paul who really stole the show. His hair had grown again and he made a striking figure in his new white gym shoes and his specially tailored black Mao suit with dark red piping.

Coming so soon after his release, the wedding was inevitably something of a media event, with the Italian press and television out in strength. Far from disliking this, Paul obviously loved to be the center of attention—so much so that when a photographer from the London *Daily Express* was delayed and missed the ceremony, Paul insisted on going through with it again for the photographs.

Those who knew him insist that this was not exactly vanity. In his longing for media attention he was seeking something that he desperately needed—a true identity, which he hoped to find in the role of some sort of cult celebrity.

Just before Christmas he and Martine left Italy for Los Angeles, where they planned to live, and in January 1975, in the suburb of Tarzana (whose founder, Edgar Rice Burroughs, was the author of the Tarzan novels), Martine had a son. Resisting the temptation of naming him Tarzan Getty, they called him Balthazar. Balthazar was one of the Three Wise Men in the Bible, and if the family was going to survive, a little wisdom wouldn't come amiss.

In wedding Martine, Paul made something of a sacrifice: Having married before the age of twenty-two, he had disqualified himself from any income from the trust his father had set up in 1966, after the divorce from Gail. This age bar was originally inserted to protect Aileen and Ariadne from potential fortune hunters, but now it ruled out Paul as well.

He made a virtue of despising what he didn't have, but from now on lack of funds was to be one of Paul's perpetual problems. He found it particularly galling to have the Getty name without the Getty money. He knew that one day he would inherit a fortune from the Sarah C. Getty Trust—but in the meantime he had trouble getting by.

IT was around March 1975 that Paul Junior began pressuring Gail to bring the children back to England. Whenever they spoke on the telephone he sounded so depressed and lonely that she was genuinely worried about him.

Sensing that there was little hope of marrying Paul or bearing his children, Victoria had left him, undergone a cure, and gotten married for the second time, to Oliver Musker, an amusing young London-based antique dealer who was in love with her.

After her departure Paul really hit rock bottom. The only person looking after him by now was a former minicab driver called Derek Calcott, who did his best to ensure that there was something in the house for Paul to eat—generally chocolate chip cookies and chocolate ripple ice cream, both of which were bad for him but amply satisfied his addict's craving for something sweet. Feeling helpless and abandoned, Paul Junior was otherwise completely on his own in a house that had become as gloomy and neglected as himself.

He was also out of money. He was financially incapable and the relatively small sums he had been receiving from the Sarah C. Getty Trust had been going to buy quantities of street drugs he was using in addition to his prescription drugs.

All this had made him wretchedly vulnerable. So-called friends had started taking his possessions, and he had sold off much of what remained—including the burgundy MG from Rome, for which his sister, Donna, gave him $2,000. He could no longer support the children in Italy and was begging Gail to bring them back to Cheyne Walk.

She was of two minds over this. Part of her dreaded leaving Italy, and she was wary of getting too involved with Paul again. On the other hand she thought that setting up house in Cheyne Walk might be good both for the children and for their father. Since she and Paul were both alone and were still fond of each other, it also made good sense for them to be together.

So Gail flew to London for a few days for the first time since the kidnaping, only to find things even worse than she expected. She arrived over the weekend. Paul was alone in the house; since he was out of money yet again his dealer had left him without drugs, and he was already showing signs of acute withdrawal.

That night he was in such desperate straits that Gail made up a bed in the study to be near him. She stayed as the sweating and the writhing started. When he told her that all he wanted was to kick the habit, she promised she would stay and help him.

There was a drug clinic at Elephant and Castle, one of the poorest areas of South London, which offered addicts treatment every Tuesday, so the following Tuesday she took Paul there. He started on methadone instead of heroin and began cutting back on alcohol. Only when she was thoroughly convinced that he was serious about his treatment did she agree to bring the children back to England.

It was a dreadful wrench leaving Italy, and the children hated it. But by now Gail had convinced herself that it was for the best, and the children all seemed glad to be reunited with their father.

It was decided that Tara should remain in France with her grandparents, and the girls were sent to separate boarding schools—Aileen to Hatchlands, a finishing school for smart young ladies near Godalming in Surrey, and Ariadne to a boarding school near Lewes.

After creating consternation by announcing—as a practical joke—that she was pregnant, thirteen-year-old Ariadne settled down and accepted the routine of an English girls' boarding school. But Aileen found the whole idea of Hatchlands very odd indeed. Like a true Italian, she hated being forced to sleep with the windows open, and always seemed to have a cold. She was taught fencing, contract bridge, and etiquette, all of which struck her as absurd. So did the trouble that was taken over teaching her to curtsey properly to royalty. Bored and resentful, she kept a secret stock of alcohol, truanted to London, and used to tell horrifying stories, generally concocted, to her more gullible fellow pupils. Far from turning Aileen into a socially accomplished young lady, a year of Hatchlands was enough to make a rebel out of her for ever.

At the same time, finding a school for Mark proved more of a problem. As it was hard to get him into a major public school at such short notice, a friend of Gail's introduced him to the less oppressive world of Taunton School in rural Somerset. Here he came to feel very much at home, was popular with the other boys, loved the countryside, worked hard enough to get a scholarship to Oxford, and became a very self-possessed, reflective human being.

MEANWHILE his brother Paul was having problems as a married man of eighteen with an older wife and two young children—Martine's daughter, Anna, as well as Balthazar—to support. Craig Copetas, a journalist from *Rolling Stone* who saw a lot of him around this time, recalls that "he was obviously extremely strong, and physically appeared to be scarcely affected by the kidnap."

But this healthy look was deceptive. Beneath the surface, five months of physical and mental torture had played havoc with a personality already at risk; Gail is convinced that Paul's nervous system had been seriously affected by his sufferings.

He was finding it nearly impossible to sleep—and when he did sleep he was a constant prey to nightmares and a never-ending sense of dread. He often woke up screaming. But his real problems came from the brandy the kidnapers had fed him in captivity. Paul had inherited an addictive nature from his father, and soon it was clear that the kidnapers had left Paul Getty a hopeless alcoholic.

It was not surprising that he found it impossible to settle down or maintain a close relationship with anyone. Martine often couldn't cope with him, particularly when he turned to drugs—legal and illegal—to help him through the day and enjoy a few hours' sleep at night.

In her practical way, Martine kept her small family together in Los Angeles, making a home for Anna and Balthazar—and for Paul too, when he needed it. When Grandfather Getty offered him a small allowance on condition that he study at a university, he enrolled at Pepperdine University in Malibu and opted to study Chinese history. But academic life was as difficult for him as married life, and he was rarely in the lecture hall or at home.

When he could he came to England; according to Gail, he continued to adore his father and romanticize his life. Although he rarely saw

Paul Junior, he was as eager as ever for his approval, and still hoped to gain it by becoming an important figure in the counterculture.

This was what really lay behind his continuing obsession with prominent members of the Beat generation. Copetas was able to introduce him to some of the high priests of the movement, such as William Burroughs, Allen Ginsberg, and Timothy Leary. He remembers Paul trying to impress Burroughs by giving him one of the earliest Polaroid instant cameras. "It was quite a present in those days. But Burroughs just looked puzzled and embarrassed and obviously hadn't the faintest notion what to do with it."

As the author of *Naked Lunch*, Burroughs was a hero to young Paul, while, as Copetas puts it, "the only thing that made Paul interesting to Burroughs was that his name was Getty and he'd been kidnapped by the mafia and had his ear cut off."

LATER that year the trial was held in Lagonegro of seven men accused of varying degrees of involvement in the kidnaping of J. Paul Getty III. In Italy it is rare for kidnap victims or their families to risk attending trials that involve the Mafia. But Gail and Paul were determined to confront their ex-tormentors.

Worried by the risks they would be taking, Paul Junior insisted that they consult the former SAS man he himself had been using as a security expert since the kidnaping. As a professional the SAS man was so worried by the prospect of a Mafia trial in the heart of Mafia-dominated country that he seriously suggested having Gail and Paul flown into Lagonegro from Naples each morning by helicopter. To Gail this seemed excessive; mother and son settled for staying in Naples during the trial and traveling to court by car each morning.

Paul was now wearing his hair longer than ever to hide his lost ear, and many commented on how well he looked. But he and Gail found the trial more upsetting than expected—particularly when they had to encounter the seven sullen faces of the accused staring at them from the iron cage where they were kept inside the court.

They were dangerous-looking characters, but since the kidnapers had always worn their masks, Paul could not recognize any of them. Nor, when she heard them speak, did Gail recognize the unmistakable voice of Cinquanta. None of the ringleaders seemed to be among the accused; as usual in Mafia trials, the godfathers had gone wherever godfathers go when trouble comes. According to police, one of the chief suspects was a leading figure in the N'drangheta. He was said to have been in charge of the affair, but the police could never catch him, this despite the fact that he appeared quite openly to get married in church at the nearby town of Gióia Táuro just before the trial.

Nor was the ransom money ever found, apart from a small sum discovered on one of the accused. This meant that more than three million Getty dollars, in carefully marked Italian lire, were currently helping to equip Mafia laboratories producing heroin and cocaine.

Those of the accused who were found guilty received between four and ten years' imprisonment in conditions of maximum security. But Gail felt that no punishment could match the cruelty the kidnapers inflicted on her son. Some years later a member of the gang who was still in prison wrote to her begging her forgiveness and saying that a word from her would help his chances of release. She didn't answer.

THROUGH most of 1975 Gail and Paul Junior seemed to get on well together in Cheyne Walk, partly because the house was big enough for both to live relatively separate lives. Gail found the house more beautiful than she remembered, but also faintly sinister—"a living tomb," she would later call it.

No, she assured one interviewer, she and Paul had not remarried, nor did they intend to do so.

Now that they were back together, she was shocked by how much he had changed and by the damage his way of life had caused him. But thanks to his regular Tuesday visits to the Elephant and Castle, he was showing signs of definite improvement, and during that summer he actually spent a two-week vacation with Mark, taking him to stay with friends in Ireland. It was the first time he had been away so long from Cheyne Walk since Talitha's death.

THROUGHOUT this period the aging Jean Paul Getty had been trying not to think too much about the future. He had spent his lifetime building Getty Oil—but what was to become of it? "I'm a bad boss," he admitted gloomily in a moment of rare candor. "A good boss develops successors. There is nobody to step into my shoes."

Theoretically the whole purpose of creating the enormous fortune in the Sarah C. Getty Trust had always been to enrich what he liked to call the Getty dynasty. But here again Getty had been having doubts. What hope could there be for a dynasty riven by disaster and dissent? Penelope told Getty's biographer, Ralph Hewins that at times the old man was haunted by the thought that "the Getty dynasty would end with him, and his empire would be divided up, never to reach the same peak again." Sometimes Getty even went so far as to blame himself for what had happened. Having sacrificed his family to success in business, he wondered if the sacrifice was worth it.

To counter such gloomy thoughts, during the summer of 1975 he tried becoming something he had never been before: a loving grandfather at the center of a big, united family, "Mr. Family himself," as Gail called him. At different times all the grandchildren would be invited to Sutton Place together with their parents.

At one time Gordon and Ann brought their four boys, Peter, Andrew, John, and William. On another occasion George's first wife, Gloria, brought her daughters, Anne, Claire, and Caroline. And Ronald and his blond wife, Karin, came with Christopher, Stephanie, Cecile, and Christina. Gail and her children were regularly invited to Sutton Place for the weekend. Naturally they went, for money is a great healer.

Gail found her ex-father-in-law as charming to her as ever. It was as if the kidnaping had never happened, and by avoiding the subject he and his grandson Paul began to get on rather well together.

Later the old man seemed surprised at how much he had actually enjoyed this novel exercise in family togetherness, and would write of how these visits had made 1975 "a most reassuring summer for Grandfather J. Paul Getty." Trying to convince himself of what he wanted to believe, he added that the warmth of family affection showed that "despite everything—be it wealth (sic), divorce, tragedy or any of the other myriad conditions and tribulations of life—the Getty family *is* a family and will continue to be one."

Brave words—but they seemed distinctly forced when checked against reality. For the truth was that few families could have been more disunited than the Gettys, and it was impossible to regard them as an American dynasty in the making, like the Kennedys or the Rockefellers. And ironically, the truth was that most of the family disunity had been caused, directly or indirectly, by J. Paul Getty himself.

Even at eighty-two he could not resist playing one son off against another. His current favorite, to the extent that he had one, was the previously despised and frequently ignored Gordon. Gordon had been appointed along with Lansing Hays as a trustee of the Sarah C. Getty Trust, and he and Ann were the only members of the family whom his father had seen fit to invite to London for his eightieth birthday party. Gordon's show of independence in suing his father in that long and hard-fought battle over his income from the trust continued to work wonders both for his morale and his personal prestige, and relations steadily improved.

From having been, by Getty standards, on the edge of poverty, Gordon was now distinctly affluent. The increased income of Getty Oil was reflected in the earnings of the Sarah C. Getty Trust, and Gordon and his brother Paul Junior apparently received $4,927,514 in the twelve months prior to their father's death.

This meant that Ann and Gordon were both free to live the life they wanted, and almost from the start they made it clear that they would not be following the penny-pinching-billionaire existence exemplified by Gordon's father.

Ann had a strong flamboyant streak, which Gordon shared, so that when they found themselves a place it was one of the largest, most spectacular private houses in the whole of San Francisco, a four-story Italianate mansion on the peak of Pacific Heights, designed in the early thirties by the prestigious California architect Willis Polk. Like Ann and Gordon, it was considerably larger than life. It had a courtyard with Italian-style frescoes, more than a dozen bedrooms, and unrivaled views across the bay from the Golden Gate to Alcatraz. It had been something of a white elephant, and they got it fairly cheap, since a lot of money would be required to make it habitable, let alone the sort of house that Ann had set her heart on.

So buying it had been a sort of proclamation of intent. Gordon and Ann were rich, they were literally at the top of San Francisco, and they were going to enjoy themselves.

RONALD'S life remained considerably less enviable than absent-minded Gordon's during that summertime of 1975. Indeed, Gordon's growing affluence emphasized still further the gross unfairness of poor Ronald's continued disinheritance. While Gordon was drawing his millions from the Sarah C. Getty Trust, Ronald was paid his bare $3,000.

On top of this, the business he had set such store by—his grandly named Getty Financial Corporation, a conglomerate of property and fast-food restaurants—had yet to show a real profit.

But after that summer's visit to Sutton Place with Karin and the children, Ronald was more hopeful than he'd been for years. Father had mellowed, and they got along better than they ever had before. Indeed, Getty had personally assured Ronald that justice would be done. He had also made his son a trustee of the museum at Malibu and an executor of his will. All this seemed to point to one thing and one thing only: that at his father's death Ronald would be placed where he always should have been, in a position of equality beside his brothers as a full beneficiary of the Sarah C. Getty Trust

*

THE only member of the family not to be invited down to Sutton Place that summer was the old man's former favorite son and namesake, J. Paul Getty, Jr. During the worst moments of the kidnaping Getty had refused to speak to him, and now, as old age took its toll, he still stood firm.

Paul Junior became deeply upset by this, and still telephoned his father's friend Penelope from time to time, begging her to intercede on his behalf. But it was always the same reply: "Not until he comes off drugs."

Although his father wouldn't see or speak to him, there was no way Paul Junior could be displaced as a principal beneficiary of the Sarah C. Getty Trust. As a drug addict, he was not considered fit to be a Getty, but J. Paul Getty, Jr., was already set to be a multimillionaire.

CHAPTER SEVENTEEN

Posthumous Pleasures

IT was odd how little consolation Getty actually derived in his old age from the enormous fortune he had spent his life creating. There had always been something curiously unreal about the vast amounts of money he had conjured from the earth, and because he was always so determined to preserve the fortune from extravagance and taxes, it was as if he had never entirely possessed it. And just as he had never known quite how large his fortune was, so he had always been uneasy when using it except for the business that preoccupied him even now: making even further vast amounts of money.

Over the years, money had taken on various aspects for him: money as power, money to make more money, and in a deeper sense, money to justify himself before his parents and his conscience. But there was never cash to be enjoyed as any normal person might have enjoyed it, by the simple act of spending. Because of this, it was as if Getty's money cheated him; and since he had made the fortune in his own image, this meant that he was finally cheated by himself.

He couldn't change his nature any more than he could change his face, and here he was, trapped in the persona he had carefully created in order to create the fortune. In the past he had made himself an isolated figure in the interests of secrecy and strength—but now his isolation merely left him lonely. His face, which he had trained so carefully to reveal nothing of his feelings, had become a mask incapable of registering anything at all, even the terror of mortality, which never left him. He had made himself immune to love and pity—and now, at the age of eighty-three, he was incapable of feeling love for anyone. As some are color-blind, so he was people-blind, having schooled himself for years to ignore the distraction of ordinary emotions.

The result showed when his grandson was kidnaped and the emotional shutters had descended, just as it also showed in his refusal to lift the telephone and tell his drug-addicted son, Paul Junior, to come and see him. Most of all perhaps it showed in his unawareness of the wrong he'd done to his son Ronald.

Since the age of its owner in no way lessens the attractions of a vast amount of money, Getty continued to attract his women. By their eighties most men are ready for a little rest and dignity about such matters, but opportunity and habit kept him at it, and injections from his doctor enabled him to have an erection. When he was in his eighties there were women still protesting their agonized desire to marry him.

Some women had vanished from his life. Mary Teissier had more or less succumbed to drink and disappointment and retired to the house he bought her in the south of France. But there were always fresh admirers on the scene—even aristocratic ones, like the Duke of Rutland's sister, Lady Ursula d'Abo, who declared her love for Getty in the pages of the *National Enquirer*—which prompted an answering billet-doux from the emotional Nicaraguan Rosabella Burch, in an article in the *Sunday Express* saying that *she* was considering marrying him— "He's such a dear man and so amusing."

But another old Getty habit was that of playing women against each other and watching them fighting for his ancient favors. He would sit now viewing television in the evening, lost in thought and pointedly ignoring them; then, when he'd seen enough he would stagger to his feet and thoughtfully select that night's companion.

Along with concupiscence, a further habit that he couldn't break was the favorite vice of old age: anticipatory stinginess. One of the few things that could still excite him was his will. On the edge of eternity, he enjoyed paring down particular bequests as a final way of getting even with women he had once been fond of—even his ex-wives Teddy and Fini, both of whose allowances he cut, as he did that of his onetime "honorary daughter," Robina Lund, who had somehow managed to offend him. (On the other hand, he now remembered a number of very old mistresses.)

But his greatest problem was the one that had been there almost all his life: the fact that part of him had never really grown up. Even with death approaching, the financial genius was as firmly linked as ever with the emotional adolescent.

It was the childlike side of Getty that seems to have appealed to the women who were genuinely concerned about him—like his secretary, Barbara Wallace, who stayed up all night holding his hand when he was terrified of dying; or Jeanette Constable Maxwell, who had remained a friend since he gave her that monster coming-of-age party; or his "dearest Pen," Penelope Kitson, who had been too wise to marry him and was among the few who had not allowed his money to dictate her actions or affections.

One can understand why, by the spring of 1976, when he knew he had inoperable prostate cancer and refused to see the women he could use no longer, he still wanted Penelope near him, reading those never-forgotten boys' adventure books by G. A. Henty. There was reassurance in this authoritative woman treating him like a child and reading him children's stories, just as there is something particularly pathetic in the thought of this richest of all Americans, with his sad old face and his hunched figure, in his armchair with his shawl around him, dreaming of going west with Drake or to India with Clive, and wondering about reincarnation and dreading dying.

AT his death in June 1976, Getty had more than fulfilled the bargain made with his mother when they set up the Sarah C. Getty Trust together, forty-two years before. He had made absolutely sure that, as ultimate heirs to nearly $2 billion in the Sarah Getty Trust, his children and his childrens' children would want for nothing—at least financially.

In the first year after his death the trust produced an income not far short of $4 million each for Paul and Gordon, and the same sum was equally divided between George's daughters, Anne, Claire, and Caroline. Since these five beneficiaries of the trust received all its income, the payments they received would rise steadily as Getty Oil increased its cash dividends. These dividends rose from $1 a share in 1978 to $1.90 a share in 1980, and on to a record $2.60 in 1982. By the early 1980s Paul and Gordon would be receiving $28 million *each* from the trust each year, while George's daughters would share the same sum among them.

But apart from money, J. Paul Getty left the members of his family remarkably little, certainly none of the things the founder of a "dynasty" might have been expected to leave behind—no land, no appreciable heirlooms, not even a center for the family. Apart from money, which by its nature is anonymous, there was little for members of his family to remember him by at all.

Since he had only rented Sutton Place, even the house he had loved was sold, its pictures and furniture dispatched to the museum. It was as if, not trusting his descendants with his memory, Getty was making the museum at Malibu the ultimate repository of his reputation and his sole memorial.

What he had left his family was something else: too much money, a tangle of troubles, and a legacy of broken lives.

THUS one sees how important the idea of the museum must have been for Getty during the months before he died. It hadn't mattered that he never saw it, any more than it had mattered that he never visited the Neutral Zone until long after he had built it into one of the most productive oil fields in the world from his hotel room in Paris.

He was a virtuoso of remote control, of using his money and his expertise to make extraordinary things happen far away, while seeing them in his imagination. It was a most unusual talent, and for several years before he died, he had been quietly using it to build his own museum of the imagination 6,000 miles away at Malibu.

He was probably wise never to have visited it. Reality might have disappointed him—and there was always time to visit in another incarnation.

Instead, from his room in Sutton Place, he could methodically perform the tasks that he enjoyed: reading architects' reports, checking on cost estimates, and minutely following the progress of the building. (According to Stephen Garrett, one of the old man's most exciting moments came when he watched a video the architect had sent, of the concrete being poured into the foundations.) Then, when his Roman villa was complete, it had been time to start to fill it with treasures.

In his last months, one of his few remaining pleasures was to discuss its contents with Gillian Wilson, who as well as being his museum's official curator of decorative arts was also young, intelligent, and pretty. On the last occasion that she saw him he had shut his eyes and said: "I am entering my decorative arts gallery now. Tell me what I'm seeing."

Wilson talked "as descriptively as possible" about the gallery for nearly half an hour, at the end of which he opened his eyes, smiled at her, and said, "Well. Quite a spread, eh?"

By then the intial press reaction to the museum was forgotten. Attendance figures were already proving its popularity. In the year before Getty died, there were over 350,000 visitors—who, as he could not resist working out, had cost him $3.50 a head. But this had been one expense that he had not begrudged, for it was good to know that people were already appreciating what he had created.

When in Rome before the war, he had had a marble bust made of himself, and had asked that it be placed in the vestibule of the museum.

"The ideal visitor to the museum," he once remarked, "should fancy himself back two thousand years, calling on Roman friends who live in the villa." When they did, they would find the marble bust of a middle-aged man looking not unlike a Roman emperor waiting in the vestibule to greet them.

UPON his father's death, Gordon, as co-trustee with Lansing Hays of the Sarah C. Getty Trust, became the richest—and, potentially at least, the most important—member of the family. In addition to the $3.4 million income he received in 1977 from the trust, he took in an additional $1 million trustee fee, plus a $4 million fee as executor of his father's will.

But although Ann and Gordon intended to enjoy their affluence, Gordon appeared unmoved by whatever power and responsibilities accompanied it. Diffident by nature, he was no match for the lawyerly self-confidence of Hays, who, looking on himself as regent for the Getty empire after the emperor's death, treated the board of Getty Oil with scant respect—and Gordon likewise. The board of Getty Oil periodically objected to such treatment, but Gordon didn't. As Getty Oil was doing very nicely at the time, and returning steadily increasing dividends to its principal shareholder, the trust, Gordon had more important things to think about.

An unmalicious man, Gordon spoke well of everyone, even his father, on whom he published an amiable if enigmatic obituary:

> My father was a fathomless man, commanding and disarming, a philosopher and a clown. He was inscrutable, a showman, a prince of players. He was charismatic, even mesmeric. Many of his old employees, underpaid or not, would have shed blood for him. He was stoical in grief and at last jocular to the day he died. I think he meant to tell us something about courage.

Perhaps he did, although it's hard to know quite what. What *was* clear was that Gordon had no intention of learning lessons from his father over such matters as personal economy and self-denial. Money would never turn his head, but this didn't mean that he and Ann were incapable of enjoying it.

Unlike his more sophisticated brother Paul, he and Ann were not rich cosmopolitans, and their social aims were essentially confined to San Francisco, where Ann was ready to displace her memories of the Sacramento Valley by becoming undisputed queen of Pacific Heights.

So the style and quality of living at 350 Broadway rose after Jean

Paul Getty's death. They glassed in the atrium, making the house ideal for full-scale parties and receptions. Getty's butler, the solemn Bullimore, was taken on from Sutton Place, together with a household staff of six. A splendid kitchen was installed with amusing trompe l'oeil paintings of a farmyard, and the most majestic of America's interior decorators, Sister Parish, was engaged to supervise the decor in the house. It was thanks to her that the pride of the place became the dining room; there, electric light was banned, and the Gettys and their guests dined exclusively by genuine candlelight from elaborate candelabra (this despite Bullimore's grumbling about the candle wax needing to be cleared up later). With its antique blue-and-gold Chinese wallpaper and its view of the lights of Oakland glittering across the bay, it was a room of considerable beauty. Guests reported filet mignon so tender they could cut it with a fork, soufflés of virtuoso lightness, and memorable wines from France and California, although they observed that Gordon generally drank water.

On a simpler level, as a family man, Gordon was anxious not to inflict upon his children the sort of insecurity he had grown up with. He and Ann read Dr. Spock, and were relaxed and undemanding parents. "We're a close-knit family but we're not big on family meals. Everyone kind of eats when they're hungry," said Gordon. This applied to him as well. He tended at times to disappear all day to his noiseproof workroom, not surfacing until it was almost time for bed.

No longer having any need to prove himself before his father, he was able to enjoy his freedom and do more or less exactly as he wanted. But what *did* Gordon want? It was none too clear, even to himself. Later he described this as a period when he was "simply floundering around." With little formal teaching, he was already trying to write music, but was unable to complete anything to his satisfaction. He sang Schubert—*Winterreise*, which he enunciated with his eyes shut—but his voice, though powerful, was faintly but fatally off key.

According to his wife Ann, "Gordon's favorite pastime is buying CDs at Tower Records. He practically supports the shop." But apart from records, he spent little directly on himself. His dress sense was minimal. Lacking all taste for self-adornment, he wore a $40 Casio electronic wristwatch. He prefered his Dodge convertible to a Rolls or a Bentley.

Ann had started buying French impressionists but lacked the temperament and inclinations of a serious collector. Regular contributions were made to the San Francisco Opera House and the San Francisco Philharmonic but, in general, Ann and Gordon's philanthropy was done "rather mechanically" as Ann put it, in accordance with an annual list compiled by Gordon's secretary.

As a couple, they were generous but not overgenerous, not wishing to be landed with reputation for prodigality, and appeared somewhat less concerned with human beings than with animals, prehistory, and conservation—particularly "conservation of the world's resources before it is too late," as Gordon put it when setting up the J. Paul Getty Wildlife Conservation Prize in memory of his father. (He did not make it very clear what connection there had ever been between his father and conserving anything except large amounts of money.)

Gordon voted Republican and Ann Democratic, "thus cancelling each other out," as Gordon put it; they were equally impartial in lending the house to any cause they happened to approve of.

At this stage in the marriage it appeared to be Ann who set the pace. It was Ann who bought herself a Porsche, Ann who dressed in Paris. And while Ann became the most glamorous and talked-about woman in San Francisco, Gordon continued to exude the faintly baffled air of a music professor who has suddenly found himself a multimillionaire— a multimillionaire who sometimes happened to forget where he'd parked his car, but who, when he did find it, always insisted on driving his friends home after dinner.

During this period he seemed perfectly prepared to "flounder" on forever, devoted to his children, inflicting Schubert on his long-suffering friends, and ignoring what was happening in the far-off world of Getty Oil and the Sarah C. Getty Trust. At times it seemed as if he were positively inviting people not to take him seriously. Few did.

ONE will never know for certain why the old man didn't use his will to right the wrong that he had done to his eldest son, Ronald. It seems inconceivable that the ancient grudge against Ronald's grandfather Dr. Helmle still rankled. Given the somewhat bumpy history of their relationship, Getty may simply have felt disinclined to do Ronald any favors. But most probably he was wary of changing anything in the Sarah C. Getty Trust that could have given a point of entry to his abiding enemies, the tax authorities.

Instead he offered Ronald certain consolation prizes, which made things worse rather than better. He left Ronald a share with Paul and Gordon in La Posta Vecchia, which none of them wanted. Still less, in the circumstances, did Ronald want his father's diaries, which for some extraordinary reason were bequeathed him. (The diaries, which were valued at a nominal value of $1 for probate purposes, lay forgotten for years in a warehouse in South Africa, before surfacing in 1993 in a saleroom in Atlanta, Georgia. Paul and Gordon considered buying them for $300,000, then decided not to.) Apart from a legacy of $320,000, the only substantial benefit Ronald had derived on his father's death was his fee of $4 million as his executor, a role he shared with his brother Gordon.

After so many promises he was bitter and humiliated, so he went to law against the museum and the trust. Fearing that his case would delay settlement of the will and threaten the tax-free status of the great bequest, the museum settled with Ronald for $10 million. But he got nowhere in his case against the trust, although he claims that Paul and Gordon had been willing to include him in the trust until their lawyers disuaded them.

So the injustice done to Ronald festered on, leaving him feeling doubly betrayed by his father—first at the age of six when the trust was founded, and now in this will that had continued the injustice and had set him firmly against his brothers.

Of course, Ronald *was* a multimillionaire; sensibly invested, his money would have brought him enough to live in comfort for the remainder of his life. But Ronald wanted more than comfort: He wanted to prove himself against his father and his brothers and before his children. So he invested his money in business ventures, risking everything to make another Getty fortune on his own account.

APART from Ann and Gordon, George's children, Anne, Claire, and Caroline, were the most fortunate members of the family. Ever since George's death, their mother, Gloria, had carefully protected them from further scandal and from press intrusion; continuing the pattern established by their father, they kept more or less apart from other members of the family. Each received a third of the income that their father would have had from the trust; in the twelve months following their grandfather's death this approached $2 million dollars each.

Although this meant that they were great heiresses, they remained wary of the world outside their sheltered circle. It was as if all three of them had learned important lessons from their father's downfall and were determined to avoid the temptations and disasters of the very rich. They revered the memory of their grandfather. Their mother retained a strong influence on all of them, and for all their money they continued leading undramatic, very private lives.

IT seemed that the fault line in the Getty family continued through Paul Junior and his children, and by the time his father died, it was clear that Paul's attempt to repair the damage by bringing Gail and the children back to Cheyne Walk had failed.

Throughout the marriage of Paul's former lover Victoria Holdsworth to Oliver Musker, her mother, Mary Holdsworth, had kept in contact with events at Cheyne Walk. Being concerned for Paul, she used to bring him supper in a basket every Wednesday evening, which also gave her an opportunity to keep in touch with what was happening.

It is hard to be precise about the sequence of events during the spring before J. Paul Getty's death. Strains had been appearing between Paul Junior and Gail and the children, as Paul was clearly finding it hard to cure himself of his addiction and continue his treatment at the clinic. Simultaneously there had been strains in Victoria's marriage, which ended in divorce some two years later. When she decided to move back to Cheyne Walk, Gail moved out at once to a house across the river. She continued visiting Cheyne Walk to look after her family, but she was increasingly upset to see that in her absence, Paul was giving up on his cure completely and was soon as heavily addicted as before.

This was the point when Gail concluded the cause was lost. There were angry arguments, and she felt that there was nothing further she could do for him. The children were unhappy, and after one final desperate scene between her and Paul, she decided that no further purpose could be served by their remaining.

All she wanted was to take herself and the children as far away as possible from the unhappiness of Cheyne Walk, which for her meant getting to California—first San Francisco, where they stayed with friends, then Los Angeles, where they finally found themselves a house. It was the most decisive move they could make, a total break with Europe and the past. Sometimes Gail dreamed of Italy, which appeared an insuperable distance from California.

As for Paul Junior, after his father died, he made an agonized appearance at the memorial service. He was ashen-faced, wearing dark glasses and showing such difficulty walking that he seemed to need the support of Bianca Jagger, who came with him. This was the last time he was photographed in public for many years. He missed the children and bitterly regretted not having seen his father before he died; his health was beginning to deteriorate as the drugs and drink started to affect his circulation.

For a man who had suddenly become a principal beneficiary of the greatest fortune in America, he could hardly have appeared more wretched.

But the greatest casualty within the family was still young Paul. He was now a confirmed alcoholic, and financially his affairs were in such chaos that, since his father exercised no personal control, his grandfather Judge Harris filed suit in Los Angeles to be appointed his legal guardian on the grounds that Paul was "financially improvident" and "unable economically to handle his own affairs."

The marriage with Martine had effectively collapsed by now. Paul was bouncing checks and had given up on college; he was drinking more heavily than ever, mixing with lowlife characters, and buying cars on the strength of the Getty name, then charging them to members of the family. In desperation, Gail invited his old friend the journalist Craig Copetas to Los Angeles to talk to him, "which," as Copetas says, "shows how desperate she'd become."

Copetas describes how his friendship with young Paul ended. "I stayed with him for a few days at the place he was renting off Sunset Strip. He was drinking heavily, but he said he wasn't happy, and longed to sort life out somehow but it wasn't possible.

"While I was there his grandfather's application was due to be heard in court, and on the morning of the hearing I drove him and Martine to the court in an old red Chevrolet I'd bought. He seemed quite calm and reasonable, so I said to him, 'Paul, this is your chance to show a real change of attitude. Everyone's pissed off with you, and there'll be hordes of reporters at the court. Show yourself in a new light. Just for once, be responsible.'

"But suddenly he exploded and started to attack Martine. Underneath everything he had a fearful temper. I think that it was now that I realised that Paul Getty was a lost cause. I stopped the car and bawled him out. He stopped, and I got him to the court, but once again he made a scene, and that was that. I left California a few days later, and never saw Paul again."

PART THREE

CHAPTER EIGHTEEN

Drugs and Coma

AFTER his father died, it was as if Paul Junior had condemned himself to death-in-life in his beautiful unhappy house, and the years ticked by as he served his sentence for what had happened to Talitha. His grief alone could not explain his situation, which was also due to alcohol and drugs and money. The alcohol and drugs enabled him to insulate himself from life, and the effortless supply of money permitted him to go on living as he wanted.

The attraction of heroin is that it temporarily blanks out human misery. For the hour or so following a fix, there is absolute relief from any sense of worthlessness and guilt and all anxiety. Reality dissolves, and in its place comes a feeling of ineffable tranquility. The feeling does not last and in the long term the use of heroin has a cumulative effect, leading to yet more anxiety, loss of self-esteem, stifling depression, and a sense of utter isolation. When reality returns, the thought of loved ones can become a source of guilt, which helps explain why Paul saw members of his family so rarely and gave no sign of missing them. Confined within that house of many memories, he grew morbidly suspicious, and his reclusiveness increased together with his fear and his suspicion of the world outside.

For company he had his books, and books possess a sympathetic magic of their own, especially books as rare and valuable as those he was collecting—fine bindings, painted manuscripts dating from the Middle Ages to the present day, and exquisitely printed books from private presses. These were not books to read so much as talismanic objects, history, individual works of art.

Paul's books were one of the few escape routes he possessed, for they belonged to the past, and the past is safer than the present. He could enjoy the benediction of the printed page, the smell of leather and the sensual feel of vellum. Books had become his solace, the lovers he no longer bedded, the family he never saw. He was becoming increasingly well-read, and being clever and methodical he also studied bibliography, learning about the different styles of binding, printing, and the esoteric lore of rare editions. In his scholarly way he started to become invulnerable in a field that transcended drugs and money.

For anyone in his condition it was a considerable achievement, proof that his mind was still as sharp as ever. He started building up his library—one creation he would be proud of—and he was at his happiest in Rossetti's old studio, which he had made his study, the heavy curtains drawn against the light and his books around him. He was in his mid-forties now but looked older, bearded, bespectacled, full-bellied, the drink and the chocolate-chip cookies having made him put on weight, giving him an occasional resemblance to the bearded figure of his long-dead hero.

One of his few regular visitors was the kindly Bryan Maggs, king of London rare-book sellers and virtuso bookbinder on his own account. (His resplendent binding of John Gay's *Trivia, or the Art of Walking the Streets of London* is on exhibition in the British Museum.) With Maggs to buy for him, Paul's library increased, and all the while he went on sniffing heroin and drinking rum and hardly ever saw his children.

Being intelligent and rich, he was able to pursue other interests that also passed the time and brought him no anxiety. One was the cinema. He had a huge collection of old films, and a deep knowledge of the golden age of Hollywood. He also enjoyed British movies from before the war; they became an important source of his enthusiasm for a nostalgic England he had never known but which he loved and felt at home in. Films were a window into life beyond the prison he had built so carefully around him.

There was another window, too, that opened up more unexpectedly. Living the life he did, he found sleep impossible for long periods; killing time, he would watch interminable TV programs. He was doing this when Mick Jagger came to see him and inquired why he didn't watch something more worthwhile.

"What?" he asked.

"Cricket," said Jagger, switching to a test-match program and starting to explain the rules. Paul was hooked. From the days when he and Mario Lanza had attempted to establish baseball in Rome, he had always had an interest in spectator sports, and he enjoyed the subtlety of cricket, together with the drama and excitement it can offer those who take it seriously. As an increasingly Anglophile American, he also found an exotic fascination in this curiously English game. Soon he was saying that cricket was to baseball as chess was to a game of checkers.

With old films, old books, and cricket on TV, Paul could fill the longueurs of his solitary life and seemed set to continue thus until he died—which he gave every sign of being on his way to doing fairly quickly, as drink and drugs and lack of exercise undermined his constitution.

From time to time he would enter the London Clinic for a cure, which never lasted; at the same time he received treatment for damage to his circulation and his liver, and for suspected diabetes, along with other symptoms of his precarious condition.

Meanwhile, his children were growing up. Friends of the family often said that Aileen was the child who most resembled him, both physically and with the streak of wildness in her personality. She was intuitively bright and very pretty, with large brown eyes and a spritelike charm that made her mother call her "my Irish leprechaun." But Aileen really liked to think herself a rebel, and after dropping out of the University of Southern California, she did most of the things that rebellious young women did in Los Angeles in the seventies, including painting, campaigning against the Vietnam War, and using pot and cocaine for relaxation. As part of her political protest she made artistic collages, including one of photocopied thousand-dollar bills emblazoned with the message "Fight Against Capitalism." She lived for a period with a jazz pianist; he was followed by a film director. And she attempted to ignore the fact that she would one day be a great heiress, as if the whole idea appalled her. Possibly it really did.

Less of an extrovert, her sister, Ariadne, was too much a traditionalist to be a rebel. But just as she had been the tomboy of the family, so she was still comparatively wild, with a mercurial personality and emotional ups-and-downs. After studying at Bennington College in Vermont, she took up photography specializing in landscape and architecture. She was already promising enough to have acquired her own New York dealer.

Mark was the one member of the family not to have succumbed to the lure of California. After his English education, he appeared as resolutely Anglophile as his father, but his English accent and exterior were deceptive. His Italian was as fluent as his English, and having been born in Rome he regarded Italy as home. He had been young enough to be less seriously affected than Paul and Aileen had been by their parents' divorce and the ensuing dramas. Unlike his brother Paul, he seemed aged beyond his years by their father's absence, and did his best to take Paul Junior's place. He was sensible and caring and responsible, qualities whose rarity among the Gettys made them particularly valuable.

Mark was not the only family member who missed Italy. After the trauma of the kidnaping they had all kept anxiously away, but their mother, Gail, tended to regard Los Angeles as something of a place of exile. She still owned—and longed to see—the house at Orgia, which was now closed up, while Remo the gardener kept an eye on it for her.

Finally they felt that they could keep away no longer. Early in 1980, Gail and Mark and Ariadne all returned for the first time since the kidnaping. Anxious to discover what had happened to the house, they did not stay in Rome but hired a car at the airport and drove at once to Tuscany. On reaching Orgia they heard that Remo had died just before Christmas. As he had been ill beforehand for some time, he'd been unable to look after the house, and they found it had been badly vandalized.

The house's condition might have been a symbol for the family's. Yet despite the mess and filth, the occasion was still like a homecoming. This was where Gail and the children had been happiest, and despite the memory of the kidnaping they were determined to have the house restored. They sensed that they belonged here, and decided to return.

They felt safe in Orgia, for here in this open country, with the vines and the dark red soil, there was none of the closed-in atmosphere of Rome. Besides, they couldn't live their lives avoiding danger any longer. As Gail said, it was better to face the risk of kidnaping than hide away for ever.

Leaving Italy, Gail and the children were back in Los Angeles in March for Aileen's engagement party. After she tired of her film director—or he of her—Aileen had spent some time with Elizabeth Taylor's son Michael Wilding Junior, and through him had got to know his younger brother, Christopher. They had fallen in love and, having been together now for practically two years, they wished to marry. Although everyone liked Christopher, who was handsome, kind, and charming, marrying him was not that simple.

From the start it was evident that any wedding that involved a Getty and a son of Elizabeth Taylor was a forbidding undertaking. The Hollywood protocol would be as complex as at any royal wedding; the publicity could be a nightmare; and both families had problems of their own to add to the confusion. Christopher, who was still devoted to his former stepfather, Richard Burton, insisted that he would have to be present—as well as his mother, who was now married to U.S. Senator John Warner. The filming schedules of the two major film stars, if nothing else, made this difficult—and on the Getty side there seemed little chance of bringing the members of the family together in tolerable harmony. There was certainly no way of persuading Paul Junior to take his daughter up the aisle.

The marital logistics seeming insuperable, Gail suggested giving an old-style American engagement party for the couple—after which they could "elope" and marry later, at their leisure. Both rather gratefully agreed, and on 17 March Gail held a formal engagement party in their honor for a hundred and fifty at her house at Brentwood.

To give her blessing, Elizabeth Taylor made a regal appearance at the party "shimmering in pearls," and Aileen, dressed as a bride with flowers in her hair, wore a Hollywood-style engagement ring of imperial jade, surrounded by diamonds.

The Gettys were represented by Paul and Mark and Ariadne, and Hollywood by Sissy Spacek, Dudley Moore, and Roddy McDowell. Timothy Leary came to represent himself; and at the end of what Aileen called "my surrogate marriage party," the bridal pair "eloped," and married secretly soon afterward in a chapel on Sunset Strip.

THAT summer further links were forged between Italy and the Getty family when Mark returned to Rome and met Domitilla Harding. Just twenty, with the face of a Sienese Madonna, she was the daughter of an American businessman and an Italian mother. Her father's family came from Boston, but her mother, Lavinia Lante della Rovere, belonged to one of the oldest families in Rome. Domitilla's uncle was that same Prince Ladislao Odescalchi, who had owned La Posta Vecchia and sold it to Mark's grandfather, and the Lante della Roveres themselves had once possessed one of the loveliest houses in Italy, the famous Villa Lante at Bagnaia, near Viterbo, which had been in the family for generations until Domitilla's grandmother sold it in the 1950s.

At the end of summer Mark had to return to England to start studying (philosophy, politics, and economics) at St. Catherine's College, Oxford. But because of Domitilla he seemed certain to return to Rome as soon as possible.

AS the children grew up, even the disordered life of Mark's unhappy brother Paul was showing signs of calming down. At the beginning of 1981, six years after the kidnaping, he was still heavily dependent on drugs and alcohol; when frustrated or provoked he could be as impossible as ever. Surprisingly, he was still married to Martine, but he rarely saw her and had found himself a new fiancée—a chic Italian woman from a very chic Italian family, Emmanuela Stucchi-Prinetti.

It was a good sign that he was beginning to work at last—and in the one area he'd always dreamed of: the movie industry. From 1978 he worked as assistant to the film director John Schlesinger, then as an actor with an old friend of Martine's, the German avant-garde director Wim Wenders.

Wenders's early films, with their uneasy themes of alienation and male wanderlust, might have been tailor-made for Paul. He could easily identify with Wenders's characters, and after he had played several minor parts, Wenders offered him a major role, that of a writer in *The State of Things*, early in 1981.

Through his acting Paul was showing signs of coming to terms with life at last. In the past there had been his adolescent dreams of impressing his father by being a figure in the counterculture. This had never worked, despite his hippie life and his attempts to associate with some of the heroes of the Beat generation. But now, when least expected, he found himself becoming a success in avant-garde cinema. Wenders was happy with the early scenes of the film, which were shot in Portugal. More filming followed in Paris, and Paul actually enjoyed his time there. He had Emmanuela with him and seemed happier with her than he had been with any other woman; although still heavily dependent on his daily bottle of Wild Turkey bourbon, he was almost clean of drugs.

Then in March he returned to Los Angeles with gentle, dark-haired Emmanuela to shoot the final footage for *The State of Things* in Hollywood. They stayed with friends, and Paul seemed happy to be back in familiar Los Angeles. But soon he had to face another crisis. He found working in a Hollywood studio none to easy, and once shooting started he discovered that he couldn't act and drink—so he gave up drink. For a longtime alcoholic, this was a considerable shock to the system, and to help him cope with his withdrawal symptoms his doctors prescribed a formidable mixture of drugs, including methadone to help him sleep and Placidyl, Valium, and Dalmane to calm his nerves.

Despite so many pills it was still hard for Paul to sleep, and he tended to wake early, which was why Emmanuela was particularly worried when she couldn't wake him from the deepest slumber on the morning of April 5, 1981. He was inert and scarcely breathing. Thoroughly alarmed, she had the sense to call an ambulance.

Everyone suspected drink or drugs. What had actually happened was that, unable to cope with the pharmaceutical cocktail the doctors had prescribed, Paul's badly treated liver had failed to function, causing a temporary cessation of oxygen to the brain. By the time he reached the Cedars of Lebanon hospital in Hollywood he was in the deepest coma.

Someone had telephoned Gail before the ambulance arrived; she was staying in Santa Barbara, so it took her an hour and a half to reach the hospital. By the time she reached Paul he was just alive on a life-support machine, with symptoms of brain damage from lack of oxygen. When Gail asked the doctors what she could do for him, all they could say was "Wait." So once again Gail waited.

The doctors did everything they could to bring Paul back to consciousness, but couldn't hide their anxiety when he failed to respond. Then a few days later came a further cause of worry; X rays revealed water on the brain, which was causing it to swell alarmingly. As something of a last resort the doctors turned to a revolutionary technique known as deep hibernation, which had never been tried before on human beings. Drugs were employed to send the patient into an even deeper coma; then, he was gradually restored to his earlier condition.

Three days of deep hibernation cured the swelling of the brain, but Paul remained unconscious, showing only the faintest signs of breathing.

"He was alive," says Gail, "but only just—in the deepest of deep slumber, like the Sleeping Beauty. You could have pushed pins into his feet and he'd still have given no response or shown the faintest sign of waking." By now the doctors had nothing further to suggest—except more waiting. And it was then that Gail understood, as she understood when Paul was kidnaped, that it was up to her to save him.

Realizing her total ignorance of coma, she visited the university bookshop, and in the medical section bought everything she could discover on the subject. There was not a lot. Since 1981 the knowledge and treatment of coma has advanced substantially, but at that time she found just one medical journal that gave her what she was seeking: an article on ways of maintaining brain activity in coma victims. Certain methods were suggested: continual talking to such patients, reading a book aloud to them, or playing them their favorite music. The theory was that, although unable to respond, the patient could often take in much of what he heard. Maintaining mental activity is all important to prevent coma victims from lapsing into silent inactivity.

Since then this treatment has become widely accepted, but at the time the doctors tended to dismiss it. It made sense to Gail, however. More important, it offered her and the family something positive that they could do for Paul instead of hopelessly watching him become a vegetable.

She organized members of the family to give him round-the-clock attention. "The aim was to make sure that there was always someone with him, either reading or talking to him or playing him his favorite music." It was hard work; fortunately, the watchers by the bedside soon found they had another helper.

Mark was back at Oxford when he heard the news about his brother.

He did not know that by leaving the university he would probably forfeit his chance of a degree. But as with the kidnaping, he felt an obligation to be with Gail and his brother at a time of crisis. A male presence was required, and since his father was unable to provide it, it was up to him to take his place. By April 8, three days after learning of Paul's disaster, Mark was on the twelve-hour flight to Los Angeles.

From now on he took responsibility for part of the night shift looking after Paul. Gail would stay at the hospital every evening until midnight; then Mark would take over until dawn. During the day, Aileen and Ariadne took turns reading and talking to their brother. Martine joined them. Despite the problems in their marriage, she insisted that she was still Paul's wife, and that she, not Emmanuela, was the one to be with him. As usual in a trial of wills, Martine won.

There is something quietly impressive in the idea of a family asserting its presence to avert a tragedy and will a dormant loved one back to life. But as the days ticked by it looked as if it wouldn't work.

"With Paul just lying there," says Gail, "it was sometimes hard to tell that he was even breathing, but we tried ignoring this, staying as positive as possible, and talking and joking with him as if nothing very much had happened." Attempting to stay cheerful, she recounted incidents to Paul that she thought might still amuse him. Sometimes they played his favorite records, and all the time they continued talking without the faintest notion of whether he heard or understood a word they said. Sometimes it seemed a pointless exercise. But as there was nothing else to do, they continued night and day for more than five long weeks. And through it all, Paul lay still and silent as a statue.

One problem was that there was no way of telling how much damage had been done to his brain or how impaired he'd be if and when he did revive. All that the doctors knew, and the family suspected, was that the longer he remained unconscious, the worse his chances of recovery.

By the sixth week the doctors were no longer trying to disguise their feelings. With modern medical technology, there was no particular problem keeping Paul alive indefinitely—but everybody knew that past a certain point his hope of recovery fell dramatically, and that this point was fast approaching.

Typically, Gail was refusing to accept this; she still insisted that her son was going to recover. Instead, for the others what they were doing was starting to appear a sad and rather hopeless exercise. Then on May 14, nearly six weeks after Paul went into coma, there came a glimmering of hope.

It was Mark who witnessed it during one of his vigils through the small hours by his brother's bedside. Tired of talking, he had been playing Paul one of his favorite records, Wagner's "Ride of the Valky-ries," and as the loud Romantic music boomed out above the motionless figure of his brother, Mark noticed that something was happening. Tears were running down his brother's cheeks. Six weeks into his coma, Paul was weeping.

Or so it seemed. The doctor on duty was quick to dampen Mark's excitement. He had seen this before with coma victims; it was usually a speck of dust causing minor irritation to the eye.

But Mark and Gail were convinced that Paul's tears must have come in reaction to the music. This was the only thing that gave them hope that Paul still had a future. But for several days, nothing further happened. Paul was as deep as ever in his coma, and it seemed as if the doctors had been right, as usual.

TO pass the endless hours at the hospital, Gail had been inviting old friends of Paul's to his bedside; one of them started reminiscing about the practical jokes he and Paul had played at school together. Some of the jokes were quite outrageous, and the friend soon had Gail laughing. When they stopped they realized that someone else was laughing, too. From the bed, quietly but unmistakably, Paul was joining in.

This was proof at last that he really was emerging from his coma and would live. According to Gail, "none of us quite believed it, and of course we were all in tears and highly emotional. But from that point on the coma started lifting, very slowly, like a light being slowly turned up in a room." In medical terminology this process is known as lightening.

As Paul recovered consciousness, the doctors could finally assess the damage. It was as bad as the gloomiest had suspected. Although able to feel sensation in his body, he was virtually paralyzed from the neck down. He was blind except for extremely limited peripheral vision. His speech, though audible, was seriously impaired. With such appalling disabilities, it seemed a final mockery that his intelligence remained completely unaffected.

The doctors were very kind to Gail when they talked about the future. But she wanted the truth, not kindness, and they gave her their honest opinion. They told her that Paul would almost certainly have to spend what remained of his life flat on his back in a bed in an institution.

AFTER more than six weeks struggling to keep hope alive, this was more than Gail could take. She was exhausted and the strain was telling.

But just as she wouldn't give up hope when Paul was kidnaped, so she refused to give up now.

She said there could be no question of leaving her son to such a fate. But the doctors, still believing that they had to do their duty, insisted on telling her that quadriplegics as impaired as Paul were almost always better off in institutions properly equipped to look after them, and provide full-time nursing and the specialist treatment they needed. Attempts by loved ones to look after them invariably ended in disaster. However devoted relatives like Gail might be, the exhausting nature of the task ended by destroying the private life of anyone rash enough to take it on.

"Then that's a risk I'll have to take," she said. Had she had any doubts about doing this, they were now banished by Paul himself. Whenever he realized that she was in the room he'd start to weep and with an enormous effort enunciate a single word.

"Home!" he'd whisper.

Then in case she hadn't understood, he would repeat it.

"Home! Home!"

SO the work began that would occupy Gail's life for many years. Attached to the house in Brentwood was a guest house with a swimming pool. Once it was equipped with the facilities of a private clinic it would prove ideal for Paul to live in with his helpers.

In one thing the doctors were soon proved right: their warning about the strain looking after Paul would place upon her private life. Emmanuela felt this too. Her parents had little difficulty convincing her that there was little future as the fiancée of a quadriplegic, and she decided to return to Italy. Martine, on the other hand, was once again a source of strength, and the two children, Anna and Balthazar, treated Paul exactly as they always had. Oblivious of his disabilities, they were soon clambering into bed with him and loving him as much as ever.

Fortunately Gail could hire nurses to provide the expert round-the-clock attention Paul needed, together with the cleverest doctors and most practiced physiotherapists in California. None of this would have been possible without large amounts of money. But since Paul was a Getty, and money was one thing the Getty family possessed in abundance, she thought it wouldn't be a problem. But as so often in the past, where money and the Gettys were concerned, Gail was wrong.

CHAPTER NINETEEN

Recovery

WHEN her son Paul came out of the hospital, Gail was being helped financially by her father and by Paul's uncle Gordon, who had bought the house where she and her family were living and who was still providing everything his nephew needed. For the long term this was clearly wrong. Gordon was immensely rich but so was Paul's own father, and Paul Junior, not Gordon, should be paying for the treatment of his stricken son. He could obviously afford it countless times over. However, when Gail began sending the bills to Cheyne Walk, they were returned—unpaid. Angry telephone calls ensued, and Paul Junior made his extraordinary position absolutely clear. Although a multimillionaire, he was adamantly refusing to meet his son's medical expenses.

To begin with nobody could quite believe it, and Gail's lawyer sent a calming letter trying to explain the situation—only to produce a fresh refusal. As Gail explains, "Along with Gordon a group of us were paying for Paul's treatment and after a while it just seemed crazy and unjust to go on doing so. The very last thing any of us wanted was the publicity of suing, but with Paul refusing to listen, there was finally no alternative."

As Gail expected there was much unfavorable publicity for J. Paul Getty, Jr., when, in November 1981, he instructed his lawyers in Los Angeles to oppose Gail's court application for payment of $25,000 a month toward their son's medical expenses. The presiding judge was sufficiently shocked to rebuke Paul in court: "Mr. Getty should be ashamed of himself spending far more money on court obligations than living up to his moral duties."

Even as close a friend as Bill Newsom described Paul Junior's behavior as "bizarre," adding that he had "books in his library that cost more, much more, than it would have cost to look after his son for years."

So what was going on?

*

THE truth was that young Paul's coma had come at a bad time in his father's life. During a cure in Switzerland, Victoria had met and fallen in love with Mohammed Alatas, a young Saudi businessman. She had once again given up hope of a satisfactory married life with Paul, so when Alatas proposed, Victoria accepted.

This had left Paul feeling more alone than ever back at Cheyne Walk. His intake of drugs and alcohol increased, and the more isolated and drug-dependent he became, the more his anxieties and fears grew. During young Paul's coma, his brother Mark was telephoning back to England almost every day with news for their father, who became as painfully affected by his son's ordeal as he had been in the early days of the kidnaping. And once again he tried blanking out the anxiety and the pain of thinking.

What happened then provides a good example of how drink and drugs can actually distort reality, leading to emotional disruption and personal disaster. Without making spurious excuses for Paul Junior, it is possible to discern a sort of addict's logic in his behavior over the medical bills. His refusal to pay them was generally seen as a recurrence of his father's stinginess, but this was not the case at all, and his actions were really not concerned with money.

They were partly the result of a typical addict's neurosis over what he thinks is happening behind his back. They were also his own strange way of attempting to play down what had happened to his son. For once Paul could convince himself that he was being cheated over these medical expenses, he could shift his sense of guilt for what had happened onto those he told himself had done the cheating. Stuck in his fastness in Cheyne Walk, he could even make himself believe that his son's appalling disabilities weren't as appalling as the dishonest doctors said they were. They had simply been exaggerated to extract money from him; by challenging them, he could expose those lying doctors, and prove that his son's condition was far less serious than they claimed. He wasn't the fool they took him for. And if he refused to pay a penny, he might even force them to admit that his son wasn't really sick at all.

Predictably, when matters didn't work out like that, Paul felt more rejected and guilt-obsessed than before—which made him more drug-dependent than ever. After the judge's remarks in the courtroom in Los Angeles, his lawyer, Vanni Treves, flew specially to Los Angeles to see young Paul on his father's behalf. Treves confirmed everything Gail and the doctors said, and described the pathetic state that Paul was in. Paul Junior, finally convinced, paid what he should have paid from the beginning. There were no more arguments, but the damage had been done—principally to Paul Junior himself. As a result of what had happened, his family inevitably turned against him.

"Gordon is light, and my father is the dark side," Aileen told a journalist. Even Mark, loyalest of sons, was firmly on the side of Paul and Gail after so many bitter, angry things had been muttered over the telephone from London.

And locked away in the house on Cheyne Walk, Paul Junior became more wretched than ever and determined to have done with his family. The abrasive contact with them and their sufferings brought further threats to his precarious stability, and he reacted as he always did—by relying more heavily on his trusted sources of relief, which produced the inevitable relapse, followed by a further lengthy stay in the London Clinic, which was becoming his home away from home.

WHILE what was left of Paul Junior's health and self-esteem was undergoing yet another battering, Gail and the children in America were doubly grateful for level-headed Uncle Gordon, who, in contrast with his brother, was happier than he'd ever been.

In a Paris bookshop just the year before, Gordon had found a copy of the poems of the great nineteenth-century American mystical recluse Emily Dickinson, some of which struck him as ideal to put to music. Inspired by the poems, he overcame whatever had been holding him back as a composer, and in a fevered period of work, produced settings for thirty two of them, from which he finally created the song cycle he entitled *The White Election*. (The title came from a phrase of Dickinson's.)

The White Election marked the beginning of a whole new life for Gordon and of his true ambition—to become a serious composer. All his enthusiastic energies went into it, and this was the point at which he always claimed his life had really started.

As a composer he had great ambitions. As he put it, "composers are remembered by posterity when businessmen are forgotten," and he staked his claim in no uncertain fashion: "I should like to be a composer who is remembered alongside the masters of the past, like Bach, Beethoven, Schubert, Wagner, Mahler, and Brahms. Maybe it's hubris to put my name in that group. And maybe hubris is a damned good thing."

Gordon's confidence and newfound creative happiness formed the greatest contrast to his brother Paul's addictive misery. Gordon was a genuinely happy man, with everything he wanted as well as money. For Gail and the children, he was what they would have loved his brother to have been—supportive, kind, and quietly concerned about them all. But Paul Junior had started to suspect his brother of usurping his family's affections, and grew jealous of everything he represented.

It was typical of Gordon to be the only one who didn't seem to notice his brother's change of attitude or take offense at it. Gordon continued treating Paul as if nothing very serious had happened. It was here that the brothers' shared passion for the opera took on a particular importance as a slender bridge between them. Gordon would send Paul information about the great singers whom they both enjoyed.

"Domingo greater than ever at La Scala," he would say.

"Pavarotti greater still," Paul would answer.

AFTER the dramas of the year before, 1982 started with a period of calm throughout the family and witnessed the beginning of a partial recovery for young Paul Getty.

At first he had seemed so terribly afflicted that his grandmother Ann's first words on seeing him had been "They should have put him down to end his misery." Muscular cramps were causing him excruciating pain, and his body was so rigid that even the touch of bedclothes on his limbs was intolerable. Agony, tears, periods of deep depression followed, but after a while something miraculous began. To almost everyone's surprise, Paul started showing extraordinary willpower as he struggled to make something of the little that was left him.

It was now that the Getty money really helped. Just as it had been the origin of so many of his problems, so now it helped relieve his ghastly situation; for without it the specialized nursing and equipment he relied on would have been impossible. However, Gail insists that there was more to Paul's treatment and recovery than money. "It included not being afraid and negative. It called for courage and perseverance. It was about never giving up."

And beyond this lay the most important fact of all—that the lost boy had found himself at last; that, thanks to the disaster, the self-destructive urges that had nearly destroyed him had been replaced by their opposite, a clinging to life, which in turn was followed by a resolute will to live.

Finding himself with nothing, Paul was being forced to fight to be a human being, which he did with increasing power as his stamina improved. Everything in life that had previously been boring, gratuitous, taken for granted, had to be struggled for now. Since the kidnaping there had been few challenges in his life. Now everything became a challenge.

Although he couldn't see, he asked to be taken to his grandfather's museum at Malibu on a day when it was closed to visitors. While he was pushed around the empty galleries on a gurney, he had the paintings described to him, and they became precious to him as paintings never had been when he could see them.

Every morning he exercised with his physiotherapists in the pool beside the house—boring, repetitive exercises, but he endured them, and gradually his strength improved. His speech remained a problem, as the motor damage to the brain had caused a condition known as aphonia, making that it was hard to pronounce consonants correctly. (In 1983 Gail would take him to work with the speech therapists at New York's Rusk Institute of speech and hearing, which brought a slow but definite improvement.)

He became hungry for books, and his friends took turns reading to him. Martine was a lifeline, as were the children, giving him yet further strength to carry on. Gail's devotion was unstinted.

One of his heroes from the past, Dr. Timothy Leary, came to visit him. "His willpower is like Niagara. He is a miracle," Leary said.

NINETEEN eighty-two saw another marriage in the family.

When, just before Christmas, Mark married Domitilla Harding in Rome's ancient Basilica of the Santissimi Apostoli, he became the third generation of the Getty family to marry in the Holy City. Unlike the other weddings, his was a very grand affair, which not only guaranteed that the Italian connections of the Getty family would continue, but also linked the family with Italian history. Along with its famous relics of St. Peter and St. Paul, Santissimi Apostoli contained the tombs of numerous Riario and della Rovere cardinals, all of them antecedents of the bride. Part of the church itself had been built by the most famous member of her family, the warlike della Rovere Pope Julius II, who patronized Michelangelo, was painted by Raphael, and was played by Rex Harrison in *The Agony and the Ecstasy*.

Although the bridegroom had now made peace with his father, Paul Junior was unable to attend, as he could barely walk and was still unwilling to return to Italy. And on the day of the wedding, in spite of all the detailed preparations, things soon started going wrong. First the bride failed to arrive at the church. Her grandfather John Harding had flown all the way from Boston to give her away. But owing to a typically Roman muddle, he went all the way to the family's summer house along the coast at Fregene to pick her up, although she was actually staying in her apartment in the Roman neighborhood of Parioli. By the time John Harding found the right address and got his granddaughter safely to the church, the bridegroom and the congregation had endured two anxious hours wondering what had happened to the bride.

She arrived looking beautiful and quite unflustered, but this did little to resolve an even more disturbing mystery—where was the bridegroom's aunt, Gordon's wife, Ann Getty? Since she wasn't there, the service had to start without her.

When Mark and Domitilla had announced their intention of marrying in Rome, Uncle Gordon put his foot down rather firmly. Worried by the memory of Paul's kidnaping, he had reluctantly decided that it was still too big a risk for him or his family to attend. But Ann, by nature less anxious than her husband, thought otherwise. She was on a trip to Europe at the time, and without informing Gordon had flown to Rome to be present at her nephew's wedding.

She was staying at the Excelsior Hotel on the Via Veneto, and Bill Newsom had arranged to meet her and bring her to the church. But once again something had gone wrong. Somehow they missed each other, so Ann took a taxi to the church alone, only to discover that while she spoke no Italian, and the driver spoke no English, she had forgotten what the church was called. For the next three hours she and her taxi driver toured Rome, visiting every church where a wedding might be taking place.

With the memory of young Paul's kidnaping never far away, Bill Newsom, Gail, and several members of the family were alarmed that the worst might well have happened. Gordon could have been right. Ann should have never come to Rome alone.

She and her taxi driver never found the church. Eventually they returned to the hotel, where she was reunited with the family when the service was over. Only then, with the nightmare of a second potential Getty kidnaping behind them, could all the guests enjoy the party.

Next day, while Ann was flying safely back to San Francisco, Mark and Domitilla were en route for their honeymoon in Switzerland. Elizabeth Taylor had invited Gail and the family to spend Christmas with her at her chalet in Gstaad, and the newlyweds joined them. The snow was thick, the threat of kidnaping was forgotten, and even with Elizabeth Taylor as their host, Christmas in Switzerland proved a far more peaceful proposition than a Roman wedding.

CHAPTER TWENTY

Gordon the Peacemaker

GORDON Getty was a late developer—and rather proud of it. "You know, for me it's true," he used to say, beaming at the world around him, "life really did begin at forty"—for it was then that he had begun to realize his true potential, as a composer, an intellectual, and a businessman.

Unlike most other members of the family, Gordon had always seemed to keep his fortune from obsessing or distracting him by the simple expedient of ignoring it. He still loved his enormous house at the top of Pacific Heights, he was as devoted to his family as ever, and he obviously enjoyed the freedom from the daily grind that his money gave him.

But he also insisted that he'd "scarcely notice the difference in my lifestyle if I didn't have my fortune. I think I'd drive the same car I'm driving now, watch the same TV shows, the same movies. I might not have had the luxury of being a composer, but I'd probably have taught literature in a college somewhere and been just as happy."

Perhaps he would, for currently his greatest problem was that of being taken seriously for anything except his money. Reactions to *The White Election* had been mixed, but Gordon showed a commendable unconcern about the the words of critics. "My philosophy has always been that the next guy's taste is just as good as mine, but I won't defer to his." What was difficult was to know how much critical reaction either way was influenced by the fact that he was a multimillionaire.

"I'd describe Gordon Getty as the best millionaire poet in the language," the Irish poet Seamus Heaney told Bill Newsom after reading some of his extraordinarily fluent, highly polished and romantic poetry. Much the same applied to Gordon's music and his economic theories, which tended to be placed in a special category just because he was a Getty.

This was not entirely fair, for Gordon, far from being a wealthy dilettante, worked immensely hard at anything he did. Unlike his brother Paul, he had always been a workaholic, a tendency inherited, like his money, from his father. And like his father, when the mood possessed him Gordon would work in massive waves of energy, rising at 6:30, confining himself to his workroom, and laboring throughout the day without pause for food or exercise or conversation, until as he put it in typical Gordonese, "I'm bushed."

Apart from his record collection—by now probably the largest in private ownership in America—he remained entirely unacquisitive. It was Ann who had recently bought the three Degas paintings of ballet dancers that hung in the bedroom, and who had chosen the furniture in the spectacular drawing room. Ann loved jewelry and grand furniture and impressionist paintings. Gordon preferred ideas. At around this time a visiting friend noticed that a painting of a dog was propped against a sofa; remembering that Ann had recently bought a Manet painting of a dog, the friend asked if this was it.

"Gee. I wouldn't know," said Gordon. "Ask anyone but me."

Someone described him as "opaque," a quality due partly to his apparent vagueness and also to his size, which gave him a sort of massive impenetrability.

But as the next few months would show, Gordon could be made to care as deeply about money as the next multimillionaire. And anyone who challenged Gordon would be ill advised to place excessive store on his naïveté and absent-mindedness. Opaque he might be, but for all his talk about ignoring money, in a financial battle Gordon was someone to be taken seriously.

BY the time of Mark's wedding, trouble was already brewing between Gordon and the board of Getty Oil.

A few months earlier had come the death of Gordon's solitary fellow trustee of the Sarah C. Getty Trust, the all-powerful lawyer Lansing Hays. Since the trust owned 40 percent of the capital of Getty Oil, Hays had been dominating the company management on the trust's behalf ever since J. Paul Getty died in 1976. Hays had made no secret of his contempt for the head of Getty Oil, the ex-accountant Sid Petersen. Now, with Hays departed, Petersen felt freer to assert himself.

But it was unwise of Petersen to have been so tactless in his dealings with Gordon Getty. For now that he was sole trustee of the trust, Gordon felt a need to know more about the state of Getty Oil, in which all the trust's money was invested. Petersen however, like others in their time, regarded Gordon as something of a simpleton and treated him accordingly.

By that autumn, Petersen's behavior was seriously annoying Gordon, less on account of his affronted dignity than because he felt that Petersen and the board of Getty Oil were insulting his intelligence. Since he effectively controlled the great family trust, Gordon felt he had a duty and a right to know why Getty Oil had reached an all-time low of less than $50 a share. But, as he complained to Bill Newsom, "Whenever I ask about it, Petersen treats me as a nonentity."

Unable to get the information he required from Petersen, Gordon turned to others who might help. He flew to New York to consult a firm of Wall Street investment bankers. Were shares in Getty Oil, he asked them, seriously undervalued—and if so, what could be done about it?

He was being just a touch naïve to act in such a manner. With takeover warriors like Ivan Boesky and T. Boone Pickens on the prowl, such inquiries by anyone as unmistakable as Gordon Getty would inevitably suggest that Getty Oil was ripe for their attention. So when Petersen caught wind of what was happening, battle between him and Gordon was inevitable.

It was a curious fight, for while Gordon continued to pursue what he felt to be the interests of the Sarah C. Getty Trust with a sort of rugged innocence, his opponents went to extraordinary lengths of cunning to thwart him. Their action took the form of a secret plot to persuade some member of the Getty family to petition the court in Los Angeles for the Bank of America to be appointed as an additional trustee on the grounds of Gordon's incompetence.

The plotters were not over-clever when they did this. Apart from underestimating Gordon, they also made a bad misjudgment in their first choice for a family petitioner. In October 1983, Mark Getty was so surprised to be asked to present the petition against his favorite uncle that he flew to San Francisco especially to ask him what was happening. Gordon himself was baffled, at least to start with. But Mark's query served to warn him that something was afoot, so when the lawyers representing Getty Oil persuaded Gordon's brother Paul Junior to petition the court on behalf of his fifteen-year-old son Tara, Gordon was prepared.

The fact that Paul Junior hardly ever saw his child by Talitha made this appear a fairly cynical maneuver. And from the point of view of Getty Oil, it was also singularly inept. As Gordon's opponents might have foreseen, he possessed one weapon they couldn't beat. Aware of what was going on by now, the bumbling Gordon used it—and the fate of Getty Oil was sealed.

Gordon's strength lay in the fact that most of the money that J. Paul Getty had left to his museum at Malibu was in the form of a 12 percent holding in the shares of Getty Oil. Until this point, the museum chairman, Harold Williams, had purposely remained aloof from what was happening. But now, thanks to the behavior of the board of Getty Oil, Gordon had little difficulty persuading Williams that the museum's best interests—especially its financial interests—lay in helping him defeat the board. Together, the shareholders of the Sarah C. Getty Trust and the J. Paul Getty Museum formed a majority able to dismiss the board of Getty Oil, which they duly did.

This was the point at which a takeover of Getty Oil became inevitable. The medium-sized Pennzoil Company promptly offered a cash bid of $110 a share. This offer suited Gordon, who reached an understanding with Pennzoil's chief executive to become chairman of the reconstituted company.

Now, however, completion of the Pennzoil deal was delayed by a lawsuit from one of the Georgettes (as someone had recently christened George's daughters), his second child Claire, who was sentimentally opposed to this impious attempt to break up Grandpa Getty's precious company and petitioned the courts accordingly.

"Why, Uncle Gordon, does a trust already worth $1.8 billion need to be increased in value?" she had asked him.

"A very interesting philosophical question, Claire," said Uncle Gordon, scratching his curly head and searching for an answer. "It is my fiduciary duty to maximize the wealth and income of the trust."

Maximize he did, and largely thanks to Claire. For while her lawyers were arguing the legality of the Pennzoil deal, the oil giant Texaco slipped in a higher offer of $125 a share for Getty Oil. And in January 1984, when Gordon accepted the Texaco offer on behalf of the Sarah C. Getty Trust, the value of the trust doubled overnight, going from $1.8 billion to nearly $4 billion.

Even this was not the end of it. To forestall yet another legal intervention from yet another quarter of the family—this time from Ronald's children, claiming that the price was still not high enough—Texaco actually increased its offer to $128 a share, and that was that.

If the word "awesome" can properly be applied to a financial deal, then the sale of Getty Oil was awesome. By paying a total of $10 billion for the whole of Getty Oil, Texaco had just made what was then the largest corporate acquisition in American history.

Some of the results were less than beneficial. With Getty Oil now swallowed up by Texaco, the family company lost its identity—and 20,000 Getty Oil employees lost their jobs. For Texaco, too, the monster deal proved ultimately disastrous: Pennzoil successfully sued it for $10 billion over the affair, and bankrupted it in the process.

Within the family few seemed happy at the outcome; the legal battles rumbled on. Ronald used the sale as the occasion for one more attempt to right the injustice that had dogged his life; he petitioned the court to "equalize" his share of the trust with those of his three siblings. (Two years later, Los Angeles Superior Court Judge Julius M. Title would finally express his sympathy for Ronald's situation, but reluctantly rule that "in law there was no proof that his father ever promised to correct the inequity.")

George's daughters, Anne, Claire, and Caroline, also went to court, hoping to punish Uncle Gordon for what he'd done to Getty Oil by forcing him to pay all taxes due on the sale. And the earlier attempt in Tara's name to have a co-trustee appointed to the trust continued. Despite the anger and upheavals that ensued from this earthquake of a sale, one thing was undeniable. While the Sarah C. Getty Trust had been under the solitary control of an absent-minded would-be poet, composer, and economic theorist, its capital had more than doubled and now, as has been mentioned, stood at something over $4 billion.

Whether by extraordinary cleverness or by the luck that guides the innocent, Gordon in this one traumatic deal had made almost as much money for the Sarah C. Getty Trust as his father had within in his lifetime. This time, *Forbes* was proclaiming a Getty the richest human being in America. This wasn't strictly true, as Gordon didn't own the trust money he controlled, and he was limited to an annual income as its principal trustee of a mere $200 million.

Left to himself, Gordon would almost certainly have stayed exactly where he was and worked on composing his opera based on the character of Shakespeare's Falstaff, which the Globe Theatre Trust in London had recently commissioned. Apart from finding fame as a composer, Gordon truly craved little in life, and San Francisco suited him to perfection. "I can go down into the street and get into my own car and don't have to call the chauffeur as I have to in New York," he said. Besides, his friends were there, along with his precious workroom with his two computers, his Macintosh loudspeakers, and his Yamaha piano.

But Ann felt differently. Under California law, she was theoretically entitled to half of Gordon's income, and within the family it was she who had the role of mover and spender. Even so, she had a problem over what to do with such a massive sum of money. For, like Gordon, she appeared to have more than enough of almost everything.

They already had their private Boeing 727, with Ann's initials painted on the tail, and its own bathroom with a real shower, which for some reason seemed to fascinate her husband. She had been known to redirect the plane to Paris on a sudden whim to do some shopping, but by now she had sufficient scarves from Hermès, bags from Gucci, and shoes from Ferragamo to last a lifetime.

She and Gordon made donations to causes they believed in, still principally concerned with conservation. The Leakey Anthropological Trust was supported in its work on human origins, as was Jane Goodall for her work on the behavior of chimpanzees. When Gordon gave $5 million to the Leakey Trust, he said: "There is a now-or-never quality to anthropological research, as human encroachment and deforestation threaten sources of fossil data base."

Simultaneously Ann decided to rebuild her family home in the Sacramento Valley for her mother. Although inclined to refer to her mother as a "tough old bat," Ann was a good daughter, and hoped she'd please her with this brand-new home in the style of a Tuscan villa, complete with courtyards, flower beds, and tower. But the "tough old bat" stayed fairly cool about it all. And the building used up only $2 million out of all that money.

It was around this time that a glamorous-looking Ann, interviewed on television by Barbara Walters, tempted fate by setting out her current credo. "Not at all," she replied to a suggestion that too much money was an instant recipe for misery. "I think it's possible to be very rich and happy, and, I suppose, very poor and happy. But it's easier to be very rich and happy."

Determined woman that she was, she now set out to prove this to her private satisfaction.

Ann is the sort of woman who likes challenges as well as money, and since there was little left to challenge her in San Francisco, she decided it was time to focus her attention on New York. Having made herself the undisputed social queen of Pacific Heights, she now planned to do the same from the large apartment she and Gordon had acquired on New York's Fifth Avenue.

It was a spectacular, expensive operation, an adventure into what is sometimes called "the regality of wealth," with Ann, if not exactly Gordon, apparently set to become the nearest thing to royalty for America. She entertained lavishly, dressed superbly, and soon acquired courtiers such as Jerry Zipkin, famous for his friendship with the Reagans, and the Greek financier and socialite, Alexander Papamarkou. It was Papamarkou who introduced her to a real king—or rather ex-king: Constantine of Greece, and when she decided to convert to Greek Orthodox Christianity, King Constantine stood beside her as her godfather.

But despite this royal connection, Ann remained at heart the girl from Wheatland, California, and to satisfy her conscience, she attempted to become what is known as working rich, by joining the boards of Sotheby's and Revlon and becoming a trustee of the Metropolitan Museum and the New York Public Library.

It was not enough. What she secretly craved was not so much work as self-improving culture—the subtle conversation of philosophers, evenings with distinguished authors, enriching contact with gigantic minds. All of which were suddenly on offer, thanks to an unlikely friendship with a portly, polyglot, cigar-loving publisher of Austrian Jewish origin who happened to be a member of the British House of Lords.

SINCE the early 1970s Ann and Gordon had been flying regularly to Europe in their Boeing 727, doing the rounds of the music festivals—Salzburg, Spoleto, Bayreuth—which they thoroughly enjoyed. It was at Salzburg back in 1972 that they first met the Baron Weidenfeld of Chelsea, and the friendship subsequently flourished.

Although a publisher by profession, George Weidenfeld is essentially an old-style Central European cultural magician. Everything about him has a touch of magic, including his barony, conferred upon him by the socialist premier Harold Wilson, and the equally magical survival of his London publishing house, Weidenfeld and Nicolson. Meeting Ann now to discuss her aspirations, he suggested that the answer to her problems was to become a publisher.

It was an original suggestion, but it was not impossible for the wife of the richest man in America, particularly as Weidenfeld knew that Barney Rosset of the Grove Press, famous publisher of Henry Miller, Jean Genet, and the Marquis de Sade, was eager to sell his business and finally retire with $2 million.

Ann had always been an eager reader—though whether of books from the Grove Press is another matter—and the idea captured her imagination. "I love to read all day," she said. "But as I'm of Puritan stock and grew up believing that you have to work all day, I decided to make reading my work."

Buying the Grove Press suited her, for as well as reading for her living, she could now begin to meet those strange Houyhnhnm-like characters, famous living authors. She even went on a promotion tour with one of them, Nien Cheng, author of the best-selling *Life and Death in Shanghai*.

The purchase also suited George Weidenfeld, who had persuaded Ann to become a partner in Weidenfeld and Nicolson in London, and simultaneously help finance a new and independent branch of Weidenfeld and Nicolson to operate from New York, in close cooperation with the Grove Press.

For Ann Getty and Weidenfeld, publishing now became a game that two could play. He would fly the Concorde to New York, where they would get together to discuss the publishing conundra of the 1980s: could they encourage Joseph Heller to create a proper sequel to *Catch-22*, or J. D. Salinger to do likewise with *Catcher in the Rye*? Could Ann entice the susceptible Norman Mailer or the saturnine Philip Roth to their imprint, or should they go for less expensive, lesser known authors? They also planned to enter films, preparing to bring Weidenfeld's old hometown, Vienna, to the screen "in all its intellectual and cultural splendour," as the publicity put it. There was talk of an impressive cultural magazine. A TV series on 2,000 years of archaeology was commissioned.

"Everything I do is related to everything else I do," said Ann as she set up the Wheatland Foundation to encourage her various interests in the arts. The foundation went to Venice to discuss the future of opera, and to Jerusalem to discuss the symphony. Writers were taken up the Nile to discuss literature, and others brought to talk about their books beside the Tagus.

And through it all Ann paid large advances to her authors, which is the best and noblest way for anyone to offload fairly large amounts of money.

At the Getty apartment on Fifth Avenue, there were also dinner parties for authors and their agents the likes of which have not been seen before or since in the world of publishing, with exquisite food, exotic flowers, twenty-four sitting down to table—all this together with the aroma of George Weidenfeld's Corona Corona and his fluent conversation in five European languages.

Throughout these dinner parties Gordon, being Gordon, sat in the background, smiled his Gordonesque smile, said "Heck" and "Gee," and tried working out the latest puzzle that had started to obsess him, an odd one for a billionaire. How can modern capitalist society operate without money? Money causes such a lot of problems. Surely, he told himself, there had to be a better way.

*

BUT Gordon couldn't meditate for long, since the fallout from the sale of Getty Oil continued. In all, Gordon found himself facing fifteen separate lawsuits, most of them filed by members of the family. This genuinely disturbed him. "There's nothing more rancorous and upsetting than a family lawsuit," he said sadly. Besides, he was longing to return to his composing.

As a close witness to the effects of past family dissension, Gordon wanted peace. According to Bill Newsom, he was "astonished at the way the sale of Getty Oil had gone" and confessed to him, "Bill, I just don't *want* four billion dollars." Nor did he want the trouble that accompanied his position as sole trustee of the Sarah C. Getty Trust. Nor, for that matter, did he see much mileage in prolonging the existence of the trust from loyalty to his father. It had done its work. It had played a major part in creating and preserving the family's amazing fortune. Its usefulness was over.

So, acting like the philosopher billionaire he was, Gordon Getty bowed to the inevitable and killed the Sarah C. Getty Trust stone dead. First, he paid practically $1 billion in taxes, then, Solomon-like divided up what remained of the corpse four ways. Each part was of roughly $750 million. One went to his brother Paul, another to "the Georgettes" the three daughters, of his half-brother George, yet another to the heirs of his half-brother Ronald—and the fourth part he kept for himself and his family.

As Ronald's exclusion from the fruits of the trust continued, this brought a certain complexity to the situation. Apart from George's daughters, none of the grandchildren of J. Paul Getty would inherit until the death of the last of his three remaining sons, which by actuarial computation could be expected around twenty-seven years hence. In the meantime the money that would go to Ronald's children was in turn divided into three separate trusts, the profits from which would go to Paul, to Gordon, and to George's daughters until the next generation was in a position to inherit.

The dismembering of the Sarah C. Getty Trust was an important moment in the history of the Gettys. In giving each section of the "dynasty" control of its own finances, it offered the family the possibility of peace at last. The immensely profitable sale of Getty Oil had already freed the family from its dependence on the uncertain future of the oil business. Now the family possessed this vast new acreage of wealth, which with appropriate investment could last virtually forever, with the capital within the trust steadily increasing and the income beneficiaries living immensely well off the interest.

At the same time, Gordon made one further contribution to the future well-being of the family. Appreciating the danger of having vast amounts of money locked away within the separate trusts for years, to gush forth only on the death of the last of the older generation, he devised a way of ensuring what by Getty standards was a relatively modest income for younger members of the family in return for their participation in the workings of the different trusts.

He personally gave up the 5 percent trustee fee to which he had been entitled, in order to provide annual fees of around $150,000 for younger members of the family, who were to be appointed co-trustees of the family trusts at the age of twenty-five. In this way, he hoped, his children and their cousins would gain experience in the financial affairs of the family and have an early stake in its prosperity.

Already he was looking forward to a future for his children free from the disasters that had dogged the Gettys in the past. He put his hopes for them into a poem which he wrote around this time and entitled "My Uncle's House." It ended thus:

> I wish my sons no finer birth;
> I wish them this, to find
> How patience and the generous earth
> Make life, how work makes wealth and worth,
> And song the graced mind.

CHAPTER TWENTY-ONE

Knighthood

THE $750 million Paul Junior received from the division of the Sarah C. Getty Trust made him overnight the sixth-richest man in Britain. The capital was credited to his Cheyne Walk Trust, where it was expertly invested by fund managers across a whole range of investments to guarantee security and growth—which, with interest rates at an all time high in the early 1980s, meant that while the core capital would steadily increase for the benefit of future generations, Paul would immediately receive more than $1 million every week in interest. In terms of disposable income he was even richer than most other hyper-rich. With his children and grandchildrens' inheritances taken care of by the capital in the Trust, and with no extraneous demands upon his income, he was free to spend entirely as he wanted.

But it would have been hard to find a neater parable on the futility of excessive wealth. What use was $1 million a week to someone who despised himself, who barely left his home except to enter a clinic, who derived no pleasure from family or food or travel, and who was suffering acute phlebitis, impending diabetes, suspected cirrhosis of the liver, impaired lung functioning, brittle bones, and dreadful teeth?

The poverty of Paul's desires made the richness of his inheritance seem pointless. Yet by an unexpected twist of fate, it was the arrival of this vast inheritance that marked the beginning of Paul's personal salvation.

The arrival of the money, coincided with a personal crisis. Paul was very ill indeed; Victoria was still married to Mohammed Alatas—and now the mother of two sons, Tariq and Zain; it was particularly hard for him to remain at Cheyne Walk without her. With his health in ruins he reentered the London Clinic for what would clearly be a lengthy stay.

It was around this time that his thoughts returned to the Catholicism to which he had been converted at sixteen by the Jesuits of St. Ignatius. He had subsequently lapsed, but during this period in the clinic he was influenced by the Jesuit chaplain, Father Miles, from nearby St. James's, Spanish Place. Under his guidance Paul returned to the church.

Restored to the faith, and having severed most connections with possessions and the world outside, he was living rather like a monk within the London Clinic. Here he had no responsibilities and was blessedly free from fear and worry.

So his first reaction to his money was a Christian one. He remembered Christ's remarks comparing rich men's chances of heaven to a camel's odds of getting through the eye of a needle, and was prepared to follow Christ's advice. Having no need of so much money, he was perfectly prepared to give the greater part of it away. But it wasn't easy. As a onetime hippie, Paul was uncomfortable with very large amounts of money anyhow, and had few clear plans of what to do with it—apart from wanting to see it used to good effect.

His first large donation went to a cause he personally believed in. As a lover of the cinema, he had discovered that the whole legacy of early British movies was in danger. The only copies of countless British films in the archives of the British Film Institute were on perishable nitrate stock, and the institute lacked the funds for the expensive process of transferring them to modern media. Paul financed this—very quietly, as he wanted no publicity—finally contributing to the tune of nearly £20 million. So it is largely thanks to him that the early history of the British cinema has not been lost forever.

Shortly afterward he offered £500,000 to the Manchester Art Gallery to prevent a small painting of the Crucifixion by the Sienese master Duccio from being purchased by the J. Paul Getty Museum. This aroused speculation in the press that he was getting even with his father's memory—or alternatively with his brother Gordon, who was a trustee of the museum. But his own explanation for his gift was simpler. He remarked that "I'm fed up with everything streaming to Malibu. It's time that someone stopped it."

Influenced by Father Miles, Paul now made a firm commitment to give up drugs forever. But he had made the same decision many times before, and was painfully aware of the difficulty of sticking to it. Because of this, he intended to continue his treatment, supervised by his doctors in the safety and obscurity of the London Clinic, for as long as possible.

He would in fact stay fifteen months—but his desire for obscurity was not to be respected.

*

BY the beginning of 1985 the government of Margaret Thatcher was facing problems over its policy toward the funding of the arts, a minor but potentially embarrassing area where supply-side economics, as practiced by her monetarist administration, patently failed to function. In theory, as the state cut taxes and the rich grew richer, the so-called trickle-down effect would start, with grateful multimillionaires offering up their surplus capital to fund the arts rather as wealthy donors had been doing in America for years.

But England's greed decade was so extremely greedy that things hadn't worked like that. (More to the point, perhaps, contributions to the arts were still not tax-deductible, as they had long been in the United States.) And the fact was that by the mid-1980s many of the country's great museums and galleries, endowed in more civilized eras, were strapped for cash in a world of monetarist plenty.

Ironically, the Getty Museum at Malibu—itself the product of private benefaction, and with its wealth increased, like Paul and Gordon's, from the recent sale of its stock in Getty Oil—was making the situation worse by pushing up the prices of major works of art and being able to outbid any major gallery in the world. In the absence of serious funding by the government—which would have upset the prime minister and her spending limits—the National Gallery would be pauperized, left unable to bid for further acquisitions in the marketplace of international art.

There was one notable bright spot in the gloom of the artistic-patronage scene: the gift to the National Gallery in London by the Sainsbury family to construct a brand-new wing on a neighboring site which would ultimately bear their name. The prime mover had been the artistically enlightened scion of the Sainsbury family, Simon Sainsbury, who coincidentally happened to be the business partner of Christopher Gibbs. While the Sainsbury gift was being finalized, one of the gallery's trustees, the Marquis of Dufferin and Ava, had talked to Gibbs about the gallery's need for "an equivalent great endowment," which it could invest to provide an annual income for its major purchases.

Gibbs pondered—but he can't have pondered very long. For it was shortly after this that some influential members of the government and the world of art became extremely interested in a previously neglected hermit billionaire currently residing in the London Clinic.

IT had been nearly twenty years since Christopher Gibbs first met Paul, and he was one of the few who had continued seeing him regularly through the bleak years following Talitha's death.

During this period, Gibbs himself had prospered. With Simon Sainsbury as his partner, he had become a successful West End art dealer, with a rich clientele and a fascinating shop in Mayfair. At the same time he had transformed himself from the wunderkind of 1960s Chelsea into a serious social figure, with a house beside the Thames at Abingdon, an apartment in Albany, and a wide range of influential friends.

During his own ascent, there had been little he could do to halt his friend's decline, but now he detected in the current situation a chance for Paul to help himself while helping the National Gallery solve its problems. If Paul could be persuaded to make the gallery the sort of grand donation it required, the result might well work wonders for his public image—and thereby for his private self-esteem and precarious morale.

Despite his gifts to the Manchester City Art Gallery and the BFI, Paul still had far more money than he knew what to do with. So when Gibbs described the plight of the National Gallery, Paul agreed in principle to a £50 million gift without demur.

But Gibbs wanted to ensure that Paul received full credit for his generosity. With so much money—and such dubious publicity from the past—the gift could easily backfire if handled badly. To prevent this, Gibbs relied upon a number of strategically placed allies who understood the situation and would be able to ensure that the gift became a coup for the gallery—and something more than this for J. Paul Getty, Jr.

The most important of these allies was the newly appointed chairman of the gallery trustees, the financier and art collector Lord Rothschild. A perceptive human being as well as a successful banker, Jacob Rothschild was swift to appreciate the irresistible nature of the gift, and what it would entail.

"It just never happens that you get an offer of £50 million even for the National Gallery," he says. "So when it *does* occur, you go for it with everything you've got, and throw in the whole boiling—support from politicians, from royalty, from anybody who can help. It's your job to be an opportunist, and do everything you can to make it happen. I knew that Christopher was seeing this as part of Paul's return to life, and hoping it would change the perception people had of him. That was something I was obviously prepared to go along with."

Another of Gibbs's influential friends, Thatcher's minister for the arts, Lord Gowrie, felt much the same once he heard what was on offer. As a member of the government he had a stake in ensuring that the donation went ahead, and he was fully aware of the political significance of so much private money for the arts. So, like Lord Roth-schild, he visited Paul Getty, Jr., in the London Clinic to express his gratitude and finalize the details of the gift.

He was quick to tell "the Boss," as he referred to Thatcher, who was equally delighted at the news. High art was fairly low on the Thatcherite scale of values, but an unsolicited gift of £50 million to the nation brought out the gentle side of the Iron Lady, and her immediate reaction was that she should thank Paul Getty, Jr., in person.

In the United States it would have been unthinkable for the head of government to associate with a well-known addict with a history such as Paul's, but for Prime Minister Thatcher it would have been unthink-able not to. She liked rich people, and was particularly moved that one of them was showing such patriotism to his adopted country. Since he was in the London Clinic, what else could a caring premier do but don the mantle of Florence Nightingale, come to the bedside of the invalid billionaire, and thank him warmly for his generosity.

Before this happened, Gowrie felt it prudent to inquire of Paul how he felt about meeting Margaret Thatcher. He relates that he found him "rather excited by the idea, but being a very shy man he was also wary and asked me to brief him over what would happen. I told Paul, 'Just don't worry. You'll find that she'll be very charming and very easy to talk to and as soon as she sees you, she'll say, "Now, my dear Mr. Getty. What on earth's the matter?" Then before you know where you are she'll have taken over your case medically.' "

When Lord Gowrie brought Thatcher to the London Clinic a few days later, he was understandably relieved to see that "Paul had spruced himself up and was sitting on the edge of his bed like a schoolboy waiting for Matron." Once introduced, the prime minister treated Paul almost word for word as Gowrie had predicted.

"My dear Mr. Getty," she began. "Now, what's the matter? We mustn't let things get us down, now, must we? We must have you out of here as soon as possible."

Gowrie saw Paul looking worried—for, as he says, "He was obviously as happy as a clam in the London Clinic, where he was taken care of and had no intrusions on his privacy, and had everything he needed— his records and his books and television." The thought of being forced to leave this haven must have shocked him deeply.

Otherwise the visit went off admirably. Everyone was very charming, and Paul himself was genuinely touched by the prime minister's con-cern. When a signed photograph arrived from Downing Street it was given pride of place beside his bed; and during the months ahead, Paul and Mrs. Thatcher met several times and got on splendidly together.

Later, meeting Paul's half-sister, Donna, in America, Margaret Thatcher told her that her brother had one of the most remarkable minds in Europe.

DESPITE the prime minister's desire to get him out of the London Clinic as soon as possible, Paul had nearly nine more months of clamlike bliss within its pricy portals. According to his lawyer, Vanni Treves, he was treating it "more like a hotel than a hospital," but this did not belie the fact that he had been extremely ill and that the process of recovering from such long and deep addiction required time.

Fortunately there was no pressure to economize on the £250 a day (plus treatment costs and incidental extras) that his room was costing. Methadone could take the place of heroin, lager in the icebox could become an acceptable substitute for rum—but there were no short cuts to help his wounded spirit to recover.

In the meantime, since Paul was still determined not to spend his enormous income on himself, it was announced that he was placing much of it in a charitable trust and keeping "only what is necessary to maintain a relatively modest lifestyle."

It was now that he contributed £20 million to establish the J. Paul Getty, Jr., Charitable Trust. The trustees were Christopher Gibbs, Vanni Treves, and James Ramsden, a former Conservative minister and chairman of the London Clinic. Paul was careful to designate the sort of groups on which the annual income should be spent.

Two key categories were to be conservation and the environment, but the rest of the money was to go to what Paul termed "unpopular causes," generally involving "poverty and misery." Most of the grants would be between £5,000 and £10,000 and would go to small community and local projects, such as work with the mentally ill, drug addicts, ethnic minorities, and the homeless. The trust would also "offer support for people under stress," such as battered women, victims of sexual abuse, and families in difficulty. Most of the suffering Paul was hoping to relieve had definite connections with his own experience. He had never known poverty, but otherwise was fairly well acquainted with most other forms of human misery.

The trust being established, Paul continued giving on the widest scale, often on the spur of the moment to something he had seen on television. Hearing that the virtuoso pianist John Ogdon was so short of money that he had been forced to sell his piano, Paul told him to choose a new one and send him the bill. (Ogdon did, and it cost £18,000.) Touched by the plight of a group of breakaway striking miners, he sent them £50,000. Another £250,000 went to preserve the environment of Ely Cathedral from the threat of building, and £10,000 to conserve a medieval field in Somerset. Since then he has made large donations for famine relief in Eritrea, medical supplies for Poland, the Special Air Service, and the Imperial War Museum. He also paid $1 million for Claus von Bülow's legal fees for his successful defense against charges of attempting to murder his wife, Sunny—"because my father would have done so."

By giving he was generating great goodwill. Britain is not a generous country, and gratitude was palpable around him. Meanwhile, from his room within the London Clinic, he continued to adhere to that "fairly modest lifestyle" he apparently enjoyed. His only personal extravagance that year was the purchase for £3.4 million of Wormsley Park, a run-down country house with a more or less derelict estate thirty-eight miles from London.

Built in 1720, Wormsley had been home to the Fane family for two centuries until they found it too expensive to maintain. The house needed rebuilding—or demolishing; and its greatest asset was its romantic position in an upland valley on the edge of the Chilterns, surrounded by 3,000 acres of meadowland and seriously neglected beechwood.

Why Paul bought the place is anybody's guess. Had he needed a country house—which currently he didn't—why a derelict edifice like Wormsley when he could have purchased almost any stately home in Britain? To make his attitude toward the purchase clear, a spokesman told the press that the house and the estate would be restored "regardless of cost—and then given to a charitable trust for deprived children."

Perhaps it would. But as with his gift to the National Gallery, the initiative behind the Wormsley purchase came from Christopher Gibbs, who cheerfully admits to having "bullied" Paul into it. Gibbs was a man of many interests, but creating homes at great expense for deprived children was not among them.

WHEN Paul's gift to the National Gallery was announced, the establishment united to express its gratitude.

"Maecenas has come among us," hymned Gowrie's deputy, William Waldegrave, as he brought the news to an awed and grateful House of Commons. Simultaneously a missive of considerable rarity arrived for Paul at the London Clinic. It was from the secretary to the cabinet, and conveyed the news that "the Cabinet agreed that the standing of the Institution and the munificence of the gift combine to render this an occurrence of national significance, and express their warm appreciation of, and profound gratitude for, your magnificent generosity."

Meanwhile from America came congratulations couched in less tortuous vernacular. "Three cheers for your magnificent support," Gordon cabled. "If that means Britain can keep art works that might have gone to the J. Paul Getty Museum, that's fine. If you personally were to target Getty Museum acquisitions for retention funds, picking on us and not on other purchasers, I don't see how I could find much fault with that either."

Since Gordon was a trustee of the museum it was generous of him to write like this. And against the background of the treatment he had been receiving from Paul until quite recently, his note seems positively saintly in its attitude. But Gordon was wanting bygones to be bygones. So was Paul. A new and unaccustomed mood of reconciliation had started in the family.

At the same time, public approval was beginning to have the effect on Paul's morale that his friends had hoped for, encouraging him to stay off drugs and be worthy of the glowing reputation he was gaining. He had tried to break the habit many times before, but failed to sustain the resolution. This time however, he was revealing unsuspected strength of will.

Even so, it wasn't easy, and his cure was by no means completed. He had been addicted now for nearly twenty years, and the psychological dependence developed over such a period is often more difficult to break than the purely physical. Prolonged addiction can inhibit emotional development so that former addicts find themselves subject to relapses and panic attacks; they are painfully at risk.

Strong-willed though he was, Paul remained vulnerable, and his damaged psyche needed reconstructing rather like an injured body. In the process much of his former self was being quietly replaced by something very different.

This explains why J. Paul Getty, Jr., onetime hippie, heroin addict, and unemployed billionaire, was getting on so well with Margaret Thatcher, who as a person and a politician stood for much that he would once have almost certainly derided: middle-class morality, hard work, and family values.

Paul was changing. He was now fifty-two, and in place of the Pre-Raphaelite hippie of the early days in Cheyne Walk, an increasingly conservative middle-aged Englishman was emerging.

*

THAT autumn came his biggest test of all: reunion with his son Paul. This was young Paul's first flight to Europe since his coma. He flew from Los Angeles with his two male nurses, and once in London the first thing he wanted was to see his long-lost father; or rather, since young Paul was all but blind, to hear his father's voice, be with him again, forget the past, and start a new life with his blessing.

It would have been hard for any father to cope with such a situation. Inevitably there were tears, especially from Paul Junior, whose sense of horror and regret when faced with what had happened to his broken son can only be imagined. It was a harrowing ordeal for him, particularly as he could no longer dull his sense of guilt with drugs or alcohol. But there was also joy, and the chance of making restitution in the future. He was learning his first lessons in coping with his guilt unaided; with every day that passed, the future seemed more hopeful.

BY the second week of March 1986, Paul was sufficiently recovered to take Thatcher's advice and leave the London Clinic. He had stayed hidden away so long that despite the fame his generosity had brought him, he was regarded as something of a mystery by the general public, and bizarre rumors of his physical condition prompted Vanni Treves to assure reporters that "his health is now actually very good."

Like most lawyers' assurances, this was true to a point. Paul was off heroin and booze, his circulation had improved, as had the condition of his liver, and his general health was certainly better than it had been eighteen months earlier. But his physique remained impaired. He tired easily, and was liable to fall and break bones if he wasn't careful. To Lord Gowrie he appeared "as if he had received a bad wound sometime in his past, and had never quite got over it."

Wise for once, Paul decided against returning to Cheyne Walk to live, his excuse being that the house had been so seriously neglected that it needed renovating. But the truth was that Cheyne Walk contained the dead weight of his past—regret for his children, guilt for Talitha, drugs, drink, the influence of Dante Gabriel Rossetti—and to leave now was to make a break with all that it had represented.

His new abode could not have been more different: a flat in a modern block created for the very rich just behind the Ritz. There were no ghosts here. It was quiet and discreet and somewhat clinical, its principal features being the views from its plate-glass windows of trees ad infinitum in Green Park, and the occasional presence of Rupert Murdoch as a neighbor. Paul had actually purchased the flat some months earlier for his mother, but as she was now dying of cancer and her doctors were in America, she had little use for it.

THE final accolade for Paul arrived in early June with the Queen's Birthday Honours List. Not entirely unexpectedly, he was appointed Knight of the British Empire, "for services to the arts."

For a man suffering low self-esteem there is nothing like a knighthood, and it was touching to observe Paul's obvious delight at what was happening. This was the final seal of acceptance by the British establishment, proof that as far as Britain was concerned, the past was over and the slate wiped clean. However as a foreigner he could not style himself "Sir Paul"—which would have rather suited him—because foreigners are given only honorary knighthoods. To enjoy the curious pleasures of a title, he would have had to change his nationality, something he had already contemplated doing, having come to the conclusion years earlier that "Britain is Utopia."

But he reluctantly explained that "my advisers have asked me not to, because of the enormous tax consequences. [The change would have involved him in double taxation, by the United States and Britain.] If I became a British citizen it would prevent me putting my money where it is needed."

One sees his point. His knighthood had already cost him £50 million. To pay yet more money to the British treasury for the right to use it would have been excessive. So he remained plain Mr. Getty K.B.E., joining a distinguished group of his fellow Americans including Ronald Reagan, Gerald Ford, Henry Kissinger, and Douglas Fairbanks, Jr.

Receiving the K.B.E. insignia from the queen at the official investiture at Buckingham Palace was Paul's first appearance at a public event since his fraught arrival at his father's memorial service with Bianca Jagger ten years earlier. In its way this was even more of an ordeal, given the forbidding nature of the palace and the fact that he was still far from well and had grown even shyer and more reclusive with the years. But he had to go, not only because the queen had summoned him, but because his mother and his half-sister Donna had flown in from America to be present at the great occasion.

In place of the bustling Auntie Mame figure, Ann was now skin and bone, so ill that her daughter, Donna, had had to accompany her. Ann had borne witness to the troubles that had hit the Gettys, and to the pain and disappointment Paul had caused her. But now for the first time in many years, she could be proud of him, and could die having seen the Queen of England honoring her son.

*

B Y now Paul was following several paths toward salvation. His Catholicism was one, his philanthropy another—and the third, and most pleasurable, was cricket.

Ever since Mick Jagger had introduced him to the game, he had continued watching it on television and, given his addictive nature, he was soon a dedicated fan. Cricket can have extreme effects on grown men. Harold Pinter once seriously insisted that "cricket is the greatest thing that God ever created on earth, certainly greater than sex, although sex isn't too bad either." Paul would have probably agreed.

Scholar that he was, he began studying the history of the game from the days in the 1790s when the members of the Marylebone Cricket Club adjourned to Lord's Tavern to codify the "laws" of the game. In love with England, he loved the Englishness of cricket, and the way it had been patronized by the aristocracy when they played it with any laborer from the estate who could hit a ball for six. He learned all he could about cricket's famous players, past and present, rather as he had once learned everything he could about the greatest opera singers.

So it was that when James Ramsden, chairman of the London Clinic, introduced him to a distinguished-looking fellow patient who was recovering from an operation, Paul knew exactly who he was and felt honored.

Sir George "Gubby" Allen was one of the grandest of the grand old men of English cricket. The son of a former police commissioner, educated at Eton and Trinity College, Cambridge, he was one of the last of the great amateur all-arounders. He captained England against Australia in 1936, and is remembered for refusing to indulge in Douglas Jardine's ruthless "bodyline bowling" against the Australians in 1932, on the grounds that it "wasn't cricket."

Gubby came to be Paul's ideal Englishman, and after his death in 1989, someone suggested he had been like an elder brother to him.

"More like a father," Paul answered.

It was a telling remark from someone who had missed out badly in a father. Gubby became something Paul had always wanted, the sort of father figure who exemplified the virtues he needed, self-discipline and courage in particular.

For any cricket lover, election to the Marylebone Cricket Club is one of life's golden pinnacles, taking much time and influence to reach. If one is very lucky one is put down for the MCC at birth, and might just get elected in one's thirties. But with Gubby president of the MCC, and Gibbs's brother, Roger, a committee member, Paul's election proved what everybody knows—that in England most doors open in the presence of extremely large amounts of money and the right connections.

For Paul, election to the MCC was like acceptance into Paradise. Outcast no longer, he was entitled to wear one of the marks of English upper-class acceptance, the maroon-and-gold MCC tie (known among cricketers as "rhubarb and custard"). He also had entrée to one of the last male bastions of England, the historic Long Room in the MCC Pavilion.

Sitting beside his friend the great Gubby Allen in this cricketing Valhalla, Paul could participate in the ritual of the national game, watching the batsmen pass through the Long Room as they strode out to bat, following their innings from the vantage point of the pavilion, and then applauding—or sitting in commiserating silence—on their return.

The Long Room experience did more than anything to draw Paul out of the isolated world he'd lived in for so long. Old cricketers will always talk about two things—cricket and themselves—and for Paul the idea of a cricket bore was inconceivable. Before long he was numbering among his friends some of the greatest names in cricket: the fine Australian all-arounder, Keith Miller; Dennis Compton; and the oldest surviving English test-match captain, R. E. S. "Bob" Wyatt. These great men treated Paul with the easy camaraderie experts tend to show wealthy seekers after truth, and his natural shyness didn't seem to matter.

Gubby continued to be very kind to Paul, but it would be pointless to pretend there wasn't method to his kindness. He had been a crafty bowler in his time, and as a successful stockbroker and former treasurer of the MCC, he was not financially naïve. Cricket was seriously underfunded, and Gubby had long had plans to improve the standards of the game and the amenities at Lord's cricket ground.

Paul soon agreed with him, and with Gubby to advise him, he felt honored to become the self-appointed godfather of English cricket. Soon he was dispatching anonymous donations to hard-pressed county sides, paying for schools for youthful cricketers, and helping a group of Britain's worthiest recipients—old and needy cricketers—with pensions. Then in 1986 Paul crowned his benevolence to cricket by donating £3 million for a badly needed new spectator stand at Lord's.

His £50 million donation to the National Gallery had earned Paul his knighthood and acceptance from the British establishment, but his support of cricket brought him something different—genuine and lasting popularity. And paradoxically, while establishing his popular appeal, cricket also endeared him to the English upper classes.

He understood the game and genuinely loved it, and from his private box in the new stand he had paid for, he could watch its arcane rituals as he sat in splendor, offering excellent champagne to his friends among the cricketing fraternity and alleviating the boredom of the English summer. But as far as Paul's private future was concerned, something more important still was taking place beneath the beechwoods in a long-forgotten valley in the Chilterns.

CHAPTER TWENTY-TWO

Wormsley

EVEN in the lost years of Paul's addiction, when Christopher Gibbs was making weekly visits to Cheyne Walk, he had always found his friend "a very clever, funny, erudite man"; and despite the anguish and the heroin, Gibbs insists that it was during these years that Paul had taught him "most of what I know about books and the book arts, and everything I know about the movies, and much, much else besides."

Having known each other so extremely well for many years, they had developed much in common—interests, tastes, a shared sense of humor—so that once his friend received his monster fortune after the sale of Getty Oil, Gibbs could see, better than anyone, how this vast amount of money could be used to rescue Paul and steadily enrich his life.

One of Gibbs's many passions is the English countryside, and even when Paul had seemed stuck in the London Clinic, he was already planning how to introduce him to the serious pleasures of country living.

When Paul left the clinic, it was obvious that, for all the talk about that "fairly modest lifestyle" he intended to lead, he would not reside exclusively in his flat beside the park for ever. Gibbs knew Paul well enough to understand that in his present mood he had no interest in buying a stately home like Sutton Place, which would have worried and constricted him. It was because of this that he had pushed him into buying Wormsley.

At the time of the purchase, Gibbs saw Wormsley as little more than "a dullish house in a romantic setting," but he could also see how something extraordinary could be made of it. The "romantic setting" could become the ideal background for what he was envisaging for Paul, a place so perfect that it would satisfy his every need and whim and speed his recovery.

In fact the whole idea of creating such a house had been haunting

Gibbs for years. He had always been deeply interested in architecture, and had become fascinated by a recurrent architectural fantasy, of an earthly paradise whose occupants could effortlessly find true happiness. In the past, the would-be paradises of the very rich have had many names—Xanadu, Shangri-la, Schiffanoia, Sans Souci—but Gibbs had become particularly intrigued by an English version of this dream, that of re-creating Adam's house in Paradise in the English countryside.

It was an idea associated with an unlikely figure who had come to fascinate both Paul and Gibbs because of his close connections with Rossetti and the Pre-Raphaelites: William Morris, the artist, typographer, and early socialist, with whose wife Rossetti was in love.

Gibbs says that he has "always had a vision (which comes and goes like all things mystical), of an English paradise like the one in William Morris's novel *News from Nowhere*." Paul was acquainted with this vision, too. And here in this upland valley of the Chilterns, an area he had known since childhood, Gibbs saw how Wormsley could become a sort of rural paradise on earth. It could bring back Paul's appetite for life, reunite him with his family, and make him happy. And once the house was bought, a few visits were enough to make Paul equally enthusiastic, thus putting paid to his hermit life for ever.

Once started, work on Wormsley soon built up its own momentum, which would last for more than seven years, keep over a hundred men permanently employed and cost around £60 million. The result would be such an extraordinary creation that, having seen it, one recent writer claimed that, "as the expression of one man's taste on a grand scale, Wormsley has no equal in modern Britain."

Even from the start it was obvious that more would be involved than just transforming "dullish" Wormsley into the "fine country house" Gibbs had wanted for his friend. The house would virtually need rebuilding, but above all, Paul was concerned about housing his precious book collection. He had bought so many books by now that the bulk of them were in storage in London warehouses, and he couldn't wait to bring them all together in one building with a perfect library. But what was the perfect library?

The simplest solution would have been to have built an extension to the house in a style to match its eighteenth-century architecture, but, as Gibbs put it, the place "would have ended up looking like a nursing home." He remembered seeing eighteenth-century houses in Ireland and on the Scottish border built close beside much older castles. A castle would also offer just the touch of fantasy that Wormsley needed, and someone suggested building it from local flint. No one had built a flint castle in England since the Normans, but Paul agreed to the proposition.

He also wanted the most up-to-date modern cinema, along with un-obtrusive garages, a nuclear-bomb-proof shelter, an indoor swimming pool, a deer park, and a four-acre lake. Wormsley had no lake, but Gibbs believed that any proper country house just had to have one. So an artificial lake would have to be created. And since there was no water for it, boreholes would have to be sunk and water pumped from depths of over 400 feet through the chalk to fill it.

The 1,500 acres of beechwood also needed careful reforestation. The fields required hedging, as the estate had been terribly neglected, and Paul had set his heart on having a herd of his favorite long-horned old English cattle at Wormsley. But the first priority was to put the house and cottages in order. Paul desired a center for his family, for now that relations with them were improving, he was already picturing himself with his children staying on the estate. Picturesque New Gardens Cottage was needed urgently for young Paul's visit in December, which meant a rush to build a heated swimming pool where he could continue his exercises.

For the future there still remained one all-important matter to consider: the creation of a cricket pitch, which Paul had also set his heart on. He was excited by what he'd read of the great days of English country-house cricket—hot summer afternoons, white-flanneled figures at the crease, and the effortless pursuit of the best game in the world. Before Wormsley was complete, it would need a perfect cricket pitch to match.

THE creation of a billionaire's Shangri-La in the Chilterns might all too easily have ended as a nightmare or a joke; for Paul, either would have been a personal disaster. It was really Gibbs who kept this from happening, thanks to the guidance he exerted and the experts he produced to work upon the project. Just as it was largely through his friends that he had helped Paul get his knighthood, so now he turned to other friends to bring his hopes for Wormsley to fruition.

With the wrong architect, the library castle could all too easily have become something from Disneyland, but Gibbs had in mind an architect he knew and trusted. This was Nicholas Johnston, a man with a talent for interpreting the whims of wealthy clients. Gibbs had known him even before he made his name by designing a mock-Georgian extension to the Ian Fleming house near Swindon, and had grown to admire his taste and ingenuity. As Gibbs expected, Johnston got along well with

Paul, and the Wormsley library is one of his most successful creations. From outside it is essentially a happy castle, living benignly with its next-door neighbor, but once inside, one sees what a sophisticated building Johnston and his collaborator, Chester Jones, have created for its owner's fabled book collection.

Ever since the sale of Getty Oil, Paul had been stepping up his spending on priceless books and manuscripts. Apart from buying Wormsley, this remained his one authentic self-indulgence, but even with virtually unlimited resources and an expert like Bryan Maggs to advise and buy for him, the days were over when one individual, however rich, could build a comprehensive major library. The books are simply unavailable today.

However, there remain individual treasures to be bought—and Paul had been assembling a collection of what he calls milestone books in the history of book production to enrich his library. Among them were a priceless twelfth-century Gospel from the monastery of Ottobeuren in Germany, Flemish illuminated books of hours, and elaborate nineteenth-century French *livres d'artiste*, luxuriously printed and produced editions illustrated with original paintings by contemporary artists. The strength of the library consists in great bindings (a passion of Paul's), English aquatint books, and wonderful examples of the private press movement.

Such books are a most recherché way of spending large amounts of money, and must have formed a very private source of pleasure to their owner. When converted into books, capital acquires a semi-sacred aura, and Johnston's library, with its scholarly interior and carefully controlled humidity and temperature, has something of the atmosphere of a secular chapel built to serve the house beside it. On the ceiling are painted the stars in their courses as they were on the night of September 7, 1932, above the Ligurian Sea when Paul was born. When some of the treasures of the library have been brought up from the vaults and placed on display they make a splendid sight.

Once it was completed and the precious books had been reverently set in place on their barathea-covered bookshelves, Paul was soon pottering between the book-strewn sitting room where he habitually watched television, through the conservatory, and into the leather-scented silence of his library, which soon became his favored place for reading.

As well as designing the library, Johnston also supervised the transformation of the run-down country mansion into an up-to-date vision of a perfect eighteenth-century country house.

Once again there was a danger of Wormsley exhibiting what Gibbs himself once called that "frightful uniformity of richness where everything shrieks that Mammon's worshipped." To avoid this outcome he introduced another friend whose work he trusted, the interior decorator David Mlinaric. An amiable charmer, Mlinaric is essentially a scholar who has made himself the pope of the English classical interior—and, like the pope, he tends to be infallible, as he has shown in his work for the Rothschilds at Warwick House, at the National Gallery in London, and for the British embassy in Paris.

At Wormsley the result of his extensive operations has been a very gentlemanly blend of comfort and understated opulence, together with a touch of the atmosphere you sometimes sense in great historic houses. The priceless carpets underfoot are very slightly worn. The new oak floors have been artificially distressed as if by generations of the feet of gentry. And the furniture, mostly found by Gibbs, manages to look as if it had arrived at Wormsley over the last 250 years.

PERHAPS the most interesting thing about this curious period when Wormsley and Paul Junior were being reinvented was how effortlessly he became accepted by the English upper classes.

This was something that his father had desperately wanted, having been infatuated with the English aristocracy, who were perfectly prepared to visit Sutton Place and eat his food and take his hospitality. But although intrigued by the old man and deeply fascinated by his money, the English upper classes never saw him as or remotely belonging to their own subspecies of humanity.

With Paul Junior it was different. Times had changed and his previous vices could be easily forgotten. In a way this seemed unfair, since until quite recently he had been exhibiting a much wider range of human failings than his father. But it is important to remember that while his father had become notorious for a particularly déclassé brand of stinginess, none of Paul's vices was particularly shocking to the British upper classes. Drink, drugs, marital carelessness, and being beastly to one's children are largely endemic to the English aristocracy, where they tend to be accepted on the grounds of eccentricity.

Paul had also made himself accepted through his love of cricket, which is widely taken as the purest proof of love for England. Indeed, at a time of faltering national self-confidence, there was something reassuring in the thought of this wealthy Californian taking England quite so seriously. His philanthropy also showed how genuinely he cared for his country of adoption, and there was a certain grandeur to his generosity. At a time when the native aristocracy had, by and large, abandoned the remotest interest in philanthropy, he was giving on a scale traditionally reserved for princes.

Another element in Paul's acceptance lay in Wormsley. Had the house revealed that fatal touch of Mammon as Sutton Place had done, he'd not have stood a chance. But because Wormsley was so understated and romantic, with the correct class connotations in the decor and the furniture, it could not be faulted. Nor, by association, could its owner.

One must remember, too, that at Wormsley Paul was indulging in a massive exercise in pure nostalgia, and attempting what the English aristocracy had been doing since the Reformation, but because of the expense can do no longer: creating a classic nobleman's establishment in its entirety, complete with its castle, its mansion with its pillared portico, its home farm, deer park, lake, and cricket pitch, together with one of the richest libraries in the country, crammed with treasures held in trust for future generations.

The final element in Paul's acceptance was the way that members of the royal family gave him their seal of personal approval. This had started when the queen awarded him his K.B.E., but in 1987 there came a setback in his royal progress, making one realize just how delicate was his recovery.

Early that May he was due to be presented with the prestigious National Arts Collection Fund's Art Benefactor of the Year Award by Prince Charles at a dinner at the Dorchester.

Paul had already shown that he was not averse to honors, but receiving them in public was a form of torture. On this occasion he was unable to go through with it and cried off, pleading toothache, shortly before he was due to arrive. Luckily, seventeen-year-old Tara was staying with him and, being commendably relaxed about such matters, collected the award for his father.

Three weeks later one more chance to meet another member of the royal family nearly failed as well. One of Gibbs's friends and neighbors, Lady Katherine Farrell, had invited him, Paul, and Victoria to a small luncheon party she was giving for her friend Queen Elizabeth the queen mother, whose curiosity had been aroused by what she'd heard about this strange American philanthropist. While Paul was waiting for the queen mother's arrival, panic overcame him, making him feel so unwell that he had to lie down in a room upstairs.

"Such a pity," said the queen mother when informed of Mr. Getty's indisposition, but, practical as ever, she added: "I suppose we'd better have a little something and begin without him."

Luckily Paul had recovered by the time the meal was over, and he was able to accompany the queen mother and show her Wormsley. Her Majesty was fascinated—by Paul as much as by his house—and they met later on a number of occasions.

LIKE almost everyone, Victoria fell in love with Wormsley, as did Tariq and Zain, her two children. Hardly surprisingly, her marriage to Mohammed Alatas wasn't working now that she was seeing Paul again. His health was improving, and the stronger and more confident he became, the happier he seemed when with Victoria.

Now in her mid-forties, she was still an elegant, rather nervous English beauty. As he was haunted by Talitha's memory, her role with Paul had never been particularly easy, and had been complicated by her diversionary marriages and romances. But by now she knew and understood him better than anyone, and he was particularly relaxed and comfortable in her company. He bought her a comfortable house in Chelsea, but for Victoria, Wormsley was the house that really mattered, and inevitably she became its chatelaine.

Rossetti had gone, except for his famous painting *Proserpine*, which hung in Paul's London flat like a souvenir from Cheyne Walk. Talitha's portrait by Willem Pol still hung in his dressing room. Queen's House itself would soon be sold to Gibbs's partner, Simon Sainsbury and his friend, Stewart Grimshaw.

Occasionally Paul would venture forth incognito into the world outside, sometimes bearded, sometimes not, and apparently enjoying the newfound freedom of his anonymity.

That autumn he spent £4 million buying *The Jezebel*, a wonderfully elegant motor yacht built in Germany before the war for the head of the Chrysler car company. He would spend more than twice as much again restoring her, and although she would lie for several years in lonely luxury on the River Dart, her presence was a promise of foreign lands and travel and a more exciting life around the corner.

It was as if his life was slowly starting up again after a massive interruption. Paul was building up an inner circle of extremely faithful friends. He was also rediscovering his past by bringing over some of the old members of "the Getty Gang" from San Francisco, like James Halligan and John Mallen, and having them to stay at Wormsley.

Among his children, there seemed to be surprisingly little bitterness about the past. Tara was particularly relaxed and seemed to have inherited his mother's happy nature. Although devoted to the Pols and spending much of his time with them in France, he was also seeing more of his father now, and got along well with him and with Victoria just as he got along well with almost everyone. The two daughters had remained in California, (Ariadne would marry the actor Justin Williams in 1992). Paul was hoping to see his daughters at Wormsley in the near future.

As far as the family's future was concerned, the most important of Paul's children was turning out to be his second son, Mark. Realizing how important the control and direction of the family finances would inevitably become, Mark decided on a career in high finance. Because of this he had taken Domitilla to New York, and had landed a job with the banking house of Kidder Peabody & Company. He admits that "the fact that they'd recently made $15 million out of the sale of Getty Oil might have helped."

In 1982 Mark and Domitilla had a son; wanting a name that sounded equally good in English or Italian, and thinking there had possibly been sufficient Pauls in the family, they called him Alexander. But they disliked the idea of bringing up a family in New York and, wanting to be nearer to Italy, moved to London, where once again Mark didn't find it difficult to get a job, this time with the influential merchant bank of Hambro's.

The only person who was none too pleased by this was Mark's father, who wanted him to return to Oxford to finish his degree (something he had never done himself). "For someone who has been so unconventional himself, he was getting very conventional about it all," says Mark, who as a married man was not particularly eager to become an undergraduate again. Largely to please his father, he did return, earned a degree in philosophy and politics, and then returned to Hambro's.

But the more he learned of banking and finance, the more concerned he was becoming for the future of the family. It was clearly going to be of great importance how the Getty resources were managed as the rest of his generation grew to adulthood; and what particularly concerned him was the human problem of avoiding the misery and wastage he had witnessed in the past.

Already he was becoming something of a bridge between the different sides and generations of the family. He had remained extremely close to his uncle Gordon and his cousins in San Francisco, and also with Uncle Ronald's eldest son, Christopher. He remained as devoted as ever to his mother. Two more sons were born—Joseph in 1986 and Julius two years later—and Mark was happiest when staying with his own small family at his childhood home in Orgia.

After the bitterness and battles of the past, what he wanted most was peace among the Gettys so that his children could grow up unscarred and unaffected by the past and free to make the most of all they would finally inherit.

For him the Christmas of 1987 was a very special one. At Wormsley the covered pool had now been built beside New Gardens Cottage, so that everything was ready when his brother, Paul, and his nurses flew in from California to join the family for Christmas. Paul was still paralyzed and his speech and sight remained impaired, but he had now transformed himself from the hopeless, totally dependent invalid he had been in the aftermath of his coma. Mark had not seen him so optimistic or so full of life for many years.

Paul had made up his mind to live as if his disabilities didn't matter—and to an extraordinary degree he had succeeded. He had recently been taking classes in English literature and history at Pepperdine University, the school he had flunked out of before his coma. Once a week he attended classes at the university, and one of his nurses made tapes of texts for him and interpreted his answers for his tutor.

He loved concerts and the cinema, and had made himself something of an expert on San Francisco restaurants. He had even started skiing once again, strapped to a metal frame on skis, with a ski instructor fore and aft. He dreamed of someday returning to Orgia.

In the meantime, in preparation for the Wormsley Christmas, Gail had arrived, and was delighted to be with her sons and her grandson, Alexander. Remembering how hopeless her son Paul had seemed after the coma, at times she still found it hard to believe all that he'd accomplished. The recovery of her ex-husband, Paul Junior, was almost as miraculous in its way, and she was glad to see him happy and relaxed at last—and able to enjoy a traditional English Christmas in his own home. He was now fifty-five and it seemed as if the family's troubles could be over. But even then the past could not be so easily evaded.

CHAPTER TWENTY-THREE

Aileen

TOWARD the end of 1985, Elizabeth Taylor, as president of the American Foundation for AIDS Research, had gone to Paris on a short fund-raising trip. Earlier that year her daughter-in-law, Aileen, had finally given birth to a son, Andrew. Afterward she had been seriously depressed; thinking that a holiday in France would do her good, Elizabeth decided to take her along.

For Aileen the holiday became more of a nightmare than a treat. The constant discussion of AIDS made her suddenly aware of risks that she had taken in the past. There were things that she would rather have forgotten. After a sleepless night in her hotel, she told Elizabeth that she might well be HIV-positive herself.

As something of an expert on the dread disease, Elizabeth did her best to reassure her daughter-in-law, but the blood tests Aileen took on returning to America proved positive. It was like a sick joke. Apparently the daughter-in-law of the president of the American Foundation for AIDS Research was in danger of developing AIDS herself.

After the first shock of the discovery, Elizabeth was the only person able to comfort the terrified Aileen, who seemed to dread other people knowing as much as she dreaded dying. She clung to Elizabeth pathetically, and to help her start the painful process of adjusting to the situation, Elizabeth let her stay in the privacy of her Bel Air mansion. Aileen's fears were worst at night, and the star would calm her terror by letting her share her bed.

For Elizabeth the situation was complicated by the fact that Aileen was mother to her two grandchildren (Aileen and Christopher had already adopted a son called Caleb before Andrew was born), and that her problems didn't end with being HIV-positive. The illness was in fact the culmination of a series of dramas and disasters in her private life.

*

AILEEN had become the last of the sacrificial children, the latest victim of the great fortune. She was extremely pretty, with her heart-shaped face, her nervous manner, and enormous dark-brown eyes; but she was also flighty, and the combination gave the impression of a nervous animal about to bolt, like a faun on speed. For several years she had been increasingly desperate and depressed, and had seemed heading for disaster.

Her fate still mystifies her brother Mark: "One could have expected my brother Paul to have broken up, but not Aileen, who always seemed the liveliest and best-adjusted of the children. She seemed so full of life, and had so much going for her. Perhaps she just wanted everything too quickly and grew up much too fast as a result."

As usual in such situations, it is difficult to know exactly where her troubles started. Aileen has claimed that her insecurities began when her parents parted. She has also said that her rebelliousness started after her brother's kidnapping when she learned to distrust the Getty family, fearing that it would destroy her and isolate her from reality.

"I see money as a toxic element," she said. "I think it separates those with it from knowing what it's like to be without it. This takes much that is important out of life." More to the point perhaps, she could see the trouble which the Getty money had brought to those she loved: the difficulties of her parents, the horror of her brother's kidnaping, and the suspicion and unease that she, like many of the children of the very rich, had learned to adopt against the world around them.

Even in England, during her time at Hatchlands, Aileen was already starting to reject what she saw as the obligations of "being a Getty." But it was not until she returned to California that she became a full-time rebel. As a rebel, she could go with unsuitable companions if she felt like it, sleep with them, drink with them, and take drugs with them. Above all she could assert the one thing Gettydom denied her: freedom.

There was no shortage of drugs or sex in California in the middle to late 1970s, and she used them as weapons in her battle to be free. The drug she turned to was that favorite standby of the famous and the rich, which can become the most insidious of all—cocaine.

She had clearly inherited a strongly addictive nature, sniffing cocaine in such quantities that by the time she was in her early twenties her nose required medical treatment. By then drugs were giving her what she called emotional overload—principally, horrendous panic attacks and sleeplessness. By the time she "eloped" with Christopher, she had already had the first of several nervous breakdowns.

Marriage to Christopher, far from sorting out her problems, helped to make them worse. Part of the trouble was her husband's kindness. He was a gentle man who happened to be in love with her. Cocaine addicts can react cruelly to those who love them, and Aileen's mood swings made their existence a misery and normal married life impossible.

Overshadowed since childhood by a mother who was one of the most famous women in America, Christopher was hardly likely to stand up to a character as strong as Aileen. With nothing particular to do with their lives, they first tried gold prospecting, then photography, neither of which succeeded.

Aileen had several miscarriages, followed by further periods of deep depression, during one of which she vanished to New York for several weeks. On her return she had a full-scale nervous breakdown requiring electric-shock therapy.

Soon, as a friend remembers, "Christopher was getting sick of acting as a nurse to Aileen"—and of overlooking her absences. In a last attempt to save the marriage, they adopted Caleb; as often happens, no sooner had they done so than Aileen discovered she was having a baby of her own. Their son Andrew was born early in 1985. Eight months later Aileen was sobbing out her fears to Elizabeth Taylor in Paris.

AILEEN has a strong touch of drama in her makeup. After the initial shock of discovering she was HIV-positive, and knowing she could not remain with Elizabeth indefinitely, she fled once more to New York, where she tried to lose herself in drink and drugs on the Manhattan nightclub circuit. Dangerously self-destructive, she was taking what she calls "extreme measures to deal with an extreme situation," and adds that "funnily enough, I thought it would be more acceptable—this shows how unacceptable the virus was—if I died now of an overdose."

But Aileen didn't die. Instead, she returned to Los Angeles, where the two children were waiting for her. Christopher was talking of divorce. And there was, of course, one further problem, her greatest fear. Thankfully blood tests showed that baby Andrew was uninfected by the virus.

For a time she tried confining the truth about her illness to Christopher, Elizabeth, and herself, and said nothing about it to the rest of her family. They were finding it increasingly difficult to help her while she was on cocaine, and were hoping she would reach a crisis point from which she could finally be cured of her addiction.

She underwent several cures, without success. And when her family were starting to despair of her, she broke the news to them that she might well be getting AIDS as well.

What particularly upset her was the contrast between Elizabeth Taylor's instant warm reaction to her plight, and what she felt was cold indifference from those who should have loved her.

"When I told Elizabeth, she had just cried and cried—and when she hugged me I could feel she was giving me something special." But there were no hugs for Aileen from the family, and she bitterly complained that "no one in my family spared a tear for me."

She was exaggerating, as she often did. Gail was desperately worried about her, as was her sister, Ariadne. The fact was that, after so many recent tragedies, most of the family was finding it hard to face another—particularly one involving Aileen. They had heard too much about her troubles in the past. As Martine said, "Aileen had a long history of drug abuse. So at first everybody thought she'd made it up— or just didn't want to believe it."

Besides which, AIDS was so terrifying that, as Gail admits, she wanted to "shy away" when Aileen first informed her that she was HIV-positive. The real problem was that at this stage almost everything to do with AIDS was something of a mystery, particularly as the disease affected women, who still formed a small, virtually unresearched minority of its victims.

Trying to find out what was really wrong with Aileen, Gail asked her doctors, but none would say, on the grounds of her right to privacy; they refused to discuss anything to do with AIDS in even the most general terms. "It can be a hideous thing trying to comfort somebody who thinks they're dying, when you can't even get the truth of what they're suffering from," says Gail.

Elizabeth Taylor, on the other hand, as head of an AIDS charity, and having recently seen her friend Rock Hudson die of it, knew exactly how to deal with the situation; also, as an actress, she was able to give Aileen the sort of emotional reaction she wanted. The Gettys couldn't. Only when Gail found a sympathetic doctor who calmly and unemotionally explained the facts about her daughter's illness could she and other members of the family start to come to terms with what had happened.

THE news was kept from Paul Junior as long as possible, but finally he had to know. When he did, he became disconsolate, as those who knew him had predicted. All the old tragedies revived, together with the inevitable guilt and bitterness dating back to the divorce and even earlier. Would unhappiness never end?

Feeling he needed to talk things over with his oldest friend, but really needing consolation and reassurance, he asked Bill Newsom to fly over to discuss Aileen with him.

The worst thing was that there was little to be done, except to wait. In contrast with young Paul's situation, with Aileen the Getty money could make little difference. And once again there was the uneasy feeling that in some strange way the disaster was connected with a primal flaw within the family, and the chain of continuing unhappiness which seemed to follow them.

The one thing Paul could do was to see Aileen again. He had to see her, and not long afterward, Bill brought her over. Thus illness and the threat of death had reunited yet another section of the family.

IT was hard to see that Aileen had a great deal left to live for after Christopher Wilding divorced her and remarried in 1987, taking the children with him. Elizabeth Taylor, whom she called Mom (Gail was "Mummy") continued to offer personal support, but wisely refused to be involved when Christopher gained custody of the children.

That loss hit Aileen badly. She was desperate, and it was hard to tell which would get her first, AIDS or her drug addiction. She was always in and out of clinics, trying to be cured but not succeeding. Then, at the end of 1988, she suddenly informed her family that she had met the man she wished to marry. He was a good-looking young man whom she had met in her rehabilitation clinic. Gail advised caution. "What's the hurry, and why marry straight away? Take your time."

Aileen, impetuous as ever, insisted she was free of drugs and had set her heart on the marriage, which took place soon afterward at the Monte Cedro Ranch near Gail's home in Santa Barbara. Gail, Ariadne, and Martine attended, together with patients from the rehabilitation clinic. Afterward Aileen and her husband left on a three-week honeymoon.

The day after they returned from their honeymoon, a friend of Aileen's stopped by their apartment and was alarmed to find her lying on the bed unconscious. Aileen was rushed by ambulance to the hospital, and suspecting a bad overdose of drugs, her stomach was pumped out.

Gail arrived as she was coming around; the doctor said he was horrified by the sheer quantity of drugs that Aileen had taken.

It was soon after this that Aileen's second marriage ended.

IN contrast with Paul Junior's family, Gordon and Ann enjoyed reasonably untroubled relations with their children, for which they were profoundly grateful. Peter had just left college, where he had won a prize for a play he'd written. Having had it published, he was hoping to become a playwright. His brother Bill was enjoying a year at the university in Florence. Gordon remained an easygoing father, and all his sons were very much California boys—relaxed and amusing, and not really interested in living anywhere but San Francisco. This suited Gordon.

He always said how much he'd love the excitement of another major business deal. In retrospect he felt he had enjoyed the drama of the sale of Getty Oil, even the sleepless nights, the lawsuits, and the need to cope with all those possible disasters. It had been Gordon's time of living dangerously.

When he did find himself involved in another business deal, it rarely seemed to work; it was clear that his coup with Getty Oil would never be repeated. On the other hand, his own creative work was flourishing. The series of songs on the theme of Falstaff that the Globe Theatre had commissioned had grown into a full-scale opera entitled *Plump Jack*, which received its first performance in 1989. Some critics liked it; others didn't; and, as with all Gordon's work, the reception almost certainly received the attention it did because he was so extremely rich.

But Gordon's enthusiasm was unbounded, and at times he could hardly believe he'd done it. Hearing his own music professionally performed was more exciting than the sale of Getty Oil. One day perhaps the name Getty might really be remembered more for music than for money.

He was also excited by the economic theories he had been working on long before the sale of Getty Oil, and which, like Gordon himself, could be regarded as eccentric or as highly original, depending on one's point of view. The first, on which he worked for several years, was a brave attempt to apply his interest in biology to economics. Starting from the proposition that the market operates upon economies much as natural selection does upon a species, he worked out a complex theory to account for the way this functioned.

The result, which he published in 1988 under the title *The Hunt for R* ("R" being the rate of return on an investment), is a highly esoteric exercise in economic theory calculated to scare off all but the most highly qualified of professional economists by the sheer complexity of its mathematics alone. This may account for its lack of impact so far in the rarefied world of higher economic theory.

Gordon was also trying to devise an answer to a more pressing economic problem: inflation. Starting from the obvious fact that inflation tends to follow an increase in the supply of money, he began wondering

if some other form of "money" could be found which would not automatically fuel inflation in this way.

He reasoned that if only money could be made to have the same rate
of return as that on other investments, an increase in its supply need
not automatically raise inflation, for the simple reason that people
would rather hold on to it than spend it. Even as he said this, Gordon
realized that a sort of interest-bearing "money" exists already, in the
form of units in mutual funds; and his proposal, developed at length
in the article "Fertile Money," published in 1992, was that funds of this
sort could easily become a form of currency, and that if only govern-
ments adopted Gordon's ideas, inflation could be cured.

In the real world, as opposed to the worlds of opera and of economic
theory, the only apparent setback encountered by the thrice-blessed
Gordon and Ann Getty at this time involved Ann's New York ventures
following the sale of Getty Oil. It was becoming clear that they weren't
working—and never would. Gossip had inevitably started—and back-
biting and reproach, as Ann's publishing career was clearly not going
anywhere.

She had originally thought that her son Peter might be interested,
and one day even take over the enterprise. But although he, like his
brothers, had literary ambitions, Peter wasn't driven.

It was unfortunate that Grove Weidenfeld was showing signs of becoming a failure. Losing money makes the rich nervous, as they sense
the fragile nature of their great possessions.

The situation of the publishing house inevitably meant the end of
all the exciting ideas that Ann and Weidenfeld had so enjoyed dis-
cussing, and that now would have to remain just ideas—her precious
Wheatland Foundation, the projected glossy magazine on the arts, the
sponsored performances of great operas, and the conferences for writers and intellectuals: all might-have-beens, as was the role she once
envisaged for herself as a figure in the world of art and literature.

The sad truth was that for all the dinners she had hosted, all the
advances she had funded, for all the discussions, conferences, committee meetings she had attended, the publishing house had not produced
one genuine best-seller.

Barney Rosset, working for years on the literary equivalent of a
shoestring, had published success after undeniable success. He was like
a virtuso gardener, with publishing's equivalent of the greenest of green
fingers. Barney had had the knack. Ann had only had the money.

Ann seemed to bear out the truth of Scott Fitzgerald's famous dictum
about the rich being different—but in a way he'd not intended. The

very rich, like Ann, are different because money deprives them of a role—except the role of being very rich, which keeps them from being taken seriously in any other way. They are flattered and indulged, but things they undertake can have a way of ending badly.

Having lost an estimated $15 million on Grove Weidenfeld, the Gettys tried to sell it, but, finding no adequate offers, left it in a state of suspended animation. And the whole affair had left behind a sour taste among many of the people Ann had wanted to impress.

Harry Evans, former editor of the London *Sunday Times*, had worked as an adviser to the company before becoming president of Random House. He felt bitter at the way the whole affair was handled. "I didn't like the rich picking up a publishing house like a plaything, and then dropping it when they got bored. It's part of the vast carelessness of the rich. It's something maybe money does to people. They just get a little casual."

Casual or not, Ann returned gratefully to San Francisco, where she licked her wounds and started at the University of California as an ordinary student majoring in chemistry. Weidenfeld once described her as "a perpetual student." (So, in his way, was Gordon. Out of interest he once spent a few weeks studying the university physics textbook by Halliday and Resnick, took the first-year undergraduate physics exam at Berkeley, and passed.)

Ann had also been fascinated by prehistory ever since Gordon backed Richard Leakey's researches into the origins of man in Kenya. As well as studying chemistry, she also soon became involved in field research in Ethiopia under the direction of the anthropological archaeologist Professor Tim White. White was a colleague of Dr. Donald Johanson, who in 1974 found fame by discovering the fossilized remains of "Lucy," a 3.5-million-year-old female hominid, in a rocky site 100 miles northeast of Addis Ababa. Johanson believed Lucy to be the oldest human ancestor ever discovered. Subsequently, with a $15 million grant, Gordon had helped Johanson create the prestigious Institute of Human Origins at Berkeley. And Ann was currently hooked on Ethiopia and the prospect of discovering even older fossilized remains.

Soon her life was becoming one of bizarre contrasts: between the great house on Pacific Heights, together with her personal Boeing, which was being refitted at extraordinary cost—and the bleak valley in the Ethiopian hinterlands where she searched among acres of rock and shale for fossilized hominid remains. Life in Ethiopia was tough, amenities nonexistent, the climate dreadful, but Ann preferred it to New York.

*

THROUGHOUT this period, all three daughters of Gordon's brother George, were sticking firmly by their original decision to avoid the limelight. Given who they were, and how rich they had become, this was a considerable achievement. They refused to be interviewed or photographed in public. They avoided gossip and avoided scandal. "If you want a story, try my uncle Gordon. He enjoys publicity. We don't," said the second daughter, Claire, to one of the few reporters to reach her on the telephone. Even when Claire unexpectedly gave birth to a son in 1979—christened Beau Maurizio Getty-Mazzota—as the result of a love affair with an Italian she had met during a university program for foreigners at Perugia University, no further details reached the media.

The three girls also also kept their distance from the other branches of the family. Indeed, it was as if they could never quite forgive their relatives for what they saw as the betrayal of their grandfather's achievement by agreeing to the sale of Getty Oil. They would keep in touch with members of their grandfather's entourage, such as Penelope Kitson or Barbara Wallace; but when George's daughters were invited to Mark and Domitilla's wedding, the invitations went unanswered.

RONALD'S life continued to be ruled by his exclusion from the ever expanding Getty fortune, and it is only now that one can see the full extent of the damage this had caused him. By disinheriting him his father had made him a sort of exile—from the family and from life itself—and he was spending an increasing amount of time with his wife, Karin, and his four children in their house in South Africa. Ronald and the family enjoyed Cape Town. He loved the climate, while the countryside around the Cape was beautiful and free from all associations with a past that haunted him. In South Africa Ronald wasn't constantly reminded of what he'd lost in California.

The children went to school there, but Ronald's exclusion from the fortune was having its effect even on his relationship with them. There was always a subtle difference between himself and them: The children were destined to be included in the wider Getty family, from which it seemed that he would for ever be excluded.

Despite his efforts to ignore this, he could already detect a different attitude developing among them—particularly in Christopher, the eldest. He was a sturdy boy, shorter and less retiring than his father, and already he had that touch of confidence the certainty of money brings. At the age of twenty-five Christopher would become a paid trustee for the money that would one day come to him and his sisters—and that by rights should already have come to Ronald on his father's death.

But Ronald hadn't given up, and had decided that if he couldn't inherit what he felt was morally his due, he would try to earn it. He was thinking big, just as his father always had, and as part of his plan to make that elusive fortune, he invested in a company building a luxury hotel, the Raddison Manhattan Beach, close to Los Angeles Airport. The general partner, managing the company was a friend and he joined him as a nonexecutive partner.

It was a promising project, but by the early eighties there were problems. The California building boom had produced several other hotels in this once exclusive area, and when the recession followed, some went bankrupt. To prevent this happening with the Manhattan Beach, Ronald joined his three other partners to guarantee the debts. In spite of this the company finally collapsed as well.

Neither Ronald, nor the other partners could meet their guarantees, but because his name was Getty, Ronald was the one the creditors pursued for their money. When he discovered the astronomical sums for which he was liable, Ronald Getty's private nightmare started.

CHAPTER TWENTY-FOUR

Survivors

IF there was a curse upon the Gettys, it seemed to be lifting with the new decade in 1990. At last the old man's influence, which had brought such trouble in the past, was waning, and it was clear that Gordon— the least practical but most effective of his sons—had put an end, for good, to the conflict and litigation in the family when he divided up the Sarah C. Getty Trust. The sale of Getty Oil had more than doubled the combined resources of the Gettys. And by dismembering the trust and arranging for the young trustees to have an income, Gordon had done his best to ensure that the younger generation would have enough to keep them happy and to become involved in the work of their respective family trusts while they waited to inherit, probably fairly late in middle age.

At the same time, the great fortune that J. Paul Getty spent his life creating shows no sign of disappearing as have so many famous fortunes in the past. On the contrary, the way the separate trusts are structured guarantees that, with interest steadily accruing, and barring unforeseen accidents and revolutions, the capital will safely go on accumulating. As the younger members of the family start producing children of their own, the number of Getty heirs will also go on growing, but it is hard to imagine a situation in which the family will ever cease to be extremely wealthy.

Thus by 1990, the future was already looking rosy—at least financially—for the younger generation of Gettys. But what of those still suffering from past disasters?

IT was Aileen, possibly the most self-indulgent of the Getty casualties, who produced the bravest answer to her situation when it seemed most hopeless.

Early in 1990 came the first of the symptoms—in her case painful blisters in the mouth—signaling the onset of full-blown AIDS, and the doctors gave their verdict. With luck she might have six months more to live.

From Aileen this produced a reaction few expected. She was still terrified of dying and knew that she could not evade her fate, but Aileen the rebel started objecting to the way that she was being treated. It was bad enough having people pity her; what was worse was their refusal to address the subject of her illness, and she realized that she was being treated as a source of shame. This angered her, and out of her anger grew something that began to change her life. She says that AIDS gave her something positive to live for.

For a period she was very ill; her nervous system was affected, making it difficult to walk. Physically and emotionally she had always tended to be fragile. She fell a lot, and hurt herself, so that for days on end she had to stay in bed.

But one thing Aileen didn't lack was courage, and she refused to hide behind some bland denial of her situation: "What I wanted was to bring dignity to myself and to the disease." With this in mind, she openly admitted to the press that she was suffering from AIDS. Her family supported her, and with the Getty name—and Elizabeth Taylor—behind her, she gained maximum publicity for her fight "to give a human face to the AIDS plague for a world that didn't want to see it."

What particularly incensed her was the plight of other women sufferers in the United States, where women and children had recently become the fastest-growing segment of the population testing HIV-positive. So she made no secret of the true cause of her own infection—which was not a blood transfusion, as she originally stated, but "unprotected sex, out of fear of rejection" with someone she later discovered to have been HIV-positive. The point Aileen made was that however AIDS was contracted was irrelevant, and that all its victims should be treated like sufferers from any other major illness: with care and dignity. Thanks largely to her name—and to her natural sense of drama—Aileen became a powerful voice speaking out for female AIDS victims everywhere.

Soon she was on television pleading their cause. She worked with AIDS sufferers in Los Angeles. She visited and campaigned for them, and planned a special hospice for afflicted women. With her name and looks she was becoming something she had never been before: a national celebrity.

This brought the challenge of putting her personal life in order. She did her best to come off drugs, and having reestablished good relations with Christopher, who had now remarried and was living near her in Los Angeles, she was granted custody of her children four days a week.

Caleb was eight and Andrew seven, old enough to know what was happening; she was open with them, answering their questions as truthfully as possible. She told them about her illness and taught them how to cope with an emergency. Soon Caleb and Andrew were giving their mother the will to go on living—which, by a miracle, she has continued doing ever since.

Her life today is full, with her children and her work. Thanks to the Getty money she receives the best possible treatment—in her case so-called aggressive therapy, with the most powerful drugs available: the anti-HIV drug AZT and three other, separate antiviral drugs taken simultaneously. Along with this she has regained her self-respect through a cause she totally believes in. This, together with her willpower and determination, has clearly played its part in her survival.

She has periods of relapse, but on good days is unusually pretty and serene. She counsels other women sufferers, works for them, and does all she can to publicize their plight and help them. She says she now has little fear of dying, and that for the first time in years she's happy.

Aileen's situation provides her with an answer, however desperate, to what she had long seen as a problem associated with large amounts of money: its tendency to isolate the very rich from normal life and ordinary people. In her case, as an AIDS victim, she has discovered a sense of genuine companionship with other sufferers.

In practical terms, her illness has had the effect of impoverishing her, by limiting her freedom and threatening to shorten her existence. But by concentrating all her interests and efforts on her struggle to survive, it has given her something in exchange—an overwhelming sense of purpose, and an urge to go on living.

DISASTER has had a similar effect on another of the Getty casualties, Aileen's brother Paul, who after the kidnaping was practically destroyed by misery and drink. But now those closest to him think that the effects of the coma, however cruel, may well have saved his life. Until stricken, he had been locked in a never-ending cycle of disaster through drink and drugs—"hanging," as Gail puts it, "above the abyss."

Now, like Aileen, Paul insists that he is happy, and his friends confirm this. As with Aileen, the fight against his disabilities has given him a total sense of purpose. His days are underpinned with Getty money, but anything he wants requires extraordinary effort, forcing him to do something else the very rich are normally excused from doing: struggle hard for his existence.

Willpower drives him forward, and each day has the constant slog of physiotherapy, along with exercises to improve his speech. The work is laborious and painful, but Paul has slowly grown stronger. Fourteen years after the coma, his speech is still improving, his stamina has increased, and he has even taught himself to stand upright with his nurses to assist him.

His real achievement is his resolution to live as if his handicaps did not exist. He regularly attends his favorite rock concerts; he loves restaurants; he keeps up-to-date with films and picture galleries; and by having many friends who read to him, he keeps abreast of contemporary fiction and the classics. With his team of nurses, he has devised routines for traveling. His cottage at Wormsley has become his base in England, and he stays there twice a year, including Christmas, which he usually spends with his father and the family. He is still planning to revisit Italy and Orgia, where Gail has been adapting the house to take him; but already he is telling her he'd rather stay in the center of the village where, as he puts it, "I can hang out with my old Italian friends."

His marriage with Martine (or, as she now calls herself, Gisela) ended in 1993, apparently amicably, and she returned to Germany, where she now runs a video company in Munich. They remain close friends, and speak regularly to each other on the telephone. He still falls in love as easily as ever, and has no lack of girl-friends who adore him.

Paul has continued to enjoy a close relationship with his son, Balthazar, who lives nearby in Los Angeles. Balthazar has inherited his father's old ambition to be an actor and ultimately a film director, and has had considerable success since appearing as a schoolboy actor in the film of William Golding's book *Lord of the Flies*, and with parts in films like *Young Guns II*, *The Pope Must Die*, and *Red Hot*. His half-sister, Anna, is currently at the Sorbonne, and also plans to be an actress. Recently Paul legally adopted her to make her one day eligible, like Balthazar, for her share of the Getty money.

For all the courage and resolve of victims like Paul and Aileen, the fact remains that these are human tragedies—ruined lives, which all the money in the world can only cushion. The rest of the family will forget them at their peril.

Another of the family casualties—but of a very different kind—was their uncle Ronald, who by the early 1990s was facing total ruin as a result of the debts incurred building the hotel in Los Angeles. He had been naïve and far too trusting; now he was suffering accordingly. The company's creditors were remorselessly pursuing him, and no one seemed capable of resolving anything—least of all the lawyers, who seemed to think that because his name was Getty he was made of money. In fact, by now the unfortunate Ronald had lost his home in South Africa and had few friends left and no resources.

One bright spot on a fairly bleak horizon was provided by his eldest daughter, Stephanie, who would shortly marry Alexander Weibel, son of prosperous Austrian textile manufacturer. Both Ronald and his wife would find some consolation for their troubles by staying with the hospitable Weibels in their house in Austria.

In 1993 their son, Christopher, would make an even more resounding marriage—to Pia Miller, daughter of one of the richest men in America, Robert Miller, who had made a fortune out of duty-free franchises. Neither Ronald and his wife, nor their daughters, was at the wedding.

DURING this period, the family's star survivor continued to be its most unlikely candidate for redemption, Paul Junior, who had all but completed his transformation from the sick, reclusive victim of the counterculture into a respected, cricket-obsessed, oddly conventional pillar of the establishment.

What he had done was quite extraordinary. It's rare enough to inherit a fortune as immense as his in middle age. It's rarer still to do so when you're a drug-addicted bibliophile with a passion for the cinema and for high-Romantic nineteenth-century art and literature. Like a clever film director, Paul had created for himself an intricate new role through his philanthropy, and had followed this by building wonderfully romantic scenery for himself, his family, and his friends at Wormsley.

When you can buy anything you end up buying dreams, and Paul's dreams seemed oddly reminiscent of a number of recurrent nineteenth-century Romantic episodes in which rich unhappy men spent large amounts of money escaping from their sense of doom into magical worlds of private fantasy.

The most obvious parallels were with the rich, reclusive writer William Beckford, who fled unhappiness and scandal by building his medieval palace, Fonthill Abbey (not all that far from Wormsley) in the early nineteenth century, and with doomed King Ludwig of Bavaria, seeking salvation in the dreamlike castles he built in the mountains outside Munich in the 1890s. A more interesting model may have been the hero of Jules Verne's novel *20,000 Leagues Under the Sea*: the mysterious, immensely rich Captain Nemo. Like Paul Junior, Nemo was a music-lover, a recluse and a would-be oceanographer; he used his fortune to construct an enormous submarine the *Nautilus*, in which he sailed away from the world and its troubles, finding tranquility by playing the organ to himself in the vast depths of the ocean.

From the beginning, Wormsley had a touch of the same surrealist escapist fantasy, but thanks largely to his family and to friends as practical as Gibbs and as devoted as Victoria, the air of doom around Paul Junior was kept at bay, and the whole strange multimillion-dollar enterprise was working. Paul Junior was beginning to enjoy his life at last.

He was no longer quite as rich as he had been when interest rates were going through the ceiling in the early 1980s, and having given away nearly $150 million, he now required his income to sustain his building projects and his way of life. This meant that his time of spectacular philanthropy was over; most of his current giving was limited to income from the £20 million charitable trust set up in 1985. It was carefully disbursed and economically administered.

Paul himself was increasingly enjoying life from his flat in London, where he spent the week. Victoria would arrive there from her Chelsea home each morning, act as his devoted companion through the day, and stay as late as she was needed before returning to Chelsea and her children. She was an excellent hostess, and largely thanks to her, Paul's steadily increasing circle of friends included film stars like Michael Caine, writers like John Mortimer and the poet Christopher Logue, and a rich connoisseur collector like Lord Rothschild. Paul was even beginning to be seen at one of London's most exclusive dining clubs—Pratt's (proprietor the Duke of Devonshire), of which he had recently become a member.

But it was at Wormsley that Paul relaxed and became positively benign. Here, the former recluse who once had rarely seen his own children had become an admirable father figure for Victoria's two sons, Tariq and Zain. He loved the countryside, was particularly proud of his herd of traditional English long-horned cattle and even remembered enough of his William Morrisite ideals to promise one day to establish a colony of happy bookbinders on the estate. Often he would show friends something from his great collection of historic movies in his private cinema, or play them rare recordings (such as Robert Browning reading his poetry or Oscar Wilde declaiming) from his equally great collection of historic records. At Wormsley it was hard to see how boredom could afflict him.

Yet in spite of all his current blessings, Paul Junior like a true Romantic hero, seemed fated never to discover lasting happiness. His private trip to hell was over, but the scorch marks seemed to set him noticeably apart from those around him: His middle years had been wasted, lost in the oubliette of drugs forever; two of his children had been practically destroyed by the same affliction; and he would always be a semi-invalid, condemned to live his life at one remove from everyday reality.

Nor did it seem that he could ever totally escape the death of Talitha, any more than devoted Victoria could take her place. For Talitha's beauty was unchanging. These were areas where his money could not enter, and it seemed that Talitha would always haunt him, unattainable and beautiful and young forever.

MEANWHILE, from his Italianate mansion on Pacific Heights in San Francisco, Gordon was offering the family his personal example of how to stay sane and happy with a fortune of a billion dollars.

Unlike his brother, Gordon appeared curiously untouched by time or trouble. He was in his late fifties now—his looks had actually improved with age—but he was still essentially the same gangling would-be professor who forgot where he had parked his car, the same dedicated artist who would rather be remembered for an opera than a major fortune.

Although on the surface he appeared to treat his money as a slightly tedious irrelevance, this was really not the case at all. Gordon possessed a deep appreciation of the stuff, and in particular of the benefits that it bestowed.

Foremost among them was the privilege of being Gordon Getty. One of the true advantages of very large amounts of money is the right to please oneself over almost everything—and Gordon did. He could travel as and when and where he wanted in the family Boeing 727. (When he purchased a new one, the man who did the interior decoration explained: "It's the family station wagon in terms of use.")

He could also work at whatever he desired. Since he was a workaholic, work was Gordon's greatest luxury, and it was only large amounts of money that allowed him to indulge it as he did. Most days still saw him in his study, slaving over his music or his latest economic theory. "As far as work's concerned, it's pretty much sunrise to sunset," he said.

The most important aspect of Gordon's wealth was its effect upon his personality. Thanks to his wealth, absolutely nothing ever seemed to faze him. He had always been a man who pleased himself, and his fortune seemed to free him from the jealousies and insecurities that afflict so many people out of simple lack of money.

When a journalist was unmannerly enough to suggest that he was "simply an artistic Walter Mitty," Gordon laughed and cheerfully agreed.

"Of course I am. I'm Don Quixote."

And if other economists ignored his economic theories, he laughed again. "They'll come around to accepting them in the end," was all he said. "They'll have to."

As a businessman he had to rest content with his reputation as the man who had doubled the value of the Getty fortune, for few of his subsequent business ventures succeeded. In March 1990 the Emhart industrial products corporation of Connecticut rejected a $2 billion takeover bid that Gordon tried to put together, and a month later Avon Products was trying to sue him over another hostile takeover.

But business setbacks only made him more ambitious to succeed as a composer. Much of his time was spent "polishing and perfecting" his opera, *Plump Jack*; he found composing harder work than making money. As he put it, "There is no such person as a lazy composer"; his opera was virtually a full-time occupation.

By now Gordon was becoming a strangely lovable eccentric, and his real contribution to the Gettys was something they had always needed: concern and a touch of easygoing common sense from an older member of the family. Whenever he was in Los Angeles, Gordon would always make a point of visiting young Paul and Aileen, and Mark was always staying with his San Francisco cousins when he visited California.

For families to function properly, their members need to like each other—and Uncle Gordon, with his extraordinary laugh, his latest pet enthusiasm, and his slighly rumpled sense of humor, was becoming an increasingly important source of family affection and belonging.

Hardly surprisingly, this showed most clearly in his own immediate family; in their different ways all his sons had turned out somewhat like him. All were intelligent, original, rather private individuals. And while remaining very Californian and relaxed about life in general, all four of them had stayed immune to the Getty self-destructive streak that brought such havoc to other members of the family. So far they had been living undemanding lives as bright young men of independent means, able to please themselves about their future.

The eldest, Peter, was particularly like his father, to the point of even looking like him and trying to find fame as a composer—although it's hard to imagine Gordon composing music for the pop group his son had founded and named Virgin-Whore Complex.

Peter's brother Andrew was trying to write scripts for Hollywood; Bill was on his way to becoming a Greek scholar who would opt for postgraduate research on Homer at the University of California at

Berkeley. Only John, the noisy one of the family, would cause his parents serious worry when he left for San Diego, got himself tattooed, and joined a heavy rock group. But even he finally enrolled at the University of California at Berkeley and ended up researching his father's heroine, Emily Dickinson.

As a rich boys' hobby, all four brothers jointly financed an upscale wine shop in San Francisco, and as a measure of family solidarity they asked their father if they could name it after his opera.

"Well, I won't sue you if you do," said Gordon.

So they called their shop Plump Jack. Under the management of Bill Newsom's son, Gavin, Plump Jack would start to build up one of the most interesting and reasonably priced wine lists along the coast. It would also help to launch the previously abstemious Gordon onto a new enthusiasm: vintage wine. Being scholarly and rich and surprisingly thirsty, Gordon soon became a most knowledgeable connoisseur.

In the longer term, something more than an interest in wine and a wine shop will be needed to engage the full-time interests of the younger Gettys—which is why Paul Junior's son Mark seems destined for an important role within the family. Having personally witnessed so much past unhappiness, and with three young children of his own, he is quietly determined to do all he can to prevent the troubles of the past recurring.

Not that he talks about this much. Now in his mid-thirties, Mark has a certain wariness, and for all his quiet charm and easy going diffidence, he is difficult to place. Studying philosophy at Oxford may have given him his air of rather cool detachment.

In fact the coolness is deceptive, for Mark is very serious about the family. This shows in his behavior whenever his brother Paul arrives in London. Mark is always on hand to help him, look after him, and search out the sort of places and events he guesses will amuse him. Mark has also made himself the family's unofficial peacemaker and reuniter. He stays on warm terms with his father, and is devoted as ever to his uncle Gordon, who refers to him as "virtually another son."

If there is a key to Mark's character it probably lies in Italy rather than among the Gettys. People often forget that he was born in Rome; marriage to Domitilla has strengthened his ties with Italy. For some years he has owned a house near Orgia, and it is in Tuscany that he spends his holidays, keeps the horses which he races in the Siena Palios (the historic races around the city square), and he likes to hear his sons speaking Italian and playing in the village where he used to play himself.

He still has friends there. Remo's truck-driver son, Francesco, is godfather to his eldest boy, Alexander, and Mark admits the influence these country people have always had on him. Over the years they helped him reach certain conclusions that were not apparent to the Gettys.

The first grew out of the importance the villagers attached to skill and work well done. "After all," says Mark, "whoever you are, your work is the most important thing you do. It helps define you and make you what you are."

The second article of faith he absorbed from the villagers concerned the prime importance of the family. At the time of the kidnaping, when Mark's own family, for all its wealth, virtually fell apart, he could see examples of the way Italian families seemed to offer consolation and support to all their members. Later, in economic terms, he would also see how the Italian family still provides Italy with its basic and its most dynamic business structure. When Mark married and became the first Getty of his generation to have to earn a living outside the family, what he had learned in Italy gave him food for thought.

By the time he was twenty-five, as a salaried trustee of his father's Cheyne Walk Trust he was already involved in the investment policy for a fund currently standing at around $1.2 billion dollars; and by his early thirties his banking experience was giving him an increasingly important role within the family. Since then he has worked closely with Gordon on family financial policy, and he currently runs Getty Investment Holdings. His cousin Christopher recently joined its board.

But Mark was still worried by the thought of the family's troubles returning, and concern for its future made him study how some of America's richest dynasties survived and prospered. What he learned confirmed much of what he'd learned already in his village in Italy.

The Rockefellers particularly impressed him with the way they managed to remain "a flourishing, dynamic entity," in which different members of the family appeared to have a place. To discover the secret, he spent some time at Rockefeller Center in New York, studying the organization the Rockefellers created after the sale of Standard Oil to manage their investments and business interests, and to offer something of a niche for any member of the family who wanted it. The head of the family, David Rockefeller, told him from his own experience that any member of the family who was left out "tended to become a problem."

The way the Rockefellers had organized themselves helped convince Mark that there was no inevitable decline and fall facing his own family. On the contrary, it seemed as if the younger Gettys might well benefit from much the same advantages as the Rockefellers, provided that their elders were prepared to help them. Mark felt that what was needed was a sense of family identity and purpose, along with that magical activity which was as important to the rich as to the poor: the chance to work together.

In 1990, while still at Hambro's, he organized a Getty family investment in South Africa in an attempt to involve them together for the first time in a cooperative venture. He persuaded the three separate family trusts to make what by Getty standards was a fairly modest joint investment of $5 million in the South African–based Conservation Corporation, which owns the famous Londolozi game reserve in Natal and the Phinda reserve in Zululand. This was a glamorous project, started by the visionary conservationist David Varty, who planned to turn Londolozi into the finest game reserve in Africa.

As there were few foreign investments in South Africa at the time, Mark made sure he had the full approval of the African National Congress as well as of the South African government. With majority rule still some way off, the Getty investment was seen as a risky and idealistic gesture; and the corporation has since been cited by President Nelson Mandela himself as a model of how to integrate international tourism with the needs of animals and the local population. (Mandela has stayed at Londolozi on several occasions.)

Mark denies that idealism played much part in his decision to invest in Africa, and says that his real objective was to help unite his family by using their talents and resources and arousing their enthusiasm.

When his uncle Gordon came to Londolozi together with Bill Newsom, his son Peter, and Ronald's son, Christopher, they were soon excited and particularly impressed by Varty and the corporation's various locations. Later Mark's half-brother, Talitha's son, Tara, was to work there. But for Mark himself involvement in a game reserve, however exciting, is not a big enough challenge to involve the energies and enthusiasm of the Gettys.

"Frankly," he says, "I don't see a future for us in the hotel and tourist business."

He was seeking something altogether more demanding. Backed by his father and Gordon, he has been evolving what he calls "a coherent strategy" between the majority of the trusts to spend £30 million to £40 million at a time buying a number of related companies with long-term prospects for growth. The first of these acquisitions has been the £30 million purchase of an 80 percent holding in Tony Stone Images, a leading international nonnews photo library, with 30,000 color images for use by magazines and advertising agencies for average fees of £400 a sale. With his partner Jonathan Klein, Mark is joint chairman of

T.S.I. While he is confident that his company will continue to expand, he explains that the primary purpose of this strategy is to "focus family interest and expertise in one area of investment, as happened when we still owned Getty Oil," and not necessarily to provide employment for future members of the family. However, he is quick to add that he can think of "few things more exciting than working in one's own family company," and he remains convinced that "a family business is potentially the most dynamic organisation in existence—provided the family has enthusiastic members who will work for it, a reliable source of family capital, and a common purpose and identity."

By taking his long-term view, Mark is planning to harness the financial resources of the Getty trusts and thus begin to build the sort of genuine Getty dynasty that J. Paul Getty talked so much about but never understood.

As Mark puts it, "Most of our troubles originated with my grandfather, who didn't understand families or what made them tick. Come to that, he never really understood people. It's time we did."

THE year 1992 was important for the Gettys and for Paul Junior in particular. That September he would be sixty, and when the cricket season opened he resolved to celebrate the start of play on his new ground by staging something particularly close to his heart: the perfect game of cricket.

Country-house cricket was making a comeback at the time, with Prince Philip fielding a team at Windsor, and the Duke of Norfolk doing likewise on his private ground at Arundel. At the end of May, when Paul decided to follow suit at Wormsley, it is safe to say that not since Cecil Beaton staged the Ascot scene for *My Fair Lady* had a traditional English sport been staged with such precision and alarming dedication.

The setting was idyllic. The pitch had been nursed for months by Harry Brind, the chief groundsman from one of cricket's holy of holies, the Kennington Oval. The beechwoods were in leaf, and since W. G. Grace was captaining the great game in the sky, one of cricket's living legends, ninety-two-year-old Bob Wyatt, England's oldest surviving test captain, was there to ring the bell signaling the start of play.

Paul's team was captained by the most glamorous cricketer of the day, Imran Khan, captain of Pakistan; the visitors had been organized by no less a body than the MCC itself.

Paul was enjoying one of the most enviable privileges of the very rich, that of turning an elaborate dream into reality. Since a dream demands perfection, he had taken endless trouble, even asking continual advice from a friend, the doyen of cricket commentators, the late and much lamented Brian Johnston. Everything had to be totally authentic in a world that prides itself on authenticity—from the scorers and the sight screens by the pitch, to the neatly thatched pavilion and the right sort of sugar buns for tea. It goes without saying that the lunch was faultless—cold salmon and new potatoes, followed by summer pudding, with Pimm's or cool draft beer or very good champagne. The outcome of the game was faultless, too. The visitors won with a boundary hit in the last over.

A perfect lunch, a perfect day—but the man of the match was not a cricketer, but Paul himself, who had survived the disasters that had seemed inseparable from the Getty inheritance and had put on this occasion as if to celebrate his own salvation. He did it very stylishly and without saying a word, as is his nature. As he sat there, wearing his MCC tie and blazer, watching the game from his seat in his own pavilion, he was flanked by his two guests of honor. On his left sat a self-confessed cricket fanatic, the prime minister, John Major. And on his right and enjoying every minute of the game, was Elizabeth the queen mother.

FOR Paul it proved a splendid summer. The weather was indifferent, but cricket continued to the end of August. It was then that he told the cricket writer E. W. Swanton that 1992 had been "my happiest summer since I was a boy." And summer wasn't over.

When the cricket season ended he gave orders for the marquee to be taken down, but nobody took any notice. Used to having his orders obeyed, Paul complained to Victoria, but still nothing happened, and when he arrived from London for his birthday on September 7 he was annoyed to find the marquee still in place. It was bad enough turning sixty without having his orders deliberately flouted.

What Paul didn't realize was that for almost a year Mark had been planning a party for his birthday, and that instead of the small family affair Paul was expecting, Mark had secretly brought down more than sixty guests by bus from London.

Victoria, who was in on the secret, kept Paul in the house all morning; it was only when she took him for a stroll past the marquee at lunchtime that he saw what was happening. Inside, and waiting to wish him happy birthday, were many of his closest friends and relations, some of whom he hadn't seen for years. They had been brought from all around the world. There were friends from California and from Rome. There was a couple who had once sailed up the Thames and moored their yacht opposite his house on Cheyne Walk. There were some of his school friends from St. Ignatius. And sitting on his right at lunch there was even the woman who had once been closest to his father, the elegant Penelope.

At the sight of so many long-lost friends Paul was moved to tears. "I never realized," he said, "that so many people cared."

But there was more than this to the occasion. It was typical of Mark, with his eagerness to bring the family together, to have turned the party into an elaborate family reunion.

Apart from George's daughters, who were still keeping their distance, almost all the family was there. Aileen was well enough to have flown in from Los Angeles with Gail. Young Paul had also made the journey with his nurses, his sister Ariadne, and Ariadne's husband, Justin Williams. Ann had felt unable to leave her rocky valley in Ethiopia, where she was still digging for the fossilized remains of her oldest ancestor, but Gordon had flown over in the private Boeing, bringing their four boys, Peter, Andrew, John, and William.

The disinherited member of the family was not forgotten either; Mark had made a special point of inviting Ronald and his family. By now Ronald owed so much money that he had frankly no idea of what was going to happen. But the party took his mind off his troubles, and after so many years of bitterness and rejection he was reunited with his brothers. So it was an emotional moment for him as well as for his brother Paul.

"It was," he says, "like entering the family at last."

What does one give a billionaire with everything? In Siena Gail had found an antique silver-and-ivory letter opener with a handle in the shape of a tortoise which she thought appropriate. Bill Newsom had brought a yellow taxi driver's hat from San Francisco. Penelope had found a Chelsea enamel box with a picture of a cricketer, and Christopher Gibbs a rare volume by the great Whig politician Charles James Fox. It was entitled *On Wind*, and subtitled *A Treatise on Farting*.

But it was not until lunch was cleared and the birthday speeches were over that Paul received his most important present of the day. It had been concealed behind a curtain at the end of the marquee, and when the curtain was pulled back he saw something he could not believe still existed: his burgundy-cloured MG from Rome, which he had sold years before to his half-sister, Donna. The children had traced it and had had it carefully rebuilt and repainted as a present to their father from the younger generation.

It was a present that meant more to Paul than any other, for it was also an omen for the future. There is a nostalgic feel to old motorcars, and the MG seemed part of an existence that he had long considered lost forever. It was associated with his youth and with happier times in Rome, before his troubles started. He had sold it in a moment of despair, when oblivion was all that mattered. Now, by returning it to him, it was as if the children were showing that the need for oblivion was over, and that even the past could be recovered and forgiven.

Against considerable odds, Paul's car had managed to survive, and thanks to the care of those who loved him and the expenditure of a lot of money, had been wonderfully restored. So, in his own extraordinary way, had he.

CHAPTER TWENTY-FIVE

Full Circle

ANY talk about the Gettys has a habit of finally returning to the true begetter of their story, the unpredictable old man who simultaneously created most of the family's enormous fortune and most of their troubles—that loner, financier of genius, and miser extraordinary, J. Paul Getty. The image of him that persists is of a man of supernatural business skills, immense financial power, and a personal life of utter emptiness.

His was a genuinely strange existence in which money took the place of almost everything. He was an alchemist of money. For much of his life, working from some room in a hotel and using nothing but a telephone, he had possessed the knack of summoning up money that he magically converted into oil fields, refineries, and tanker fleets, usually in distant continents; and such was his skill and such his cleverness that almost anything that he created seemed to produce yet more money, which in turn enhanced the Getty fortune and the tax-immune income of the Sarah C. Getty Trust.

That was how it went, and the essential point about it all was that for J. Paul Getty, most of life—with the possible exception of sex— took place in his truly extraordinary mind. He rarely saw the far-off marvels that he and his money had created; he didn't care to. Nor did he ever spend the money which he had piled away in such abundance in the trust; he didn't dare to. It was entirely typical of him to have built that strange museum out at Malibu which he would never see. And it was much the same with the scattered offspring he had casually produced but could not be bothered with for years on end.

So it was not surprising that problems arose when he decided that his adult sons were to join the family business and start what he liked to call the Getty dynasty. To build a dynasty, one must first create a family, and J. Paul Getty, who had spent his adult life escaping from his wives and children, had really no idea of what a family entailed.

Nor was it surprising that all his offspring in their different ways were scarred by contact with their father—that George should have destroyed himself, that Paul Junior almost did the same, that Ronald was tortured by his disinheritance, and that even Gordon had been forced to build himself a private intellectual world to take the place of what was missing in his childhood.

Mutual affection, understanding, generosity—the basis of any happy family—were not in J. Paul Getty's emotional vocabulary. Instead it was as if something of the old man's lack of feeling had been inserted in its place. This together with the vast amounts of money he was making, in theory to benefit his family, served to magnify the problem, helping create jealousy, suspicion, and mistrust among the children, together with the fatal weakness that appears to have been somewhere at the root of the old man's curious psychology: fear.

With his fear for his possessions, fear for his person, and ultimately fear for his existence, Jean Paul Getty was that most unseemly spectacle, a fearful billionaire; and since fear is contagious, by the time of young Paul's kidnapping he had turned the Gettys into a fearful family as well. Much of Paul Junior's reclusiveness had to do with fear, as had George's death and the family's behavior during the kidnaping and its aftermath. Gail was important to the family because she alone was not fearful.

But now that members of the family were emerging from the old man's shadow, fear was fading. Aileen had overcome it in her private Calvary, as had her brother Paul with his determination to go on living; so had her father when he came off drugs and faced the world again. With fear now departing, the Gettys could start living as a relatively normal family.

Back in 1960, when the old man threw his monster party at Sutton Place for the daughter of a friend of a duke he barely knew, he felt no inclination to invite a single member of his family. But now, when Mark arranged the Wormsley party for his father, he had been anxious to invite all the Gettys he could muster. And the Gettys were increasingly behaving like a close and supportive family.

ON December 18, 1992, the London *Times*, quoting an Associated Press report from San Juan, Puerto Rico, reported that a son of the late oil billionaire J. Paul Getty had filed for bankruptcy, claiming no assets and debts of $43.2 million. "The claim by J. Ronald and Karin M. Getty was filed last month in San Juan."

Although locally self governed, the Caribbean island of Puerto Rico is in union with the United States and shares its legal system and its currency. Ronald and his wife had settled there after leaving South Africa, and on December 18, 1992, both appeared before a judge of the U.S. Bankruptcy Court for the District of Puerto Rico to request an extension to file schedules and statements of their affairs. This was understandable, as Ronald owed money on behalf of his company to a formidable list of creditors. They included Merrill Lynch Private Capital, Inc., the Société Générale, the First National Bank of Colorado Springs, the Crédit Suisse, and the Security Pacific National Bank.

Ronald was personally liable for these debts, and he had recently been having nightmares with the principal creditors, some of whom had been prolonging the bankruptcy proceedings in an attempt to recover assets that he simply didn't have. He was sixty-five, a bad time of life to deal with this sort of crisis, and in the past he would have had to face the music on his own. But after his reunion with the family, things had changed. Gordon and Paul were on his side and began to help in every way they could, advising him, paying for lawyers, and finally setting up a fund to pay a portion of his debts and get a settlement. As a result, Ronald was able to discharge his bankruptcy.

By doing this, they helped their unhappy brother to recover peace of mind and a measure of self-respect; since then they have also arranged for him to have an income (an undisclosed figure) as a paid consultant to his family trust. They are also helping him and Karin buy a house in Germany.

At last there was general acceptance in the family that Ronald was unjustly treated all those years ago by his exclusion from the trust. No one could change that, any more than anyone could really make amends for Jean Paul Getty's behavior. But the family could at least ensure that after a lifetime ruined by trying to prove himself against his father, Ronald could end his days where he began and where he had always felt at home: among his mother's people in his native Germany.

IN contrast with Ronald, Gordon remained the lucky member of the family, riding high on personal success, particularly with his music. Early in 1994, after attending concerts of his work in Newark, New Jersey, and Austin, Texas, he had the unique triumph for a composer of flying in his own aircraft to Moscow to be present at a concert dedicated to his music, with the Russian National Orchestra performing *Plump Jack* and his "Three Victorian Scenes" and "Three Waltzes for Orchestra."

It was the sort of accolade Gordon had dreamed of, and he seemed slightly overcome by the occasion. As he said, "There's something very special about listening to a great orchestra like that playing your own music."

In his role as latter day renaissance man he was also gaining public recognition for his economic theories from the Nobel economic laureate Professor Franco Modigliani, who publicly praised the originality of the economic theories in Gordon's paper "Fertile Money."

Simultaneously Ann seemed to be sharing in the family success, as the money and the effort she had put into the search for man's earliest remains in Ethiopia finally paid off. That September it was confirmed that the team with which she worked had found what they were seeking. It had been established that fossilized remains discovered some months earlier were 4.5 million years old and belonged to an apelike hominid. Given the name *Australopithecus ramidus*, the creature was confidently claimed to be the long-sought "missing link," joining the families of apes and humans.

The discovery was a triumph for the team's leader, Ann's tutor at the University of California, Professor Tim White. It was also a triumph in its way for Ann and Gordon, whose financial support had helped make Professor White's research possible. But it also came in the middle of a bitter academic feud in which Ann and Gordon, in their role as financial benefactors, had inadvertently become involved.

Unlike his brother Paul Junior, who has given to a wide variety of causes without strings attached, Gordon has always tended to become personally involved with the causes he donated to, treating them, as he puts it, "just as responsibly as my business investments." This was very much the case when he helped to found the Institute of Human Origins at Berkeley under the controversial Dr. Johanson. Since then there had been a falling out between Johanson and his former colleague White, with Ann and Gordon increasingly supporting White. White's success had given extra weight to his cause, and Gordon, true to his word, decided he would cease "investing" in Dr. Johanson's institute forthwith. Since this threatened the existence of the institute, Gordon naturally incurred widespread criticism for his action. But he believes firmly that he is in the right. More to the point he has the money, which invariably means that once he has his mind made up, it takes something more than criticism to change it.

IRONICALLY, just as his philanthropy was involving Gordon in controversy, so a stroke of unexpected generosity was causing embarrassment to his brother Paul Junior, by publicly raising the long-forgotten issue of his relations with his father.

After a long and disappointing campaign to raise money to buy Canova's neoclassical sculptural group *The Three Graces* for a British gallery, it had looked as if the J. Paul Getty Museum in Malibu was going to acquire the three life-sized marble nymphs for the asking price of £7.4 million. They had been in Britain since a Duke of Bedford purchased them from the Italian sculptor back in 1820, and more than £1 million was still required to keep them in the country. At the last minute Paul Junior announced that he would personally donate £1 million to the fund, provided the remaining money was contributed from other sources.

Timothy Clifford, head of the National Galleries of Scotland, who directed the campaign, expressed his delight when interviewed live on television—but when asked why Getty should have backed a British gallery against his father's museum in Malibu, he answered brightly: "I believe that Mr. Getty never got on well with his father."

Though broadly true, this was hardly tactful in the circumstances, and one can understand Paul Junior's annoyance when he heard it. When you give away £1 million you don't expect to be reminded that you didn't like your father, particularly when this has little bearing on the reasons for your generosity. In fact the motive behind Paul Junior's gift lay, as usual, in his genuine love of his adoptive country.

Uproar ensued when Paul expressed extreme displeasure and added that he was thinking of withdrawing his offer. Faced with full responsibility for the threatened loss to Britain of Canova's *Three Graces*, the unfortunate Mr. Clifford did almost everything short of ritual disembowelment to express repentance.

He said he was profoundly sorry. He wrote to Paul saying he had made a terrible mistake. "I know nothing," he publicly lamented, "about Mr. Getty's relationship with his father."

And that, at last, was that. Placated, Paul Junior confirmed his offer, and to the relief of Mr. Clifford and the intense annoyance of John Walsh, director of the Malibu museum, Canova's three young ladies were permitted to remain in Britain.

The fuss over this relatively minor matter was a measure of the unaccustomed calm that otherwise had settled on the family, and one was left to wonder: Could it last? Was the cycle of disaster truly over? Having endured almost every aspect of the curse of riches, could the Gettys possibly avoid it in the future?

In any family things always can and do go wrong for individuals, but what seems certain is that the epidemic of unhappiness that had scourged the family for nearly four decades was over, since so much of it depended on the interplay of Jean Paul Getty with his children, the circumstances in which his fortune was created, and the existence of the Sarah C. Getty Trust.

Also, families, like individuals, learn from their mistakes, and the Gettys have been forced to do a lot of learning. There was a sort of innocence in the way Paul Junior and Talitha first became involved with drugs in the 1960s, and also in the way Paul Junior's son, young Paul, made such tragic efforts to imitate his hippie father. But the younger Gettys are innocent no longer. By force of circumstance, they have become sophisticated and tough inheritors, schooled by the discipline of family disasters.

Young Paul's son Balthazar, for instance, has always been adamant in his refusal to become involved with alcohol or drugs, and remains dedicated to his ambition to succeed as an actor and a film director.

Talitha's son Tara is similarly determined to enjoy life on his own extremely level-headed terms, steering very clear of drugs, preferring France to England, and remaining close to the person who largely brought him up, his step-grandmother, Poppet Pol. He is very good to her, has inherited his mother's charm, and gets on well with all the family.

Ronald's son Christopher is resolved to achieve the sort of business success his father didn't, and with his banking expertise and connections with the family trusts, he shows every sign of doing so.

Paul Junior's younger daughter, Ariadne, is similarly committed to her husband and her two young children. She misses Italy, but the experience of the kidnaping still makes her grateful for America and the privacy and safety of her own small family.

Ann and Gordon's children are all highly motivated, self-aware, essentially private people, who are very sure of what they're doing.

As for Mark, time alone will tell if his plans for a Getty business dynasty will work. Whatever happens he has his own life very much worked out, and seems certain to find riches as a merchant banker long before inheriting his full portion of the Getty money.

Remembering the Chinese curse "May you live in interesting times," Mark says that he feels that the Gettys have been "interesting" for long enough. "I hope that from now on we can all become a little boring."

But there is nothing boring in the situation of the younger Gettys. Thanks to Sarah Getty the money from her trust can be expected to enrich the lives of her grandchildren and great-grandchildren as she originally intended. Their interests have been taken care of; the capital is safe within the separate trusts; and after the turmoil of the past, the younger members of the family are fortune's favorites. Having drawn "a winning ticket in the lottery of life," they can look forward to the best of everything and never feel the care and anguish that afflict the vast majority of suffering mankind from lack of money.

But for them, unlike their elders, there can be no excuses if things do go wrong. So they should not ignore the lessons offered by the sufferings and errors of their predecessors—or ever overlook their own immense good fortune.

Postscript

THE Fates, apparently smiling on the Gettys, had a final blessing to bestow upon the one who in his way had suffered most: Paul Junior.

Jon Bannenberg, the Australian naval architect who designed the *Queen Elizabeth II*, had been rebuilding Paul's sixty-year-old yacht, *Jezebel*, and early in 1994 the work was finished. The gleaming boat now rode at anchor on the River Dart, awaiting her new owner's pleasure.

With his yacht, as with his "paradise" at Wormsley, Paul had been indulging his expensive passion for perfection. With a crew of nineteen looking after a maximum of twelve passengers in conditions of total luxury, the 295-foot yacht now ranked among the most glamorous vessels in her class—and was about to play a special role in the final stage of Paul's recovery.

Until now, Talitha's name had invariably been remembered with a touch of sorrow, but this changed mysteriously when Paul elected to rename his yacht *Talitha Getty*. Sailors are superstitious about changing the names of vessels, but it was as if Talitha's spirit had been reborn in one of the loveliest ships afloat, and could offer Paul something he had not experienced for years: the freedom of the seas.

Born off the coast of Italy himself, he had always loved traveling by sea, but the damage caused to his feet and legs by acute phlebitis had made this impractical. With a spectacular oceangoing yacht at his command and the chance to have his private doctor always in attendance, it was impractical no longer.

At the beginning of April he and Victoria flew the Concorde to New York and on to the Caribbean, where *Talitha Getty* was waiting to receive them both like minor royalty. For Paul, after twenty landlocked years, this was the ultimate in freedom—and in Barbados he was even able to enjoy the spectacle of Britain's test cricketers beating a West Indian eleven in Barbados for the first time in fifty-nine years.

Thanks to *Talitha Getty*, Paul was also able to revisit his beloved Mediterranean late that summer with Victoria and a few close friends for company. Then, immediately after Christmas, which was spent with the family at Wormsley, the two of them flew once more to Barbados where the yacht was waiting. On December 30, in Bridgetown harbor, on the deck of the *Talitha Getty*, Paul completed the love affair that had started so many troubled years before in Rome. Before a local minister, he married Victoria.

Before leaving for Barbados, they had told no one of their intentions, but there was a sort of rightness in the outcome of their journey. Victoria's love for Paul had managed to survive rejection, drugs, ill health, and untold difficulties—and his for her had been dogged by troubles with his father, regret over Talitha, and a good proportion of the ills the flesh is heir to. But somehow, and in spite of all their problems, they had grown closer with the years. She was devoted to him and he depended on her utterly.

"Victoria is my inspiration," he frequently remarked, which in its way was true, for she, more than anyone, had been constant through his troubles and had saved him from the depths of absolute disaster. When she was very young she had dreamed of marrying him. Now that she was young no longer, her dream had finally become reality.

Uncertainty was ended; the past was over if not entirely forgotten; and, like the family itself, Paul and Victoria had earned their chance to enjoy their fortune and their days together.

Index